Gerrymande

This book considers the causes and con ... ring in the U.S. House. The Supreme Court's de ... urer (2004) made challenging a district plan on grounds ... an gerrymandering practically impossible. Through a rigorous scientific analysis of U.S. House district maps, the authors argue that partisan bias increased dramatically in the 2010 redistricting round after the *Vieth* decision at both the national and state levels. From a constitutional perspective, unrestrained partisan gerrymandering poses a critical threat to a central pillar of American democracy – popular sovereignty. State legislatures now effectively determine the political composition of the U.S. House. The book answers the Court's challenge to find a new standard for gerrymandering that is both constitutionally grounded and legally manageable. It argues that the scientifically rigorous partisan symmetry measure is an appropriate legal standard for partisan gerrymandering, as it is a necessary condition of individual equality and can be practically applied.

Anthony J. McGann is a professor in the School of Government and Public Policy at the University of Strathclyde. His research examines the theory and practice of democratic institutions with a focus on electoral systems and the behavior of political parties. He has published *The Logic of Democracy* and *The Radical Right in Western Europe* (with Herbert Kitschelt). His articles have been featured in the *American Journal of Political Science*, *British Journal of Political Science*, *Journal of Theoretical Politics*, *Public Choice*, *Comparative Political Studies*, *International Studies Quarterly*, *Electoral Studies*, *Journal of Conflict Resolution*, *Party Politics*, and *Legislative Studies Quarterly*, among others.

Charles Anthony Smith is an associate professor at the University of California, Irvine. His books include *The Rise and Fall of War Crimes Trials: From Charles I to Bush II* (Cambridge University Press) and *Understanding the Political World, Twelfth Edition* (with James Danziger). He has published articles in the *American Journal of Political Science, Law & Society Review*, *Political Research Quarterly*, *Justice System Journal*, *International Political Science Review*, *Judicature*, *Journal of Human Rights*, *Election Law Journal*, *Studies in Law, Politics and Society*, *Human Rights Review*, and *Journal of International Relations and Development*, among others.

Michael Latner is Associate Professor of Political Science at California Polytechnic State University, San Luis Obispo, where he teaches and studies political participation, representation, and civic technology. He is director of the Master's in Public Policy program and Faculty Scholar at the Institute for Advanced Technology and Public Policy's Digital Democracy Initiative. He has published articles in *Comparative Political Studies, Electoral Studies* and *Politics and the Life Sciences*, among others. Professor Latner has served as a political consultant on candidate and initiative campaigns across California and as a civic technology and social media consultant for governments, associations, and businesses.

Alex Keena is a PhD candidate in political science at the University of California, Irvine who studies political institutions and electoral politics. His dissertation investigates the effects of constituency population size on political representation in Congress.

Gerrymandering in America

The House of Representatives, the Supreme Court, and the Future of Popular Sovereignty

ANTHONY J. McGANN

University of Strathclyde, Glasgow

CHARLES ANTHONY SMITH

University of California–Irvine

MICHAEL LATNER

California Polytechnic State University–San Luis Obispo

ALEX KEENA

University of California–Irvine

CAMBRIDGE
UNIVERSITY PRESS

32 Avenue of the Americas, New York, NY 10013

Cambridge University Press is part of the University of Cambridge.

It furthers the University's mission by disseminating knowledge in the pursuit of education, learning, and research at the highest international levels of excellence.

www.cambridge.org
Information on this title: www.cambridge.org/9781316507674

First published 2016

Printed in the United States of America by Sheridan Books, Inc.

A catalog record for this publication is available from the British Library.

Library of Congress Cataloging in Publication Data
McGann, Anthony J., author. Smith, Charles Anthony, 1961– author.
Latner, Michael, author. Keena, Alex, author.
Gerrymandering in America : the House of Representatives, the Supreme Court, and the future of popular sovereignty / Anthony J. McGann, University of Strathclyde, Glasgow ; Charles Anthony Smith, University of California–Irvine ; Michael Latner, California Polytechnic State University ; Alex Keena, University of California–Irvine.
New York, NY : Cambridge University Press, 2016.
Includes bibliographical references.
LCCN 2015039157
ISBN 9781107143258 (hardback) ISBN 9781316507674 (paperback)
LCSH: Apportionment (Election law) – United States.
Gerrymandering – United States. Election districts – United States.
Jubelirer, Robert C. (Robert Carl), 1937– – Trials, litigation, etc.
United States. Congress. House.
LCC KF4905.M29 2016
DDC 342.73/053 – dc23
LC record available at http://lccn.loc.gov/2015039157

ISBN 978-1-107-14325-8 Hardback
ISBN 978-1-316-50767-4 Paperback

Contents

1

The Unnoticed Revolution

Shortly after the 2012 elections, when all the votes had been collated, it was noticed that the Republicans had won 234 seats out of 435 in the House of Representatives, even though the Democrats had won a slight majority of the vote (50.6%). This in itself was not particularly remarkable. After all, the Republicans had won a House majority in 1952 and 1994 without winning a majority of the vote. These proved to be one-off events. However, we shall argue, what happened in 2012 was different. The result in 2012 was the result of systematic bias produced by the new districts adopted after the 2010 Census.

Furthermore, eight years earlier the Supreme Court decision in the case *Vieth v. Jubelirer* (2004) made challenging a districting plan on grounds of partisan gerrymandering practically impossible. The combination of the Supreme Court effectively permitting partisan gerrymandering and the willingness of many state governments to draw districts for maximum partisan advantage has profound consequences. It will effectively determine control of the House of Representatives for the next decade; it provides a loophole for the egalitarian and democratizing electoral reforms the Supreme Court required in the 1960s; it means that state governments rather than voters can determine the character of a state's congressional delegation; and it challenges the Madisonian principle that at least one part of government should be directly elected by the people.

The Supreme Court's decision in *Vieth v. Jubelirer* (2004) drew little attention in the popular press or even academic circles – certainly there was nothing comparable to the response to the case of *Citizens United* (2010), which reduced restrictions on independent political expenditures.

This is not completely surprising, as its significance was not obvious. It did not overturn the decision of the district court. In response to a complaint of political gerrymandering in the congressional districts of the State of Pennsylvania, the Supreme Court affirmed the decision of the lower court to not overturn the plan. The Supreme Court agreed on this decision 5–4, but it could not agree on a common opinion. Thus technically it did not overturn the court's previous finding in *Davis v. Bandemer* (1986a) that political gerrymandering was *justiciable* – something the Court could rule on. However, writing for a plurality of the Court, Justice Scalia (joined by Chief Justice Rehnquist and Justices O'Connor and Thomas) argued that partisan gerrymandering was a nonjusticiable "political question" – that is, the Court has no business entertaining political gerrymandering cases. A fifth justice, Justice Kennedy, wrote a concurring opinion arguing that although political gerrymandering cases might be justiciable in principle, there currently existed no standard for deciding such cases. Thus, although the Court did not reach a common opinion, this sent a clear signal that a majority of the Court was not inclined to overturn districting plans on grounds of partisan gerrymandering. Unless a new standard for judging cases could be found, the *Vieth* decision *effectively* (though not in principle) made political gerrymandering into a nonjusticiable political question. It was clear that challenges to districting plans on grounds of partisan gerrymandering were highly unlikely to succeed, no matter how egregious the gerrymander.

We now have a remarkable situation. Drawing districts with different population sizes is prohibited by the Constitution. However, achieving the same partisan advantage by cleverly manipulating the shape of the districts apparently is permitted. In the 1960s, the Supreme Court decided that malapportionment – drawing districts that differed in population size – was unconstitutional (*Baker v. Carr* [1962], *Wesberry v. Sanders* [1964a], *Reynolds v. Sims* [1964b]). This was held to violate the principle of "one person, one vote," which could be derived from both Article 1 of the Constitution and the Equal Protection clause of the Fourteenth Amendment. Before malapportionment was outlawed, districts could vary in population by a factor of ten; now districts have to be redrawn every ten years following the Census to ensure they have equal population. This denied the state governments a powerful tool by which they could fix political outcomes. However, if partisan gerrymandering is now permitted, this creates a loophole that once again gives state governments some of this power. It also seriously undermines the egalitarian intentions of the "one person, one vote" jurisprudence of the 1960s.

In this book, we consider the effects of ending the prohibition on partisan gerrymandering. First, there are the electoral consequences. We will see that the effects are substantial. A substantial part of the book is spent analyzing the districts adopted after the 2010 Census and the electoral outcomes these are likely to produce. Before *Vieth*, the conventional wisdom was that political gerrymandering produced only marginal effects – certainly it affected individual races, but the aggregate effects were minor (see, for example, Butler and Cain 1992). However, in the redistricting following the 2010 Census – the first redistricting round after the *Vieth* decision – state government pushed partisan advantage far more strongly than in the recent past. In 2012, the Republican Party won a majority of thirty-three seats, even though it won fewer votes than the Democrats. Our analysis shows that this is not a freak occurrence, but rather the result of a systematic bias that we should expect to be repeated through the next decade.

In addition to these electoral consequences, there are constitutional consequences. We would expect the electoral consequences to persist through the 2020 congressional elections. After the 2020 Census, the districts will be redrawn. Whereas now there appears to be a substantial pro-Republican bias, this may be completely changed with the post-2020 districts. However, the constitutional effects will persist. The composition of Congress will still be determined as much by how the districts are drawn as by how people vote. In most states, the districts are drawn by the state legislature, while the governor has a veto. The Great Compromise at the Constitutional Convention was that the House of Representatives was to represent the people as a whole, while the Senate was to represent the states. It now appears that the composition of the House will also be determined by state governments. This represents an unlikely victory for the Anti-Federalist vision of government.

We first briefly explore the electoral and constitutional consequences of the fact that partisan gerrymandering is now effectively permitted by the courts before asking whether there are grounds for the *Vieth* decision to be challenged in the future.

THE ELECTORAL CONSEQUENCES: A SYSTEMATIC REPUBLICAN ADVANTAGE UNTIL 2022

The results of the 2012 House elections – the first held under post-*Vieth* districts – certainly give the appearance of strong partisan bias, although they do not prove much without further analysis. In 2012, the Republican

Party won 234 seats out of 435, even though the Democratic Party won a slim majority (50.6%) of the popular vote. Between 2010 and 2012, the Republicans lost only eight seats, even though their share of the two-party popular vote fell from 53.5% to 49.4%. However, the Republican Party has won a majority of seats despite winning fewer votes than the Democrats before, in 1952 and 1996. These elections do not appear to have represented massive, persistent bias, but rather appear to have been one-off events. Furthermore, there is reason to be skeptical about drawing conclusions from the popular vote – this can be distorted, for example, by uncontested seats.

However, systematic analysis indicates that the 2010 districting did indeed produce a very significant bias that is likely to persist through the entire decade. This analysis takes account of both uncontested seats and the fact that in any given district in a given year, there may be local factors that are at least as important as the national vote swing. We find that there is a 5% bias toward the Republican Party in close elections – if the two parties win an equal number of votes, the Republicans will win 55% of the seats. Furthermore, the Democrats would have to win around 54% of the vote to have a fifty-fifty chance of winning control of the House. Thus it is not impossible that the Democrats will regain control of the House. However, it will take a performance similar to that in 2008, when many things were very favorably aligned for the Democrats.

When we consider bias at the state level, we see a more dramatic picture. Of the thirty-eight states that have three or more House districts (and thus where bias is possible), twenty are approximately unbiased. Of the remaining eighteen, the level of bias is often quite extreme. In numerous states, there is a 20% Republican advantage when both parties have equal votes, and the Democrats would in some cases need to win almost 60% of the vote to have a fifty-fifty chance of having a majority of the state's delegation to the House of Representatives. This kind of bias means that only one party has a realistic chance of having a majority of the representatives and that it is in effect the state government, not the voters directly, that is dictating the character of the state's congressional delegation.

Of course, it is often argued that while partisan bias does exist, it is not the result of deliberate gerrymandering, but rather the inevitable, unintentional result of demography or geography. The explanations most usually given are the urban concentration of Democratic voters and the need to draw majority-minority districts to satisfy the Voting Rights Act. While it is true that both the geographical distribution of voters and the Voting Rights Act do significantly constrain what districting plans are possible, it is simply not the case that they make the partisan bias we observe inevitable. We will show that it is quite possible to draw unbiased districts in most states, and if bias is hard to avoid in some states, it is modest compared to the bias in the districting plans actually adopted. If it is possible for a state to adopt an unbiased plan, but it chooses a biased one anyway, then that is a choice it has made, not something imposed on it by demographics. Furthermore, the urban concentration of Democrats and majority-minority districts do not even explain the increase in bias we observe in the 2010 districting round. Most of the states where bias increased did not have additional majority-minority districts, and in most of them it was the geographic concentration of Republican voters that increased relative to that of Democratic voters, not the other way around.

The one thing that does explain where we find partisan bias is politics. Partisan gerrymandering is indeed *partisan*. We will find that statistically significant bias occurs almost exclusively where one party controls the entire districting process. This occurs when districting is done by the state legislatures (often with a gubernatorial veto) and one party controls the legislature and the governorship. Where there is divided government, or districting is done by an independent commission or the courts, we do not find significant bias. However political control does not completely explain the increase in partisan bias between the 2000 and 2010 districting rounds. Partisan bias increased sharply even in those states that the Republicans controlled both in 2000 and 2010. Thus the increase in bias was not simply the result of the Republicans doing very well in state elections in 2010. Rather, after *Vieth v. Jubelirer* (2004), state legislatures were willing to district for partisan advantage far more than they had previously.

THE CONSTITUTIONAL CONSEQUENCES: THE END OF EQUALITY?

The electoral effects we have outlined can only be predicted up through the 2020 congressional elections, after which new districting plans will be adopted; the constitutional effects of the *Vieth* decision, however, may last far longer. After the 2020 Census, all states need to redraw their congressional districts. How they are redistricted will depend on the balance of power in state governments and the redistricting institutions of the various states. If the Democrats have control of the state legislature or governorship in more states, they may redraw districts to erase the current Republican advantage. If they are successful enough at the state level, they may even be able to gerrymander in their favor. Indeed, now that it is apparent that regaining control of the House probably requires regaining control of state governments, both parties will probably pay a great deal of attention to (and spend a great deal of money on) state elections. Nevertheless, even if the current partisan advantage is erased in the next redistricting round, something about American national elections has fundamentally changed.

What has changed is the balance of power between national and state government. Previously, control of the House of Representatives depended on how people voted in the previous congressional election. Now, given that there are no restraints on the ability to gerrymander for partisan advantage, there are many states where the state legislature effectively determines what the congressional delegation looks like. Furthermore, it is not the state government at the previous election that matters but the state government at the beginning of the decade when the new districts were drawn. This is particularly problematic, as we traditionally think of the House of Representatives as representing the people directly, while the Senate represents the interests of the states.

The debate about the balance between national and state government, of course, goes back to the dispute at the Federal Convention between Madison and the Federalists on one hand and the Anti-Federalists on the other. At the beginning of the Federal Convention, Madison advocated a system of government in which the lower chamber of the legislature would be directly elected by the people on the basis of population, while the upper chamber would be elected by the lower. The Anti-Federalists advocated a legislature chosen by state governments. The eventual resolution, of course, was the Connecticut Compromise: the House of Representatives was to be directly elected by population, while the Senate was to be chosen by state governments, with each state receiving two Senators.

In the reapportionment decisions in the 1960s, the Supreme Court explicitly addressed this constitutional principle. In *Wesberry v. Sanders* (1964a), the Supreme Court stated that the point of the Great Compromise was that the House of Representatives was to be directly elected by the people. Furthermore, they found that this means that all voters must be treated equally – diluting someone's vote by subtle means is as much a violation as denying them a vote. For this reason, they held it was unconstitutional to draw congressional districts with widely varying populations. It would seem that if it is unconstitutional to advantage some voters over others by having districts with differing populations, then achieving the same end by manipulating the shapes of districts should also be unconstitutional. Indeed, if political gerrymandering is allowed, it would represent a loophole that would allow state governments to get around the intent of *Wesberry v. Sanders* (1964a). However, the Supreme Court did not confirm that political gerrymandering was unconstitutional until *Davis v. Bandemer* (1986a).

Thus *Vieth v. Jubelirer* (2004) did not just challenge *Davis v. Bandemer* (1986a) but also undermined the egalitarian intent of *Wesberry v. Sanders* (1964a). In declaring that the courts could not intervene in cases of political gerrymandering, it gave state governments once again the power to advantage some voters over others. As we will see, the arguments made by Justice Scalia in *Vieth v. Jubelirer* (2004) are very similar to those made by Justice O'Connor in her dissent to *Davis v. Bandemer* (1986a). These in turn echo the arguments of Justice Frankfurter in his dissent to *Baker v. Carr* (1962). The argument in all cases is that districting is a "political question" – that is, the Supreme Court should not intervene, as districting is the business of politicians. In practice, this means leaving districting to state governments. The *Vieth* decision is not simply a technical decision about whether it is possible to detect political gerrymandering, nor is it simply a correction of *Davis v. Bandemer* (1986a). Rather, it strikes at the heart of the right to equal representation that the Supreme Court championed in the 1960s.

CAN THE *VIETH* DECISION BE CHALLENGED?

The main goal of this book is to lay out and understand the effects of partisan gerrymandering. However, given the significance of the *Vieth* decision, it is also important to consider the merits of the decision and, in particular, how it may be challenged in the future. *Vieth v. Jubelirer* (2004) was, after all, something of a split decision, decided by a 5–4 margin. A majority of the Supreme Court agreed that claims of political gerrymandering could not be adjudicated by the courts because no standard for deciding them existed. However, only four Justices out of nine joined with Justice Scalia in arguing that no such standard was possible on principle. The swing voter in the case, Justice Kennedy, agreed that no standard currently existed but held out the possibility that one could be found in the future. Thus the *Vieth* decision is certainly open to challenge.

The task of challenging the *Vieth* decision, however, is a formidable one. In his opinion on *Vieth*, Justice Scalia challenged the argument that partisan gerrymandering was unconstitutional in a fundamental way.

In the reapportionment cases of the 1960s, the Supreme Court had argued that the equal right to vote was protected and that diluting this right by clever means was just as much a violation as simply denying the vote to someone. Hence malapportionment was a constitutional violation and so, it would appear, would be gerrymandering, if it achieved the same goals. Justice Scalia, however, challenges the similarity of the two cases. With malapportionment, there is a clear violation of an individual right – some votes are effectively weighted more than others, and it is easy to observe this. In the case of gerrymandering, however, Justice Scalia argues that no *individual* right has been violated. Rather, what has been violated is a group right – the right of a majority of voters to elect a majority of representatives. The Constitution does not enumerate any such right for parties or groups of voters. Thus to challenge the *Vieth* decision, it is necessary to show either that there is a collective right to representation or that partisan gerrymandering violates an individual right.

In Chapter 7 of this book, we concentrate on the second possibility – that partisan gerrymandering can be shown to violate an individual right. A recent result in mathematical social choice theory – a result published after *Vieth v. Jubelirer* (2004) and *LULAC v. Perry* (2006) – shows that the equal treatment of individual voters logically implies the majority rule principle. That is to say, treating all voters equally means that a majority of voters must be able to elect a majority of representatives. Thus if partisan gerrymandering allows a minority to elect a majority of representatives, then a right to equal treatment by *individual* voters has been violated. Thus it may be possible to connect partisan gerrymandering to a constitutionally protected individual right.

If it is possible to establish that partisan gerrymandering does in fact violate constitutional rights, it is relatively straightforward to measure it. Political scientists have a variety of measures for testing whether a districting plan is likely to advantage one party over another. These can take account of the fact that elections are about candidates as well as parties and the fact that local and incumbent factors are often extremely important. A notable measure is the partisan symmetry measure proposed by a group of political science professors in an amicus brief to *LULAC v. Perry* (2006) – if the Democrats win a certain percentage of the seats when they win a certain percentage of the votes (say, 55%), will the Republicans get the same percentage of seats if they win 55% at the next election? The problem has been that political scientists have proposed these measures to answer political science questions – is a districting as a matter of fact biased toward one party or the other? They have not grounded any measure in terms of constitutionally protected rights. The social choice results referred to in the last paragraph actually allow us to justify standards such as partisan symmetry in terms of the equal protection of individual voters. This line of argument may provide a means to challenge the Supreme Court's contention that a standard for determining partisan gerrymandering cases does not exist.

THE EXAMPLE OF PENNSYLVANIA

The power of partisan gerrymandering to fix political outcomes becomes far clearer when we consider an actual case. Here we look at the State of Pennsylvania from 1992 through the 2012 elections. As congressional districts need to be redrawn every ten years following the Census, this covers the 1990, 2000, and 2010 redistricting rounds. There are a number of reasons for picking Pennsylvania. It is a clear example of the power of districting. In 2012, the Republicans took thirteen out of the eighteen congressional seats, even though the Democrats actually won more votes. The Supreme Court case *Vieth v. Jubelirer* (2004), which declared partisan gerrymandering unchallengeable in the courts, was the result of a challenge to the Pennsylvania districts following the 2000 Census. Finally, the three districting plans that Pennsylvania adopted over this period illustrate the progression from a more or less unbiased plan to a somewhat biased plan to a strong partisan gerrymander.

We start by considering the Pennsylvania districts that were adopted following the 1990 Census and were first used in the 1992 elections. These are illustrated in Figure 1.1. Justice Scalia noted in his opinion on *Vieth v. Jubelirer* (2004) that no one had challenged these districts for being biased. Indeed, they were the result of a bipartisan compromise – the Democrats controlled the governorship and the state assembly, while the Republicans controlled the state senate. In the elections run under these districts, the result was close to a tie, which reflects the fact that Pennsylvania was (and indeed is) a swing state. From 1992 through 1998, the Democrats won eleven of the twenty-one seats, while the Republicans won eleven of the seats in 2000. When we look at the districts in Figure 1.1, most are relatively compact, and there are fewer oddly shaped districts than we will see in the later districting plans.[1]

It is significant that we see relatively unbiased districts following the 1990 Census, because it proves that this is possible. It has been suggested

[1] In Chapter 4, we will introduce measures that give a precise meaning to "oddly shaped."

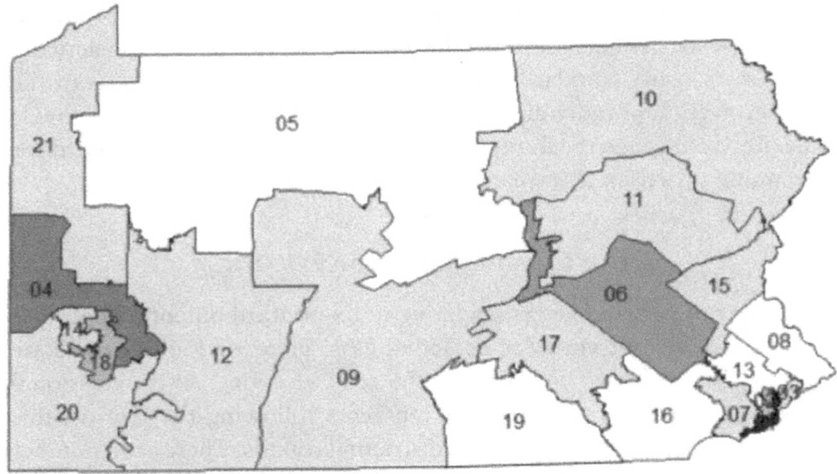

FIGURE 1.1. 1992 Pennsylvania congressional districts.[2]

by some that patterns of partisan bias are the result of demographic factors. For example, it has been argued that because there are large concentrations of Democratic voters (particularly members of ethnic minorities) in urban areas, it is inevitable that Democrats will win these districts by lopsided margins, and this wastes votes. That is, we get a naturally occurring gerrymander. It has also been suggested that the Voting Rights Act and the need to create majority-minority districts may have the same effect. However, it is clearly possible to create districting plans that do not have an obvious partisan bias such as that adopted in Pennsylvania following the 1990 Census. Indeed, as we will show in Chapter 4, the majority of states manage to be approximately unbiased between the parties. As we will argue, if there is strong partisan bias, it is because the people who drew the districts chose to create it or at least chose to tolerate it.

However, we do not wish to suggest that the post-1990 Pennsylvania districts are perfect or even that they are some kind of baseline for appropriately drawn districts. They have the merit of being approximately unbiased between the parties. However, as sometimes happens with bipartisan

[2] Source: Shapefiles provided by the U.S. Census, http://www.census.gov/geo/maps-data/data/cbf/cbf_cds.html. Shading reflects district compactness as measured using ratio of district area to district convex hull area. Darker shading reflects less compact districts. See Chapter 4 for measurements of compactness by state and redistricting plan, and category cut points.

compromise districting plans, the plan protects the incumbents of both parties. As a result, the districts are not very responsive to changes in the popularity of the parties. In spite of considerable swings between the parties in the 1990s, there was always an 11–10 split of the seats. There were also a considerable number of uncontested seats. Indeed, except for 1996, four seats out of twenty-one were uncontested in each election conducted under these districts.

The Pennsylvania districting plan that followed the 2000 Census lies between the 1990 and 2010 plans in terms of bias. There is some evidence of partisan advantage and at least one remarkably shaped district. However, the level of bias is far less than we find in the post-2010 plan. Unlike the post-1990 plan, the 2000 districts were not the result of a bipartisan compromise – the Republican Party controlled both the governorship and the state legislature. Indeed, the districts were controversial, and a group of Democratic voters challenged them in court. The district court did find that the original plan was unacceptable because of difference in the population of the various districts. However, once this was corrected, the district court approved the plan and rejected the claim that there was unconstitutional partisan gerrymandering. The Democratic plaintiffs appealed to the Supreme Court, and the resulting case, *Vieth v. Jubelirer* (2004), led to the Supreme Court finding that there was no standard by which partisan gerrymandering could be challenged.

Figure 1.2 shows the post-2000 Pennsylvania districts that were eventually adopted. These were first used for the 2002 congressional elections. There were only nineteen districts now, as Pennsylvania had lost two seats due to reapportionment. The districts mostly appear relatively compact. There are a few exceptions. District 6 in the east of the state has tendrils that curl around the districts that surround it to stretch into Philadelphia. In the western part of the state, Districts 12 and 18 are elongated and snake around each other.

In terms of partisan bias, there is some prima facie evidence that there is pro-Republican bias. In 2002 and 2010, the Republicans won twelve seats out of nineteen despite winning only 51% and 52% of the Pennsylvania congressional vote in those years. The Democrats did manage to win eleven seats in 2006 and twelve seats in 2008, but they needed to win 56% of the vote in these years. (The Republicans did win twelve seats with 56% of the vote in 2002, but this vote share was partly the result of the Democrats not contesting five seats.) It would appear that there is some bias in that the Democrats seem to need more votes to win a certain number of seats than the Republicans do. However, this bias seems to be

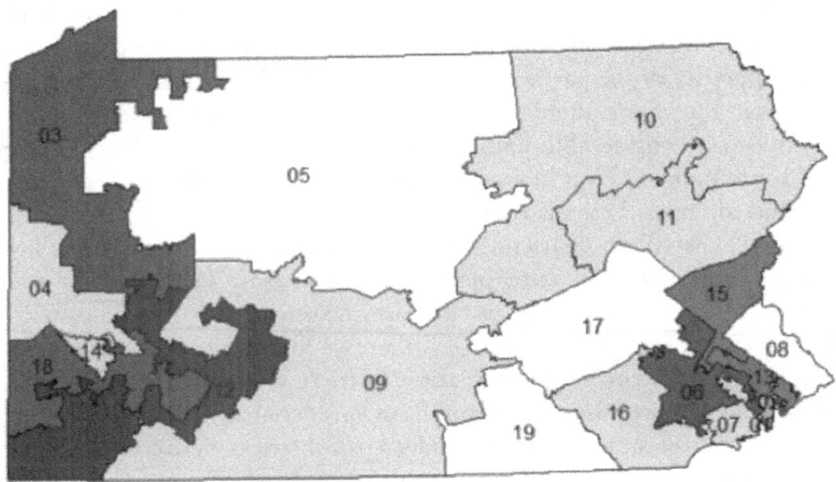

FIGURE 1.2. 2002 Pennsylvania congressional districts.

moderate, and it is certainly possible for the Democrats to win a majority of the seats. Indeed, they were about to win 63% of the seats. In Chapter 4, we use more sophisticated methods that take into account things like uncontested seats. These confirm our impression that these districts have a moderate pro-Republican bias.

It is notable that when the post-2000 districts were drawn, partisan gerrymandering could still be challenged in the courts. The case *Davis v. Bandemer* (1986a) had clarified this point, although the standards for deciding these claims remained ambiguous. This provides one explanation as to why the level of partisan gerrymandering was quite modest in the post-2000 districts compared to the post-2010 ones, even though the Republicans controlled the governorship and state legislature in both cases. If the state legislature had proposed a severely gerrymandered districting plan in 2000, there is a real possibility that it could have been struck down by the district court. Indeed, the district court did strike down the first plan proposed on grounds of malapportionment. The plan that was proposed in its place (and eventually adopted) passed muster with the district court. The district court found that the plaintiffs did not succeed in proving partisan gerrymandering under the standards of *Davis v. Bandemer* (1986a). Thus the post-2000 districting plan gives us some indication as to how much partisan bias you could get away with before the Supreme Court declared partisan gerrymandering claims nonjusticiable in *Vieth v. Jubelirer* (2004).

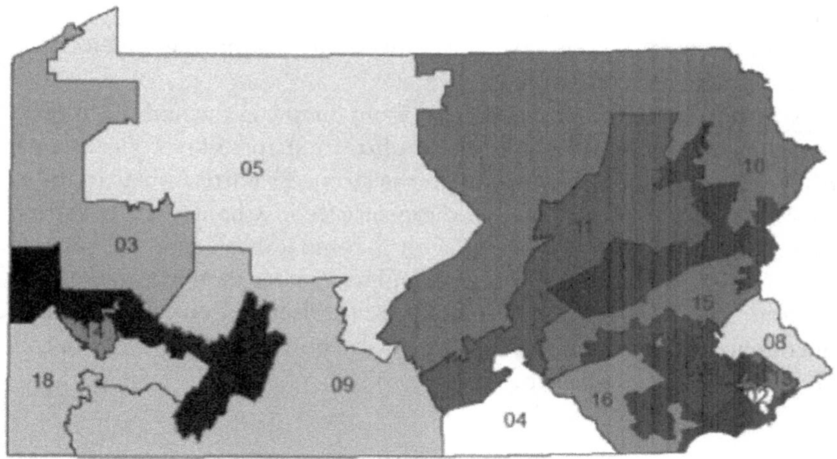

FIGURE 1.3. 2012 Pennsylvania congressional districts.

The congressional districts adopted in Pennsylvania after the 2010 Census show the full potential of partisan gerrymandering when there is no threat of judicial action. In the previous round, the Pennsylvania state government had to consider the possibility that the courts would strike down a blatantly gerrymandered districting plan. After *Vieth v. Jubelirer* (2004), this was no longer the case.

The post-2010 districts for Pennsylvania are shown in Figure 1.3. Many of the districts are not compact at all. Particularly of note is District 7 in southeastern Pennsylvania. This comprises four distinct land masses that are barely connected and that snake around the crescent-shaped District 6. Numerous other districts are either elongated or have tendrils that cut into the surrounding districts. We should note that there is no constitutional reason congressional districts need to be compact. However, if politicians choose to draw them in extremely irregular shapes, it does pose the question of why they have taken the trouble to do this.

The post-2010 districting plan has a strong partisan bias toward the Republican Party. It does not take advanced mathematics to realize that if one party wins a majority of the votes, but the other party receives thirteen seats out of eighteen, then something is up. Of course, we only have the results for one election year, 2012. However, what is striking about these results was the absence of close races – there was only one district (District 12) in which the margin of victory was less than 10%. The current results are likely to be repeated even if there is a substantial swing toward the Democrats. Using more sophisticated methods in Chapter 4, we calculate that the Democrats in Pennsylvania would have to win between 57% and 58% of the vote to even have a fifty-fifty chance of having a majority in the congressional delegation.

What we see in Pennsylvania is far from unique in the nation, either in terms of partisan bias or in terms of the bizarre shapes of its congressional districts. It is among the states with the strongest partisan bias (number four in the nation according to the measures in Chapter 4). However, there are numerous other states with a comparable degree of partisan bias. Indeed, we find no fewer than eighteen states in which the level of partisan bias is significant. From the 2012 elections on, it will not be uncommon to see elections decided not by how the people vote but by how the districts are drawn.

WHY WAS IT UNNOTICED?

We argue in this book that the Supreme Court's decision in *Vieth v. Jubelirer* (2004) was profoundly important. However, this poses the question: why has its significance for the most part gone unnoticed? The case gained little attention either in the media or in terms of political controversy. It has not received the attention from activist groups or journalists accorded to *Citizens United v. Federal Election Commission* (2010), which dealt with restrictions to campaign spending. Even when we consider specialist literature, *Vieth v. Jubelirer* (2004) is accorded minor significance. For example, it was noted in a few articles in the *Election Law Journal* (Hasen 2004; Gardner 2004), but neither gave any indication that it was of interest to anyone but an electoral law specialist. When Michael P. McDonald wrote an assessment on the likely electoral effects of redistricting in *Political Science and Politics* (a publication of the American Political Science Association) in 2010, *Vieth v. Jubelirer* was not even mentioned.

There are two reasons *Vieth v. Jubelirer* (2004) went unnoticed. The first reason *Vieth v. Jubelirer* (2004) was largely ignored was that it had no immediate or direct effects. It did not affect that following election. With the exception of Texas, which redistricted mid-decade, redistricting did not take place until after the 2010 Census.[3] Thus 2012 was the first election affected for most of the nation. It was apparent in this election that the Republican Party won a majority of the seats despite receiving

[3] It should be noted that the Texas mid-decade redistricting was challenged legally. The case *LULAC v. Perry* was eventually taken up by the Supreme Court, which reaffirmed the decision in *Vieth* that political gerrymandering was not justiciable.

fewer votes than the Democrats did. However, this in itself proves little. In single-member district elections, the smaller party sometimes wins. It is not until the results are analyzed in detail that it becomes apparent the results in 2012 were not a fluke, but rather the result of a systematic bias that is likely to be repeated for the rest of the decade.

The effects of the *Vieth* decision were also underestimated because the mechanism was indirect. The Supreme Court did not *do* anything in *Vieth*. Rather, it declared that it would *not* do something. It found that case of partisan gerrymandering could not be legally challenged (unless a new standard could be found). The effect that this has on the state governments that draw congressional districts is indirect – they do not have to worry about their maps being challenged legally. As a result, we might expect them to seek out partisan advantage more aggressively when they draw districts. However, it was not the case that the Court had been particularly active on electoral law cases prior to *Vieth* (see Hasen 2011). As Justice Scalia pointed out in the plurality opinion on *Vieth v. Jubelirer* (2004, 279–280), there were no cases of a congressional districting plan being overturned on grounds of partisan gerrymandering since *Davis v. Bandemer* (1986a) (which found that districts could be challenged on these grounds).[4]

It is straightforward to see why people should come to the conclusion that, since the Supreme Court did not overturn anything, it had no effect. However, the logic does not follow. A threat can have an effect, even if it is not carried out. For example, if states believed that the Supreme Court would overturn strongly gerrymandered districting plans, they might choose to show restraint in the plans they proposed. If that were the case, the threat of Supreme Court action would have deterred the states from proposing strongly gerrymandered districting plans. If this was the case, when the threat of Supreme Court action was removed, we would expect some states to then push political gerrymandering to its limits. We argue in Chapter 4 that this is exactly what we observe in 2012.

The second reason the effects of the *Vieth* decision were unexpected was that the consensus of the academic literature was that redistricting had only minor political effects. Incidentally, we are not challenging the consensus of this literature – there really does not appear to be much

[4] In the case of *Davis v. Bandemer* (1986), the actual districts were not overturned and were not found to be a case of partisan gerrymandering, although the Court found that districts could be overturned on grounds of partisan gerrymandering.

partisan bias in this time period. Rather, what we are arguing is that after *Vieth*, the world changed, and it became possible to take partisan gerrymandering to its limits. It was accepted, of course, that redistricting mattered greatly to individual members of Congress. However, it was believed that not much was at stake at the aggregate level, given that since 1964, all districts had to be of equal size. After all, redistricting had not produced much political bias for a very considerable time. The conclusion that redistricting *had not* led to significant partisan bias led to the further conclusion that redistricting *would not* or even *could not* lead to significant bias, given other constraints.

A significant example of this is Butler and Cain's study of redistricting (1992, 4–5). They conclude that although concern with redistricting remains as strong as ever, "the actual stakes are objectively less than they once were, on large measure because the constitutional constraints have become much greater." They argue that manipulating district shapes is a far less powerful tool than creating districts of differing sizes, which of course has been constitutionally outlawed since 1964. They go on to argue (1969, 5) that "among the alternative plans that would be acceptable to a judge applying the principle of 'one person, one vote,' the difference in most instances between the best and worst plans would alter the party balance by a handful of seats."

Other factors also constrain the pursuit of partisan advantage. In order to district completely to its advantage, a party needs to completely control the redistricting process, which in most states means it must control both the legislature and the governorship (Butler and Cain 1992, 9). It is also argued that the effects of partisan gerrymandering are constrained by the fact that if a party pursues maximum partisan advantage, it will make its incumbents vulnerable in a bad year. Thus partisan advantage has to be balanced against incumbent protection. Writing about the upcoming redistricting following the 2010 Census, Michael P. McDonald (2011, 313) argued that the Republican Party might already have reached the limits of partisan advantage in certain states (including Pennsylvania, Ohio, and Michigan) in the previous redistricting round.

The potential partisan advantage that can be produced by drawing districts has clearly been underestimated. As we have seen in the case of Pennsylvania, districting can be an extremely potent tool for producing partisan advantage, even if the districts have to be the same size. In Chapter 4, we show that if you are able to draw evenly sized districts any way you like, you can create a large advantage for one party while still leaving that party's seats relatively safe. This does require that you are able to pack the opposing party's supporters into districts where their party is very dominant. This, however, is exactly what has been done in numerous states. After the *Vieth* decision, there were very few constraints other than equal population. Certainly it was possible in the 2010 districting round to get far more partisan advantage out of Pennsylvania, Ohio, and Michigan, even though the same party controlled the redistricting process in these states in both 2000 and 2010. It is also notable that one-party control of the redistricting process was quite common in both 2000 and 2010, removing another constraint on the pursuit of partisan advantage.

Again, we are not challenging the consensus in the literature that there was little partisan bias up through the 2000 redistricting round. Rather, we are arguing that the world changed with the 2010 redistricting. States were no longer constrained by the threat of judicial challenge of partisan gerrymanders, and where one party completely controlled the redistricting process, it often took full advantage.

As we have stated, there is consensus that there was little partisan bias in congressional elections after 1964, when the Supreme Court in *Wesberry v. Sanders* (1964a) declared that all congressional districts needed to be, as near as possible, of equal population. Prior to 1964, there was considerable pro-Republican bias in the non-South, while in the South there was massive malapportionment and outright disenfranchisement in favor of rural, white Democrats (Erikson 1972; Campagna and Grofman 1990; Jacobson 1990; King and Gelman 1991; Brady and Grofman 1991; Ansolabehere and Snyder 2008). Thus by the 1980s, most studies find little or no partisan bias, with the exception of King and Gelman (1991), who find a modest pro-Democratic bias. McDonald (2006) finds a similar pattern in the 1990s and 2000s: in the 1990s, there is essentially no partisan bias, while in the 2000s, there is a modest bias toward the Republican Party (1.5%).

When we consider monographs covering the period, we find a similar story. Cox and Katz's *Elbridge Gerry's Salamander* (2002) and Ansolabehere and Snyder's *The End of Inequality* (2008) document the process whereby the "reapportionment revolution" of the 1960s changed American politics. In the 1960s, in a series of cases following *Baker v. Carr* (1962), the Supreme Court outlawed malapportionment in all elections except where it was constitutionally mandated (for example, elections to the U.S. Senate). Previously, the size of districts could vary by a factor of ten; now districts had to be, to all intents and purposes, of equal size. Partisan bias (pro-Republican in the North and pro-Democratic in the South) rapidly disappeared. There is no doubt that the disappearance of bias coincided with the reapportionment revolution, although there is a debate about the extent to which reapportionment or redistricting was the cause.[5]

Again, we do not wish to deny the force of this narrative. In fact, we draw on it to a considerable degree. The original working title of this book was *The End of Equality* – a play on Ansolabehere and Snyder's *The End of Inequality* (2008). The egalitarian position the Warren court took in the 1960s with regard to popular elections was indeed a revolutionary change to the effective constitution of the United States, having a significance comparable to the civil rights revolution that was happening at the same time. Rather, what we are arguing is that *Vieth v. Jubelirer* (2004) represents a severe rollback of this revolution. By permitting partisan gerrymandering, it offers a loophole that allows the biases outlawed in the 1960s to be reintroduced.

We note that there is a robust literature on whether majority-minority districts effectively cost the Democrats seats in Congress (Lublin 1997; Shotts 2001; Epstein et al. 2007). The argument is that majority-minority districts sometimes elect Democratic candidates by overwhelming margins, which leads to Democratic votes being used inefficiently. Regardless of whether this effect does reduce the number of Democrats elected, it cannot account for the large increase in bias observed after the 2010 redistricting round. Indeed, the 1990 and 2000 rounds managed to produce districting plans that in aggregate were approximately unbiased in spite of any effect that majority-minority districts may have had.

It is thus hardly surprising that the effects of the *Vieth* decision in 2004 were unanticipated. There were no effects at all until the 2012 elections. Even then, the effects were indirect, a result of the fact that state legislators no longer felt constrained by the threat of judicial review. Furthermore, the academic literature suggested that redistricting only had marginal political effects, as indeed had been the case for the last few redistricting rounds. What we will show in the rest of the book is that the effects of *Vieth* were indeed momentous. The 2012 redistricting round has effectively determined control of the House of Representatives for a decade. Even after that, politics will be different. Control of Congress will depend to a considerable degree on state governments and the districts

[5] Erikson (1972) and King and Gelman (1991) argued that redistricting could not explain the declining partisan bias in this period. Instead, they proposed increasing incumbency advantage as an explanation. Cox and Katz (2002) argued that once region and the strategic interaction between the states and the Court are taken account of, redistricting does explain the reduction in bias.

they draw, as opposed to the popular vote. To some degree, this turns the clock back to before *Baker v. Carr* (1962). While state governments cannot draw districts with large population differences, they can achieve similar effects through the shapes of the districts they draw. Electoral equality in the House of Representative – the chamber that is supposed to represent the people directly – is no longer guaranteed.

PLAN OF BOOK

The book consists of three sections in addition to the introduction and conclusion. Section 1 (Chapter 2) deals with the legal framework concerning partisan gerrymandering and the historical background to *Vieth v. Jubelirer* (2004). Section 2 (Chapters 3, 4, and 5) deals with the empirical analysis of partisan gerrymandering before and after the *Vieth* decision. Section 3 (Chapters 6 and 7) considers the merits of the *Vieth decision* given recent social scientific work and its constitutional consequences.

Chapter 2 lays out the jurisprudence of districting. It considers the grounds on which political gerrymandering was considered unconstitutional before *Vieth v. Jubelirer* (2004). This is based on the cases that made up the "reapportionment revolution" of the 1960s. Prior to the 1960s, the drawing of electoral districts was considered a "political question" and was not regulated by the courts (see *Colegrove v. Green* [1946]). This led to massive inequities, including some districts having many times the population of others in some states. The case *Baker v. Carr* (1962) decided that these cases were subject to judicial review, and subsequent cases (notably *Wesberry v. Sanders* [1964a] and *Reynolds v. Sims* [1964b]) interpreted the Constitution in a strongly egalitarian way to require "one man, one vote." This clearly ruled out malapportionment (districts having widely differing populations). However, political gerrymandering, if allowed, would offer a loophole through which state governments could undermine the egalitarian intent of the reapportionment decisions – political outcomes could be fixed by other means. Because political gerrymandering has been difficult to define, we will see that there has been considerable ambiguity as to how it should be treated by the courts. *Vieth v. Jubelirer* (2004) essentially decided that political gerrymandering could not be challenged judicially. In addition to considering the legal grounds for not considering political gerrymandering to be unconstitutional, we argue that the position taken by Justice Scalia is a conscious attempt to limit the effects of the reapportionment cases of the 1960s. Indeed, we can trace the arguments made by Justice Scalia in

Vieth back to those made by Justice O'Connor in her dissenting opinion on *Davis v. Bandemer* (1986a) and Justice Frankfurter's famous dissent on *Baker v. Carr* (1962).

Chapter 3 deals with the empirical effects of districting and partisan gerrymandering on congressional elections in the United States. First it explains how partisan gerrymandering works and how it can be measured. Then it assesses the degree of partisan bias in the United States as a whole and in the districting plan of each state. In particular, it looks at how much partisan bias has increased since the *Vieth* decision – that is how much greater it is for the districts adopted after the 2010 Census compared with those adopted after the 2000 Census.

Chapter 4 assesses various nonpolitical explanations for partisan bias, such as the concentration of Democratic voters in urban areas, the Voting Rights Act, and advances in districting technology. For each of these alternative explanations, we ask whether they can serve as explanations of partisan bias instead of political choice. That is to say, we ask whether they make partisan bias inevitable, whether the districting authorities want it or not. To establish that unbiased districting is possible, we consider the districting plans adopted in various states and alternative plans proposed in states where the adopted plan was highly biased. We then consider whether factors like the urban concentrations of Democrats may explain partisan bias in a weaker sense – do they make it easier for a state that wishes to draw biased plans to do so? In particular, we consider whether changes in the urban concentration of Democrats, in the number of majority-minority districts, and in the computer technology available can explain the increase in partisan bias between the 2000 and 2010 districting rounds.

Chapter 5 considers political explanations for partisan bias. We ask whether the presence of partisan bias can be explained by political variables. We would expect partisan gerrymandering in states where a political party has both the motive and opportunity to engage in it. The opportunity for partisan gerrymandering is present when one party has complete control of the districting process. A party has the motive if the state is electorally competitive – there is no point in gerrymandering a state that your party is going to dominate anyway. After considering whether we find partisan bias where we would expect it, we ask whether the level of partisan bias has changed since *Vieth* once we control for political factors. That is, we consider the alternative explanation that the increase in partisan bias we observe is simply due to the fact that the Republican Party did very well in 2010 and controlled more states than in 2000. We also consider the institutional factors that give parties the incentive and opportunity to engage in gerrymandering. We consider who has to approve the districts (state legislature versus independent commissions and also the role of the governor) and also the timing of elections (in particular off-year elections).

Chapter 6 considers the constitutional implications of the Supreme Court's decision that partisan gerrymandering is not constitutionally prohibited. The essence of the Great Compromise at the Constitutional Convention was that the House of Representatives would represent the people as a whole, while the Senate would represent the states. This was, of course, a compromise between Federalists and Anti-Federalists. However, we find that the effects of partisan gerrymandering are so strong in many states that it is the state legislature and not the people that is determining the composition of the House of Representatives. In a sense this represents the "revenge of the Anti-Federalists." It also represents a significant rollback of the egalitarian and democratic reforms advanced by the Supreme Court in the "reapportionment revolution" of the 1960s.

Chapter 7 is concerned with the arguments made by Justice Scalia in his opinion on *Vieth v. Jubelirer* (2004) and how these can be countered given recent developments in social science. Justice Scalia's opinion represents a fundamental challenge to anyone wishing to argue that partisan gerrymandering is unconstitutional. He argues that any such argument must rely on a right to collective group representation and that no such group right exists in the U.S. Constitution. Only individual rights to representation are protected. In this chapter, we show that the principle of majority rule (that a majority of voters should be able to elect a majority of representatives) is logically implied by the equal protection of individual voters. If this is so, then partisan gerrymandering can indeed violate the individual rights present in the Constitution. We also show that the principle of partisan symmetry, proposed as standard for partisan gerrymandering by a group of scholars (King et al. 2006), as in the case of *LULAC v. Perry* (2006), can be derived from the equal protection of voters. This provides a constitutional grounding for the measures of partisan bias used in this book.

2

The Jurisprudence of Districting

This chapter covers the jurisprudence concerning the drawing of districts for the U.S. House of Representatives. The Supreme Court in *Vieth v. Jubelirer* (2004) found that the courts could not intervene in districting on the grounds of partisan gerrymandering (that is, these cases are "nonjusticiable") because no standards exist for deciding them. Four justices wished to declare partisan gerrymandering complaints nonjusticiable on principle, while a fifth concurred that there was no satisfactory existing standard, although one might be found in the future. As we argued in the previous chapter, this is a decision of profound political and constitutional importance.

In this chapter, we analyze the *Vieth* decision in the context of a history of jurisprudence on districting, going back to the "one person, one vote" cases of the 1960s that followed *Baker v. Carr* (1962). In contrast to Justice Scalia, who argued in *Vieth v. Jubelirer* (2004, 290) that the one-person, one-vote standard is irrelevant to partisan gerrymandering cases, we will argue that in terms of both its judicial doctrine and political effects, *Vieth v. Jubelirer* is the latest round in a constitutional struggle over limits of states' congressional districting practices going back at least to the 1960s. Indeed, in Chapter 7, we will argue that this dispute can actually be traced all the way back to the Federal Convention of 1787. The significance of the one-person, one-vote cases of the 1960s that followed the *Baker* decision was that they severely constrained the power of state legislatures to manipulate House elections by drawing the districts (see Issacharoff et al. 2012). This was appropriately described as the "Reapportionment Revolution" (see Cox and Katz 2002; Ansolabehere and Snyder 2008). The districting plans that were overturned in these cases were examples of malapportionment – districts that varied widely in population. During this period, the Court found that vote dilution of any kind – weighting votes differently based on where someone lives – was unacceptable and unconstitutional. Nevertheless, these cases did not entirely resolve the justiciability of gerrymandering. Although the Supreme Court's rulings in *Wesberry v. Sanders* (1964a) and *Reynolds v. Sims* (1964b) explicitly forbade malapportionment and vote dilution, they did not explicitly mention gerrymandering. Of course, if the gerrymandering of districts by state legislatures were allowed, banning malapportionment would have little effect. As we will see in Chapter 3, if a state legislature is free to gerrymander, it can produce extremely biased results, even if all districts have the same population.

Although the Court did not rule on a complaint of partisan gerrymandering for a considerable time, there was, as we noted in the last chapter, little evidence of egregious partisan gerrymandering in the redistricting rounds following *Wesberry*. State legislatures, it seemed, did not try to use gerrymandering to regain the power they had before malapportionment was outlawed. It was not until *Davis v. Bandemer* (1986a) that the Court confirmed that the principles established in the one-person, one-vote cases applied to partisan gerrymandering. Thus we will argue that the effect of the Court's decision in *Vieth v. Jubelirer* (2004) is not simply to effectively overturn the decision in *Davis v. Bandemer* (1986a); rather, it is to fatally undermine the Court's egalitarian intent in *Wesberry v. Sanders* (1964a) and *Reynolds v. Sims* (1964b). Of course, it did not overturn the finding in these cases that malapportionment is unconstitutional. However, it denied that the logic in these cases could be extended to partisan gerrymandering. Thus the *Vieth* ruling gave the very powerful tool of partisan gerrymandering back to state legislatures. As a result, states today are free to use this tool to undermine the values of political equality and majority rule that the *Wesberry* and *Reynolds* rulings so strongly defend.

Although it seeks to overturn *Davis v. Bandemer* (1986a), in which the Court previously outlined standards for challenging partisan gerrymanders, the *Vieth* ruling does not take us back to the situation immediately prior to *Bandemer*. Prior to 1986, if a state legislature had attempted an egregious partisan gerrymander of its U.S. House districts, it is quite likely that the Supreme Court would have struck it down – in any case, the state legislature would have to worry about this. After *Vieth*, there is no such possibility, and states now have more power to manipulate districts than at any time since 1964.

EARLY DISTRICTING AND PRE-*VIETH* JURISPRUDENCE

The Framers of the Constitution envisioned the House of Representatives representing the people directly, while the Senate would represent the states. In the Senate, prior to the passage of the Seventeenth Amendment, state governments were free to appoint representation in the method of their choosing. In contrast, the Constitution mandates that the people directly choose U.S. House representatives through regular elections, bypassing the state legislatures. However, the Constitution does not specify *how* congressional seats ought to be apportioned within states, and state legislatures assume primary authority over how elections to the House of Representatives are conducted in the absence of specific instruction from Congress.

The precise standards for apportioning seats in the House are outlined in Article 1, Section 2 of the Constitution, which states that "The actual Enumeration [of seats] shall be made within three Years after the first Meeting of the Congress of the United States, and within every subsequent Term of ten Years, in such Manner as they shall by Law direct." Section 4 further dictates that "The Times, Places and Manner of holding Elections for Senators and Representatives, shall be prescribed in each state by the Legislature thereof; but the Congress may at any time by Law make or alter such Regulations, except as to the Places of chusing Senators," while Section 5 holds that "Each House shall be the Judge of the Elections, Returns and Qualifications of its own Members." These stipulations ultimately empower Congress to oversee the logistics of House elections and to approve states' congressional districting plans. Nevertheless, Congress has rarely acted in a concerted way to exercise these powers (not least because the existing electoral rules worked fine, as the members of Congress were elected under those rules). On a few scattered occasions, it provided instructions for redistricting, yet these instructions were limited in that they only applied to specific reapportionment cycles. In the 1842 Apportionment Act, for instance, Congress mandated that districts be "composed of contiguous territory" (491), while the 1872 Apportionment Act required "as nearly as practicable an equal number of inhabitants" per district (28). Similarly, the Apportionment Act of 1911 required that districts adhere to the principles of equality, contiguity, and compactness. Thus, for much of its history, Congress has had little to say about how districts ought to be drawn by the states. As a consequence, before the Court's intervention in the 1960s, state governments were free to use their assumed authority over the conduct of elections to manipulate

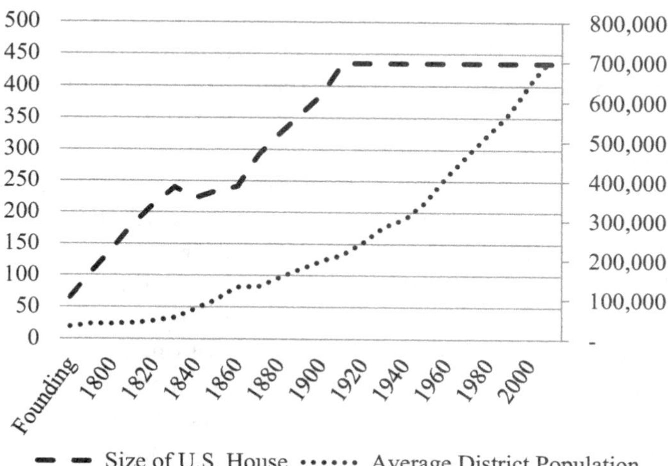

FIGURE 2.1. Population growth and expansion of U.S. House of Representatives. *Source*: U.S. Census Bureau

outcomes for partisan advantage and to disenfranchise minority groups. Disaffected citizens had few options for challenging such maps other than through these very electoral routes.

Population Growth and Malapportionment

Historically, congressional apportionment has been a contentious process, particularly in states that have lost a House district as a result of declining population growth and are forced to draw new congressional boundaries. However, before the twentieth century, the scope of districting conflict was tempered by the gradual expansion of the size of the U.S. House (see Figure 2.1). Over the course of the nineteenth century, as new states were admitted into the Union and the nation's population grew, House membership nearly tripled from 141 members after the 1800 apportionment to 386 by the 1900 apportionment (see Butler and Cain 1992).

Congressional apportionment began to take on a higher profile after Congress imposed a ceiling on the number of representatives serving in the House, set at 435, following the 1910 Census. This event had two important implications for congressional representation. First, because the size of the U.S. House was capped, the average district rapidly expanded in size over time as a result of population growth. At the outset of the twentieth century, the average district had approximately 200,000 residents, but by 1960, the average district size nearly doubled to more than 400,000 (see Figure 2.1). This expansion led to broad disparities between the large and small states in terms of the number of residents per congressional representative (Ladewig and Jasinski 2008). Second, within many states, the increase in district size did not impact all districts equally. Because growth in cities outpaced growth in rural areas for much of the twentieth century, many urban districts grew considerably larger than rural districts, particularly in states that did not periodically redraw their congressional maps. By the 1960s, the populations within a congressional district could vary by a factor of one to three (see *Wesberry v. Sanders* 1964). This had profound political effects – for example, the overrepresentation of rural, white voters was one of the foundations of the one-party, Democratic South – and led to newfound questions about the fairness of "malapportioned" districts in states' congressional maps.

Early Districting Challenges

With Congress unwilling to intervene in the states' districting practices, the courts became the primary venue for challenging the legality of malapportionment. However, from the Court's perspective, the judiciary was not the proper forum for resolving such matters. Historically, the Court refused to adjudicate redistricting complaints, arguing that the "political question" doctrine prohibited its involvement in such cases because districting was a fundamentally political affair. Although early apportionment challenges would ultimately fail to force revisions of district maps, they did initiate a dialogue within the Court on the appropriate means for addressing such challenges and provided the blueprint for challenging unfair districting practices through Equal Protection challenges.

In the case of *Wood v. Broom* (1932b), the Court initiated the jurisprudential discussion of redistricting when it considered a technical challenge to Mississippi's congressional redistricting plans. The plaintiff had argued, in part, that the new districts did not comply with the Apportionment Act of 1911 that required congressional districts to be compact, contiguous, and as equal in population as practicably possible. In its decision, the Court avoided ruling on the merits of the redistricting challenge, sidestepping an opportunity to clarify the justiciability of redistricting complaints. Instead, the Court determined that the requirements of the

Reapportionment Act of 1929 "as to the compactness, contiguity and equality in population of districts did not outlast the apportionment to which they related" (1932b, 8). The redistricting requirements pertained only to the 1910 apportionment cycle. Because the Apportionment Act of 1929 did not specifically contain these requirements, Congress had effectively repealed them.

The exploration of proper districting jurisprudence began in earnest in *Colegrove v. Green* (1946, 549). In *Colegrove*, a citizen of Illinois sought an injunction against the state holding an election because the congressional districts lacked geographic compactness and population parity. The Court noted that the relief was sought without also seeking a declaration of the provisions of the state law as invalid. The Court framed the relief sought as a request to revise a congressional district for the state of Illinois. The Court relied on *Wood* and rejected the claim for relief, stating simply that the legal merits for the case were settled in *Wood* (1946, 552). The Court held that the Illinois districts as drawn were not unconstitutional because existing laws did not require compactness, geographic continuity, or equality in population. In the plurality opinion, Justice Frankfurter, joined by Reed and Burton, argued that the Court should not engage the topic because the inherently political question presented for consideration precluded involvement by the Court. He wrote, "The remedy for unfairness in districting is to secure state legislatures that will apportion properly, or to invoke the ample powers of Congress" (1946, 556). Frankfurter explained the rationale for this approach:

> We are of the opinion that the appellants ask of this Court what is beyond its competence to grant... It has refused to do so (intervene) because due regard for the effective working of our Government revealed this issue to be of a peculiarly political nature, and therefore not... for judicial determination... This is not an action to recover for damage because of the discriminatory exclusion of a plaintiff from rights enjoyed by other citizens. The basis of the suit is not a private wrong, but a wrong suffered by Illinois as a polity. In effect, this is an appeal to the federal courts to reconstruct the electoral process of Illinois in order that it may be adequately represented in the councils of the Nation... It is hostile to a democratic system to involve the judiciary in the politics of the people. (1946, 552–554)

With the *Colegrove* case, the Court embraced the idea that redistricting issues are of a political nature and thus beyond the jurisdiction of the Supreme Court. However, the case also set the initial parameters of debate about whether in fact redistricting was a nonjusticiable issue.

Justice Rutledge concurred in the result only. He argued that the Court could in fact intervene under appropriate circumstances in part because of the jurisprudence of *Smiley v.* Holm (1932a) (time, place, manner of election provisions are justiciable). Rutledge wrote, "Assuming the controversy is justiciable, I think the cause is so delicate a character . . . that the jurisdiction should be exercised only in the most compelling circumstances" (1946, 564). Justice Black dissented and relied on equality-driven arguments. Black began with a restatement of the facts he believed were essential to his analysis. He recounted the appellants' claims as:

> . . . citizens and voters of Illinois, live in congressional election districts, the respective populations of which range from 612,000 to 914,000. Twenty other congressional election districts have populations that range from 112,116 to 385,207. In seven of these districts the population is below 200,000. The Illinois Legislature established these districts in 1901 on the basis of the Census of 1900. The Federal Census of 1910, of 1920, of 1930, and of 1940, each showed a growth of population in Illinois and a substantial shift in the distribution of population among the districts established in 1901. But up to date, attempts to have the State Legislature reapportion congressional election districts so as more nearly to equalize their population have been unsuccessful. (1946, 566–567)

Justice Black's view of the facts led him to make the following legal conclusions:

> The assertion here is that the right to have their vote counted is abridged unless that vote is given approximately equal weight to that of other citizens. It is my judgment that the District Court had jurisdiction; that the complaint presented a justiciable case and controversy; and that appellants had standing to sue, since the facts allege that they have been injured as individuals . . . The complaint attacked the 1901 Apportionment Act as unconstitutional and alleged facts that the Act denied appellants the full right to vote and the equal protection of the laws. (1946, 568)

Black further reasoned that

> While the Constitution contains no express provision requiring that congressional election districts established by the States must contain approximately equal populations, the constitutionally guaranteed right to vote, and the right to have one's vote counted clearly imply the policy that state election systems, no matter what their form, should be designed to give approximately equal weight to each vote cast . . . The purpose of . . . (Art. I and Sec. 2 of Art. XIV) is obvious: it is to make the votes of the citizens of the several States equally effective in the selection of members of Congress. It was intended to make illegal a nationwide "rotten borough" system as between the States. The policy behind it is broader than that. It prohibits, as well, congressional "rotten boroughs" within the States, such as the ones here involved. (1946, 570)

The immediate consequence of the Court's decision in *Colegrove*, which was reaffirmed in *South v. Peters* (1950), was that the Court would continue to treat districting as an inherently political matter beyond its purview. Nevertheless, the case established terms for debating the justiciability of districting matters in future cases, and Justice Rutledge's concurring opinion left open the possibility that future challenges to district plans could be pursued through alternative legal arguments under "compelling circumstances."

One such challenge occurred in a suit against a Tuskegee, Alabama, districting plan. In *Gomillion v. Lightfoot* (1960), the Court indicated that in certain circumstances, electoral districts could be challenged on the grounds of improper discrimination. The fundamental claim in the case was that the city of Tuskegee had been redrawn (from a square to a twenty-eight-sided figure) for the express purpose of disenfranchising African Americans. The redrawn district was designed and implemented to deprive African Americans of the benefits of municipal residency and deprive them of the preexisting municipal vote.

A lower court dismissed the claim of improper electoral districting, claiming it had no authority to hear the case. In reversing the lower court's ruling, the Supreme Court ruled on a claim "which amply alleges a claim of racial discrimination." In holding that the federal courts did indeed have jurisdiction over such a claim, Justice Frankfurter noted that this case was not a congressional election districting case, determining that the rights of a state to redistrict are limited by the Fifteenth Amendment's guarantee that a citizen's right to vote will not be abridged on racial grounds.

> Legislative control of municipalities, no less than other state power, lies within the scope of relevant limitations imposed by the United States Constitution.... such power, extensive though it is, is met and overcome by the Fifteenth Amendment to the Constitution of the United States, which forbids a State from passing any law which deprives a citizen of his vote because of his race. (1960, 344–345)

Frankfurter grounded the *Gomillion* analysis in a violation of the Fifteenth Amendment and thereby avoided the political question doctrine constraints he had crafted in *Colegrove*. Justice Douglas joined the opinion of the Court, but expressly adhered to the reasoning from Black's dissent in *Colegrove*. Frankfurter expressly distinguished the improper state behavior in *Gomillion* from proper state behavior and organic, or naturally arising, dilution in *Colegrove*. Although the Court appeared divided on the fundamental issue of justiciability and districting, the stage was set for the Court to revisit the debate from *Colegrove*.

DEBATE OVER JUSTICIABILITY: POLITICAL QUESTION VERSUS EQUAL PROTECTION

Since the *Colegrove* decision in 1946, the Supreme Court has wrestled with the question of justiciability and political gerrymandering, and the argument for and against jurisdiction has evolved. The cases from 1946 to 2004 indicate that the Supreme Court has determined: (1) political gerrymandering is a nonjusticiable political question; (2) in certain circumstances (i.e., race), political gerrymandering is a justiciable civil rights issue; (3) sometimes, even non–race-based gerrymandering issues may be justiciable providing the claim meets certain enumerated criteria; (4) strictly political gerrymandering issues are justiciable; and (5) strictly political gerrymandering issues are not justiciable but may be in the future, depending on certain technological advances. The germane cases represent a continuing dialogue among the members of the Court. One faction of the Court embraces the underlying jurisprudence behind the egalitarian and democratic reforms of the 1960s, while another faction of the Court prefers an analysis dependent on the political question doctrine.

Population Equality

The landmark case *Baker v. Carr* (1962) brought the debate from *Colegrove* back to the Court, which arrived at the opposite conclusion. In *Baker*, the Court overturned the *Colegrove* ruling and established that a malapportionment claim could be justiciable as an Equal Protection challenge. The plaintiffs in the case, a group of citizens who resided in an urban part of Tennessee, sought an injunction against the state's legislative district map on the grounds that it unfairly discriminated against urban residents.

As required by state law, districts were to be redrawn every ten years based on the federal census. The state of Tennessee had not redrawn the electoral districts since the census of 1901. Baker alleged the population had grown such that Shelby County residents outnumbered residents of rural districts by as much as ten to one. Thus, the value of a single rural resident's vote was equal to that of ten urban citizens. According to Baker, this disparity failed to grant him "equal protection of the laws" as guaranteed under the Fourteenth Amendment. The legislative inaction amounted to unconstitutional discrimination by the state because it had led to the "debasement" of urban citizens' votes, which had become effectively less powerful than the votes of rural residents (1962, 194).

A lower court refused to hear the challenge and ruled that the court system did not have authority over reapportionment challenges and therefore lacked jurisdiction. Although the Court agreed that the plaintiffs had demonstrated that the Tennessee legislature was in "clear violation of the state constitution," it was ultimately not empowered to offer redress (179 F.Supp. 827–828). The Court overturned the lower court's ruling, finding that it did in fact have authority to hear the case. The foundational complaint of vote dilution as a result of the state's failure to reapportion electoral boundaries was found to be a denial of equal protection. The cause of action presented a justiciable constitutional claim based on the Fourteenth Amendment's guarantee of equal protection. In holding reapportionment issues are justiciable, Justice Brennan presented a six-pronged test by which political question cases are to be determined (1962, 217):

1. "Textually demonstrable constitutional commitment of the issue to a coordinate political department"; as an example of this, Brennan cited issues of foreign affairs and executive war powers, arguing that cases involving such matters would be "political questions";
2. "A lack of judicially discoverable and manageable standards for resolving it";
3. "The impossibility of deciding without an initial policy determination of a kind clearly for nonjudicial discretion";
4. "The impossibility of a court's undertaking independent resolution without expressing lack of the respect due coordinate branches of government";
5. "An unusual need for unquestioning adherence to a political decision already made";
6. "The potentiality of embarrassment from multifarious pronouncements by various departments on one question."

Upon a determination that the issues in the case did not satisfy the conditions necessary to find a political question that could deprive the Court of jurisdiction, the Court then held that because one of the bases of the claim was the Equal Protection Clause of the Fourteenth Amendment, the case did fall within the subject matter jurisdiction of the Court. The Court unambiguously held that the claimed denial of equal protection under the Fourteenth Amendment presented a justiciable constitutional cause of action.

Justice Frankfurter vigorously disagreed in a lengthy dissent. Frankfurter reiterated his argument from *Colegrove* and asserted that what *Baker* presented was clearly a political question and, accordingly, the case should have been resolved through legislative measures. "Plaintiffs here invoked the right to vote and have their vote counted, but they are permitted to vote and their vote is already counted. The complaint being made here is that their vote is not powerful enough. They should seek relief in the legislative system, not the courts" (*Baker v. Carr* 1962, 300).

The Court's ruling in Baker established clear criteria for identifying "political questions" and opened the door for future judicial challenges of malapportionment. One such challenge, *Wesberry v. Sanders* (1964a), provided further clarification for how legislative apportionment challenges could be pursued. James Wesberry Jr., a resident of Georgia, challenged the state's congressional district maps, in which some districts had as many as three times as many residents as others. The Court agreed that the maps violated the Equal Protection Clause under the Fourteenth Amendment by unfairly and arbitrarily favoring the votes of some residents over others. After affirming its decision in *Baker*, the Court ruled the suit was justiciable and held that the Equal Protection Clause, in conjunction with Article 1, Section 2 of the Constitution, implies that citizens are entitled to equality in representation. Writing for the majority, Justice Black reasoned that because "population . . . was to be the basis of the House of Representatives," then equal population was a necessary requisite of fair redistricting:

> To say that a vote is worth more in one district than in another would not only run counter to our fundamental ideas of democratic government, it would cast aside the principle of a House of Representatives elected "by the People," a principle tenaciously fought for and established at the Constitutional Convention. (1964a, 8)

Black's opinion suggested that even seemingly insignificant cases of malapportionment would not pass constitutional muster. "While it may not be possible to draw congressional districts with mathematical precision, that is no excuse for ignoring our Constitution's plain objective of making equal representation for equal numbers of people the fundamental goal for the House of Representatives" (1964a). Thus, the decision in *Wesberry* established a new principle for legislatures drawing congressional districts: "one person, one vote." In the context of the

Court's earlier ruling in *Reynolds v. Sims* (1964b), in which it struck down an Alabama state legislative districting map with malapportioned districts, the Court signaled that legislative districts at both the state and federal levels would need to adhere to the principle of equality. Thereafter, state legislatures drawing congressional districts had to strive for maximum population equality or risk possible intervention from the courts.

The Voting Rights Act and Racial Gerrymandering

A major consequence of the *Baker* and *Wesberry* rulings was that state legislatures would be required to redraw congressional boundaries every ten years following reapportionment to ensure compliance with the new population equality standard. This development, combined with the passage of the Voting Rights Act in 1965 (VRA), marks a turning point in districting jurisprudence when the Court began to treat "partisan gerrymandering" and "racial gerrymandering" separately. Partisan gerrymandering involved the deliberate manipulation of district boundaries to achieve partisan ends. Until the decision in *Davis v. Bandemer* (1986a), the Court had not explicitly stated that such cases were justiciable, although it was clear that the Court would not accept political motivation as a compelling reason for violating the one-person, one-vote principle. Racial gerrymandering, on the other hand, occurred when mapmakers improperly applied race as a criterion for drawing district maps that segregated residents – something specifically forbidden by the Voting Rights Act. Although from the standpoint of mapmakers, each type of gerrymandering could be used to manipulate political outcomes, from the Court's perspective, racial gerrymandering would be treated as a unique issue, as it was expressly proscribed by federal law.

The Voting Rights Act prohibited any voting practices that denied or diluted the right to vote based on race or color. Specifically, Section 2 of the 1965 act states, "No voting qualifications or prerequisite to voting, or standard, practice, or procedure shall be imposed or applied by any State or political subdivision to deny or abridge the right of any citizen of the United States to vote on account of race or color." In 1975, this was amended to include language discrimination against non-English speakers. Any new districting plan, which now had to be adopted every ten years following the Census, would count as a new procedure and thus would be covered by the act. In addition, Section 5 of the Voting Rights Act requires that states with a history of discriminatory voting laws need to have any changes to voting qualification or procedures (which includes districting) precleared by a federal court.

Although racially discriminatory districting practices had occurred long before the 1960s, the enactment of the VRA in particular had major consequences for redistricting and race. The passage of the VRA dramatically increased political participation among blacks in the South. This provided new opportunities for state legislatures to draw racially homogenous districts in order to achieve politically advantageous ends. Yet state legislatures were constrained by subsequent amendments to the VRA in the 1970s and 1980s that empowered the Justice Department to prevent the states from producing district maps with racially discriminatory effects. Since then, the challenge for the Court has been to clarify when and how race ought to be taken into consideration by mapmakers. On the one hand, deliberate consideration of race facilitates minority representation and leads to "majority-minority" districts (districts where most of the residents are in a minority group). On the other hand, obvious attempts to weaken minority voters by "packing" them into irregular districts undermines minority representation and amounts to blatant discrimination.

Since the 1980s, the Court has considered several racial gerrymandering challenges in which it has clarified the conditions under which states can use race as a primary factor in drawing district boundaries. The Court interpreted the act as originally written as prohibiting practices with discriminatory intent, as opposed to discriminatory effects. In *Mobile v. Bolden* (1980), black residents of Mobile, Alabama, filed suit against the city, alleging that the city's use of "at-large" districts in city government amounted to unfair dilution of black residents' votes. The plaintiffs argued that Mobile's electoral system violated Section 2 of the VRA's prohibition of racially discriminatory voting laws insofar as it prevented black residents from influencing election outcomes and thus diluted the power of their votes compared to those of white residents. In writing the opinion of the plurality, Justice Steward held that Congress' intent in the VRA was identical to that of the Fifteenth Amendment, which does not "entail the right to have Negro candidates elected," but rather "prohibits only purposefully discriminatory denial or abridgment by government of the freedom to vote" on the basis of race (1980, 65). Because black voters in Mobile were successful in registering and voting in municipal elections, no violation of the VRA or Fifteenth Amendment had occurred.

In interpreting the Fifteenth Amendment as prohibiting only "purposeful" discrimination by lawmakers, the Court established intent as the legal standard for future cases of racially discriminatory vote dilution. Racial gerrymander challengers would need to demonstrate that lawmakers acted *deliberately* in diluting the votes of minority citizens. This created a high bar for future legal challenges and undermined the VRA as a legal remedy for combatting racial discrimination in the redistricting process.

Congress responded to the *Bolden* ruling by passing a 1982 amendment to the VRA that explicitly lowered the standards for challenging district maps on the basis of racial discrimination. The amendment included new language in Section 2 of the act to explicitly prohibit district maps with discriminatory effects. Future racial gerrymandering challenges simply needed to demonstrate that districting plans produce discriminatory outcomes rather than discriminatory intent. The Court ultimately confirmed the constitutionality of the new standard in *Mississippi Republican Executive Committee v. Brooks* (1984).

In the case of *Thornburg v. Gingles* (1986b), the Court produced standards of evidence for adjudicating challenges to racial gerrymandering under the Voting Rights Act. The case dealt with a challenge to six multimember districts and one single-member district in the North Carolina State House and Senate (although the appeal brought by the Attorney General of North Carolina that reached the Supreme Court dealt with only five of the multimember districts). The plaintiffs alleged that these districts restricted the ability of African-American voters to elect candidates of their choice. The Court affirmed the finding of the federal district court that the five districts did indeed violate Section 2 of the Voting Rights Act. However, the Court differed in its reasoning somewhat to the lower court. Writing for the Court, Justice Brennan (1986b, 50–51) laid out a three-part test: to prove vote dilution it was necessary to show that (1) there was a minority community geographically compact enough to make a majority-minority district; (2) this community is politically cohesive; and (3) there is bloc voting by the majority community that will generally prevent the minority from electing candidates of its choice. These standards were laid out in the context of a discussion of vote dilution in multimember districts; however, footnote 16 (1986b, 50) applies these standards to challenges to single-member districts.

As Grofman and Handley (1991) demonstrate, enforcement of the VRA and the success of Section 2 challenges in the Courts contributed to the proliferation of majority-minority districts after the 1990 redistricting cycle. Combined with the law's Section 5 "preclearance" requirements that gave the Justice Department the power to review changes in the voting laws of several states, the new standards forced state lawmakers to expand minority representation through redistricting in order to avoid potential legal challenges.

These standards were subsequently modified after the 1990 redistricting cycle when the Court heard *Shaw v. Reno* (1993). When North Carolina gained a congressional district after the 1990 apportionment cycle, the state legislature drew a map with only one majority-minority district. During preclearance, the Justice Department objected to the redistricting plan, asserting that the state needed to draw a second majority-minority district to comply with the Section 5 requirements of the VRA. Legislators subsequently drew a second district, but its boundaries were irregular, and the district lines cut across multiple geographic and political boundaries. White residents sued the state, arguing that the district shape was so irrational that it illustrated a deliberate attempt by the General Assembly to segregate voters on the basis of race and signified an unconstitutional gerrymander in violation of the Equal Protection Clause. In a 5–4 decision, the Court sided with the residents and held that racial gerrymandering suits could be pursued through Equal Protection challenges and that the maps would be subject to "heightened" scrutiny by the courts. The *Shaw I* decision was upheld in the Court's subsequent ruling in *Miller v. Johnson* (1995), where the Court heard a similar challenge to Georgia's congressional map brought by white voters. Writing for the majority, Justice Kennedy reaffirmed the Court's ruling in *Shaw I* and held that in future Equal Protection challenges to district maps that included irregularly shaped majority-minority districts, the states would be subjected to the standard of strict scrutiny.

The Court's decisions in *Shaw I* and *Johnson* appeared at once an advance and a setback for minority representation (see Lublin 1997 for a discussion of this "paradox"). On the one hand, insofar as the Court interpreted the Fourteenth Amendment as prohibiting deliberate discrimination on the grounds of race, the decision on its face appeared to place substantive representation of minorities above purely descriptive representation achieved through the creation of majority-minority districts. As Justice O'Connor suggested in *Shaw I*:

> A reapportionment plan that includes in one district individuals who belong to the same race, but... have little in common but the color of their skin, bears an

> uncomfortable reference to political apartheid. It reinforces the perception that members of the same racial group – regardless of their age, education, economic status, or the community in which they live – think alike, share the same political interests, and will prefer the same candidates at the polls. (1993, 648)

On the other hand, the Court's decision in *Johnson* appeared to significantly hinder the Justice Department's ability to demand that states achieve minority representation through the drawing of majority-minority districts. The ruling, as Lublin (1997, 125) argues, created a great deal of ambiguity for lower courts in adjudicating redistricting challenges. "The Supreme Court's opinion in *Shaw v. Reno* was sufficiently vague that district courts around the South interpreted its meaning in widely different and contradictory ways. The lower courts had vociferously argued over the standard of proof for racial gerrymandering and the meaning of the . . . standard invoked by *Shaw I*."

Although the Court's new standard appeared to raise the bar for states in defending the drawing of majority-minority districts, the Court provided further clarification when it applied strict scrutiny to North Carolina's congressional map in *Shaw v. Hunt* (1996b) and a Texas plan in *Bush v. Vera* (1996a). In *Shaw II*, the Court ultimately upheld the state's original plan and its use of race as a motivating factor, ruling that the state had demonstrated a "compelling" interest in drawing the second majority-minority district and affirming that state lawmakers had taken the appropriate means of pursuing this objective. In *Vera*, the Court considered a similar challenge to a Texas congressional majority-minority district with an irregular shape. The Court affirmed that although such cases would entail strict scrutiny, Texas's compliance with Section 2 amounted to a "compelling" state interest. But unlike North Carolina's plan, the Texas plan was not "narrowly tailored" to meet these interests because its irregularly shaped district could have been redrawn more compactly while achieving these ends. Thus, the *Shaw II* and *Vera* rulings suggested that although the Court would hold states to the highest scrutiny levels when adjudicating Equal Protection challenges to district maps, states could cite preclearance by the Justice Department as a "compelling" interest for using race as a factor. Moreover, an irregularly drawn district could be construed as "narrowly tailored," provided there did not exist a more logical means of drawing the boundaries.

Ultimately, the effect of the Court's consideration of racial gerrymandering in the 1990s was that state lawmakers stopped intentionally increasing the number of majority-minority districts. Unlike the 1980s, when Congress and the courts gave state lawmakers an incentive to expand the number of majority-minority districts during redistricting, the Court's clarification of racial gerrymandering after the 1990 reapportionment cycle had the effect of freezing the number of majority-minority districts after the 2000 reapportionment cycle. The Court signaled that it was willing to accept existing gains to minority representation but that further expansion of majority-minority districts and the deliberate use of race as a factor in drawing irregularly shaped districts would not necessarily be tolerated.

More recent Court decisions seem to have reduced restrictions on state governments. In the cases of *Hunt v. Cromartie* (1999) and *Easley v. Cromartie* (2001), the Court approved a redrawn version of North Carolina's District 12, the district that was found to be unconstitutional in the case of *Shaw I* (1993). The new District 12 was very similar to the old one. However, the Court accepted the argument that the district was drawn for political, not racial, reasons and thus was potentially not unconstitutional. Of course, the district could have been challenged on grounds that it was an unconstitutional partisan gerrymander, but that would have required the plaintiffs to make a very different case, presumably arguing that the district violated the standards laid out in *Davis v. Bandemer* (1986a). In some ways, *Easley v. Cromartie* (2001) may be seen as foreshadowing *Vieth v. Jubelirer* (2004) in that it indicated the opinion of the Court moving towards the position that partisan gerrymandering is not unconstitutional. This would be misleading, however, as four of the five justices in the *Easley* majority were dissenters in the *Vieth* decision. The *Easley* decision, however, does emphasize the tendency we have already noted for the Court to treat racial and partisan gerrymandering as different phenomena.

The decision of the Supreme Court in *Shelby County v. Holder* (2013) rendered the preclearance requirement under Section 5 of the Voting Rights Act inoperable. Under Section 5 of the VRA, states with a history of voting rights violations (as defined in Section 4(b) of the VRA) need to obtain preclearance for new districting plans from a federal court. Shelby County, Alabama, a jurisdiction covered by this provision, sued, alleging that both Sections 4(b) and 5 of the VRA were unconstitutional. The Supreme Court found that the preclearance requirements in Section 5 were not unconstitutional. However, it struck down Section 4(b), which laid out the criteria for determining which jurisdictions needed to get preclearance. The Court found that Section 4(b) violated the rights of states based on historical violations (use of voter qualification tests between

1964 and 1972) that the Court did not consider relevant to current performance. As a result, Section 5 and the preclearance requirement appear to be currently unenforceable.

In Chapter 4, we consider the political consequences of majority-minority districting in greater detail. For the present analysis, however, we are primarily concerned with the Court's nuanced approach toward gerrymandering and its distinct treatment of racially motivated districting and politically motivated districting. As we shall see, after "one person, one vote" and districting equality, the Court began to address the justiciability of political gerrymandering and vote dilution.

The Evolution of Population Equality

In addressing the problem of racial gerrymandering, the Court was guided by the stipulations of the VRA and its subsequent amendments that explicitly prohibited districting practices that produced racially discriminatory outcomes. Congress passed no such legislation prohibiting partisan gerrymandering, and the Court's position against partisan gerrymandering was founded on the new standard of "one person, one vote" introduced by the *Wesberry* court. During the late 1960s and into the 1980s, the Court heard a number of apportionment challenges in which it clarified the justiciability of partisan gerrymandering and affirmed its prohibition of malapportionment. During this period, the Court indicated that even small population variations in districts were unacceptable if they appeared to be driven by underlying political motives.

In *Kirkpatrick v. Preisler* (1969), the Court upheld a lower court's decision to invalidate a Missouri congressional redistricting plan that had population deviations of roughly 5%. Whereas the state argued that the deviations were insignificant and small enough to be considered *de minimis*, the Court held that the "as nearly as practicable" language in the *Wesberry* opinion foreclosed any *de minimis* standard and that states had to achieve maximum population equality unless they could provide legitimate justification for the deviations. In short, the ruling signaled that the Court was unwilling to tolerate even minor population deviations and that politically gerrymandered maps could potentially be challenged through the one-person, one-vote principle. Similarly, in *Gaffney v. Cummings* (1973a), the Court heard a challenge to a Connecticut legislative redistricting plan that alleged that the state did not adhere to the one-person, one-vote standard. The plaintiffs argued that the maps effectively constituted an unconstitutional partisan gerrymandering because they sought to divide districts that would result in roughly proportionate political representation in the state legislature. The question before the Court was whether the plan was discriminatory to citizens because its drawers adhered to a "political fairness principle" when making the state legislative districts. In other words, did the one-person, one-vote standard require mapmakers to produce the most equal map or to produce a map that was sufficient but ultimately based on political motivations? The Court overturned a lower court's earlier decision that had invalidated the maps and confirmed that redistricting plans could, in theory, be overturned on the basis of partisan gerrymandering. Notwithstanding, it could not overturn a state plan simply because it sought to achieve "political fairness" or proportional political representation in the legislature. Writing for the majority, Justice White held that

> neither we nor the district courts have a constitutional warrant to invalidate a state plan, otherwise within tolerable population limits, because it undertakes, not to minimize or eliminate the political strength of any group or party, but to recognize it and, through districting, provide a rough sort of proportional representation in the legislative halls of the State. (1973a, 754)

With the rulings in *White v. Weiser* (1973b) and *Karcher v. Daggett* (1983), the Court further affirmed its willingness to entertain political gerrymandering challenges on the basis of the one-person, one-vote principle. No amount of population inequality, however insignificant, would be accepted if it appeared to be driven by underlying political motives. In *White v. Weiser* (1973b), the Court rejected an incumbent protection scheme as a legitimate justification for small population deviances in a Texas congressional map. The Court held that Texas's redistricting plan, with deviations of less than 5%, did not meet the standards set forth in *Kirkpatrick* that required maximum equality among districts when possible. Likewise, in *Karcher v. Daggett* (1983), the Court affirmed a district court's ruling that a New Jersey congressional redistricting plan was unconstitutional because its districts could have been made more equal. Although the plan had deviations of less than 1%, they "were not the result of a good-faith effort to achieve population equality" (1983, 727). Writing for the majority, Justice Brennan suggested that

> Any number of consistently applied legislative policies might justify some variance, including, for instance, making districts compact, respecting municipal boundaries, preserving the cores of prior districts, and avoiding contests between incumbent Representatives. As long as the criteria are nondiscriminatory . . . these are all legitimate objectives that on a proper showing could justify minor population deviations. (1983, 740–741)

In this regard, the Court foreclosed the possibility that political gerrymandering could be a legitimate justification for even trivial deviations in population equality. In the wake of the Court's intolerance for malapportionment and signaled willingness to hear claims of political gerrymandering, state legislatures drawing congressional maps were forced to recognize the potential for a judicial challenge as a credible threat.

Political Gerrymandering and Equal Protection

With the arrival of new, sophisticated information technologies in the 1980s, politicians had a powerful new tool for manipulating the redistricting process for political ends while complying with the one-person, one-vote standard. It soon became clear that although the Court had taken great strides to eradicate malapportioned districts, its solution would not necessarily prevent overtly partisan gerrymandering. As Butler and Cain (1992, 33–34) note:

> Legal doctrine on voting rights in the post-1962 period gradually moved beyond the equal right to the franchise and the right to an equally weighted vote to a third political right – the right to a meaningful or undiluted vote. This line of reasoning holds that, even if an individual has the right to vote, and even if that vote is equally weighted, the districting arrangement can still be unequal and hence unfair. In particular... if the lines are drawn in such a manner as to dilute the votes of one group and enhance the electoral prospects of another, then the gains of redistricting justice brought about by the malapportionment cases can be easily nullified.

If concerns for malapportionment were appeased by the Court's action in the wake of *Baker*, the era of vote dilution signaled that unfairness in the redistricting process was far from eradicated. Indeed, by the 1980s, it was unclear whether and how politically manipulated district maps could be challenged if they adhered to the population equality mandate. With its ruling in *Davis v. Bandemer* (1986a), the Court took the opportunity to address whether partisan gerrymandering was a justiciable claim separate from population equality and formulated guidelines for evaluating such challenges.

Bandemer arose after the Indiana legislature redrew its legislative districts based on a state census in 1980. In 1982, Indiana Democrats filed suit in federal court alleging the 1981 reapportionment constituted political gerrymandering with the intent to limit democratic voting power, thereby constituting a violation of equal protection under the Fourteenth Amendment. Prior to the case going to trial, in November 1982, an election was held under the districting plan. The result of that election was that Democratic candidates in the House of Representatives captured only 43 out of 100 seats despite receiving 51.9% of the popular vote. Democratic senatorial candidates garnered 53.1% of the votes yet won only thirteen of the twenty-five democratic seats. In Marion and Allen counties, the Democratic candidates received 46.6% of the popular vote, but only three candidates were seated out of the twenty-one available posts. The 1982 election results led the district court to hold that the new reapportionment plan was unconstitutional, resulting in "discriminatory vote dilution" (*Davis v. Bandemer* 1986a, 109). The district court struck the 1981 reapportionment plan and ordered preparation of a new plan. The Supreme Court reversed the decision and held that the standard set by the lower court in finding an unconstitutional vote dilution was so stringent as to be nearly impossible to meet. "[The district court] applied an insufficiently demanding standard in finding unconstitutional vote dilution" (*Davis v. Bandemer* 1986a, 113). The Supreme Court noted under the holding, "Political Gerrymandering, such as occurred in this case, is properly justiciable under the equal protection clause. Here, none of the identifying characteristics of a nonjusticiable political question are present" (*Davis v. Bandemer* 1986a, 109–110).

Justice O'Connor concurred with the Supreme Court's reversal, but on different grounds. In her concurring opinion, joined by Chief Justice Burger and Justice Rehnquist, she took up the Frankfurter mantel and argued against the Supreme Court's conclusion that the case was "properly justiciable under the Equal Protection Clause" (*Davis v. Bandemer* 1986a, 144). Justice O'Connor instead argued that the case constituted a nonjusticiable political question because "the Equal Protection Clause does not supply judicially manageable standards for resolving purely political gerrymandering claims, and no group right to an equal share of political power was ever intended by the Framers of the Fourteenth Amendment" (*Davis v. Bandemer* 1986a, 147). Justice O'Connor urged that by granting justiciability in this case, as well as any other political gerrymandering cases, the Court would start down a "slippery slope" which would eventually not only overburden the Court, but cause undue interference in the electoral process:

> Notwithstanding the plurality's threshold requirement of discriminatory effects, the Court's holding that political gerrymandering claims are justiciable has opened the door to pervasive and unwarranted judicial superintendence of the legislative task of apportionment. There is simply no clear stopping point to prevent the gradual evolution of a requirement of roughly proportional representation for every cohesive political group. (1986a, 147)

The argument that claims of partisan gerrymandering rests on an alleged group right to proportional representation is particularly notable. Justice O'Connor argues that the Fourteenth Amendment grants no such right to groups. As we shall see, these are precisely the arguments that Justice Scalia would use to argue against the majority rule principle in his opinion on *Vieth v. Jubelirer* (2004, 288). Like Justice Scalia, Justice O'Connor equated political parties to other social groups and argued that if political parties have a right to equal representation, then so does every other social group.

In Justice O'Connor's position, we can find echoes of Justice Frankfurter's vigorous dissent in *Baker* and his opinion in *Colegrove*. It is argued that the federal courts are no place for strictly political issues to be determined and that a diminution in voting power is a strictly political issue that has no constitutional basis that allows for judicial intervention. However, the "political question" argument evolved in Justice O'Connor's hands. In particular, Justice O'Connor did not seek to overturn the position in *Baker v. Carr* (*Davis v. Bandemer* 1986a, 147) that some districting issues – such as malapportionment – can in principle be justiciable. Indeed, O'Connor used the criteria laid down in *Baker v. Carr* for an issue being a political question. She argues that these criteria are not met by complaints of partisan gerrymandering. *Baker v. Carr* (1962, 217) actually gave six criteria that could make a case a political question, but Justice O'Connor (1986a, 148) focuses on the second – the "lack of judicially discoverable and manageable standards for resolving it." She argues,

> *Baker v. Carr* reaffirmed that a lawsuit will be held to involve a political question where there is "a lack of judicially discoverable and manageable standards for resolving it," or where "the impossibility of deciding without an initial policy determination of a kind clearly for nonjudicial discretion" is apparent. 369 U.S. at 369 U.S. 217. (1986a, 148)

She goes on to argue that such a standard exists in the case of malapportionment but not partisan gerrymandering. Thus it is possible to affirm the outlawing of malapportionment in *Reynolds v. Sims* (1964b) while refusing to extend the principles of this case to partisan gerrymandering. Thus she argues,

> The Court first found a workable constitutional standard for applying the Equal Protection Clause to state legislative districting in *Reynolds v. Sims*, *supra*. But, until today, the Court has not extended the principles of *Baker v. Carr* and *Reynolds v. Sims* to test a legislative districting plan on grounds of partisan political gerrymandering. (1986a, 148)

Although the *Bandemer* ruling left substantial ambiguities as to how discriminatory political gerrymandering might be identified, the Court left no doubt that it was a justiciable claim. Indeed, the ruling left open the possibility that claims of political gerrymandering that resulted in partisan vote dilution could be pursued in court, a reality that constituted a credible threat to state legislatures during the redistricting process. This fact is evidenced by the thirteen cases of vote dilution that reached the level of the Supreme Court in the eighteen years after the Court's decision in *Bandemer*. Although none of these cases resulted in a successful equal protection challenge of vote dilution through political gerrymandering, their impact on the redistricting process is not limited to the Court's *direct* action. Indeed, the mere possibility that a map might be overturned or even challenged in courts on the basis of political gerrymandering likely prevented state legislatures from taking liberties to maximize their partisan advantages when drawing maps. As McDonald (2004, 380) notes, the mere threat of judicial intervention can foster compromise among legislators.

> The potential for court action may structure any redistricting plan or compromise. In 2001–02, Illinois faced not only a divided state government, but also the loss of a congressional seat due to apportionment. Expectations were high that if legislative action failed, a Republican-friendly federal court would do congressional redistricting (Kieckhefer 2001). Rather than risk court action and the adoption of a Republican map, the Democratically controlled state House passed a bipartisan incumbent protection plan negotiated between United States Representatives Hastert (R) and Lipinski (D) that made a concession to Republicans by collapsing a Democratic seat.

Indeed, despite the obvious challenges of presenting a successful voter-dilution discrimination case to the Court, the possibility that the Court may *one day eventually* rule in favor of the plaintiff still existed.

THE *VIETH V. JUBELIRER* DECISION

After *Davis v. Bandemer*, the Supreme Court again revisited the issue of whether political gerrymandering constituted a nonjusticiable political question in *Vieth v. Jubelirer* (1986a, 148). Whereas *Bandemer* explicitly left the door open for judicial challenges of unconstitutional partisan gerrymandering, the Court's decision in *Vieth* removed the possibility that the Court would invalidate a districting plan on grounds of partisan gerrymandering. This was because a majority of the Court found that there are no suitable standards for adjudicating such claims. In effect, this means that partisan gerrymandering is nonjusticiable, in practice if not in principle.[1] This not only effectively overturned *Davis v. Bandemer* (1986a) but has created a loophole that has allowed state legislatures to create very biased districting plans that undermined the egalitarian intent of *Wesberry v. Sanders* (1964a) and *Reynolds v. Sims* (1964b).

Background

The partisan makeup of voters in Pennsylvania regularly leads to very competitive elections. For instance, in the five statewide elections on the 2000 ballot, the Democratic candidate's share of the vote for the different positions ranged from 43% to 57% (see *Erfer v. Commonwealth* 2002, 345–348). The 2000 Census revealed a decrease in the population of Pennsylvania that was sufficiently large that the state would lose two seats from its twenty-one-member House delegation. Although at the time of the re-districting the partisan makeup of the delegation – eleven Republicans and ten Democrats – reflected the generally split partisan makeup of the state, Republicans happened to control the governorship and both legislative houses. Since at least two seats were to be eliminated, the best-case scenario for Democrats might have been a redistricting scheme that forced four Democratic incumbents into two districts, thus shedding the state delegation of two democrats.

The Republican plan went well beyond a design to reduce the Democrats by two and instead structured a map that could lead to a Republican advantage of 13–6 or even 14–5 (*Vieth v. Pennsylvania* 2002, 672–674). In addition to placing two incumbent Democrats in each of two new districts, the Republican-friendly map moved one Democrat into an overwhelmingly Republican district and formed a new district with no incumbent, thereby creating an open seat. In a challenge to the Pennsylvania congressional plan, a group of Democrats sued the state, arguing the plan was a partisan gerrymander designed to weaken the influence of Democratic voters and create a structural advantage for Republican candidates.

Although a district court dismissed the plaintiffs' political gerrymandering claim, it considered the merits of their malapportionment complaint and found that the plaintiffs had "met their burden" in proving that

[1] It did not overturn *Davis v. Bandemer* in principle because only four justices agreed that partisan gerrymandering was nonjusticiable in principle. However, a fifth agreed that no suitable standard currently existed, making a successful complaint highly unlikely.

the state's district lines could have been drawn to provide more equality between the districts. "The evidence conclusively demonstrates the population deviation was avoidable" (195 F.Supp.2d, at 675). Indeed, the plaintiffs had presented a new map with zero population deviation that cut across fewer municipalities, demonstrating that it was indeed possible to produce a map with less inequality. Having established that the state had not met its obligation to achieve the least amount of inequality possible, the district court then followed the test set forth in *Karcher* to ascertain whether the deviation was justified by the state. The court rejected the defense's explicit reason – a desire to avoid splitting municipalities – because the plaintiffs had demonstrated that it was possible to produce a map with zero deviation that did not divide municipal boundaries. Having ruled the map unconstitutional, the Court then ordered the legislature to draw a new map. A new map was subsequently passed by the Republican legislature and signed into law by the Republican governor, but it too was challenged by the plaintiffs. After the lower court dismissed both the political gerrymandering and malapportionment charges, the plaintiffs appealed to the Supreme Court.

In their brief to the Court, the plaintiffs argued that the district court had incorrectly applied the *Bandemer* standard for evaluating their partisan gerrymandering challenge. The confusion and ambiguity of the language in the *Bandemer* opinion served to insulate grossly gerrymandered districts from judicial scrutiny.

> The problem . . . is that lower courts have gutted *Bandemer* by requiring plaintiffs – who are typically affiliated with one of the two major political parties – to show not only that a map thwarts majority rule but also that they have been "shut out" of the State's political processes, in the sense of being prevented from organizing and campaigning. . . . Such a rule effectively immunizes from scrutiny any gerrymander, no matter how extreme, unless it is accompanied by separate and independent constitutional violations. (21–22)

Citing an extensive body of research and the testimony of prominent political scholars, the plaintiffs argued that the Pennsylvania redistricting scheme violated the fundamental tenets of representation in Congress and "unquestionably distorts" the relationship between the people and the government through the intervention of the states in redistricting (29). Moreover, the plan was emblematic of the entire system of apportionment and redistricting in which partisan gerrymandering was endemic and eroded the foundations of democratic representation.

While "everyone's vote still counts," that truism does little to preserve democracy when a districting scheme is carefully and purposefully arranged to minimize the political power of those holding a particular viewpoint – even where that viewpoint is or becomes the majority view. (24)

Ultimately, the plaintiffs argued, this was a problem that only the Court could redress. What was necessary was a new standard for adjudicating partisan gerrymandering challenges.

The defendants, a group of Republican state officials, asserted that the plaintiffs had failed to meet the burden set forth in *Bandemer* because they did not demonstrate that the discrimination in question was intentional and that it resulted in an "actual discriminatory effect" beyond non-proportional representation. Echoing Justice O'Connor's concurring opinion in *Bandemer*, the defense argued that Democrats do not constitute a group entitled to protection under the umbrella of the Fourteenth Amendment.

A "mere lack of proportional representation will not be sufficient to prove unconstitutional discrimination" because an equal protection violation occurs only where "a history of disproportionate results appear[s] in conjunction with strong indicia of lack of political power and the denial of fair representation." (15)

Justice Scalia's Opinion: No Judicial Standard

In writing the plurality opinion of the Court, Justice Scalia agreed with the defense in noting that the plaintiffs had failed to meet the standards set forth in *Bandemer* but went as far as to question the very existence of a judicial standard for political gerrymandering challenges. In this opinion, he was joined by Justice O'Connor, Justice Thomas, and Chief Justice Rehnquist. Ultimately, Scalia's argument is that the Court erred in *Bandemer* and that political gerrymandering claims are inherently nonjusticiable because there are no appropriate standards to decide such claims.

In his opinion, Justice Scalia defines a question as "nonjusticiable" because it is "a political question" if it is the case that "the law is that the judicial department has no business entertaining the claim of unlawfulness – because the question is entrusted to one of the political branches or involves no judicially enforceable rights." Justice Scalia cites the six criteria laid out in *Baker v. Carr* (1962) and declares that it is the second that is of issue in this case, that is, "the lack of a judicially discoverable and manageable standard." To this end, Justice Scalia argues that the burden of proof is on those wishing to argue that a standard existed for adjudicating partisan gerrymander cases and that failure to present such a standard should be taken as evidence that no such standard exists. Justice Scalia turns first to the standard proposed by the plurality in *Davis v. Bandemer* (1986a). He notes that this standard could not command the support of a majority of the Court:

> Over the dissent of three Justices, the Court held in *Davis* v. *Bandemer* that, since it was "not persuaded that there are no judicially discernible and manageable standards by which political gerrymander cases are to be decided," 478 U.S., at 123, such cases *were* justiciable. The clumsy shifting of the burden of proof for the premise (the Court was "not persuaded" that standards do not exist, rather than "persuaded" that they do) was necessitated by the uncomfortable fact that the six-Justice majority could not discern what the judicially discernable standards might be. There was no majority on that point. (2004, 278–279)

Furthermore, Justice Scalia argues, the *Bandemer* plurality standard has proved incapable of effective application and thus fails to be a judicially manageable test. He appeals both to academic sources and to the fact that despite numerous challenges, no political gerrymandering case had successfully overturned a redistricting plan in the wake of *Bandemer*. "Eighteen years of essentially pointless litigation have persuaded us that *Bandemer* is incapable of principled application. We would therefore overrule that case, and decline to adjudicate these political gerrymandering claims" (2004, 306). Justice Scalia then turns to the standards proposed by the plaintiffs. Justice Scalia argues that the plaintiffs' proposed criteria fail to provide a judicially discoverable standard with regard to the effects of political gerrymandering. That is, the standards the plaintiffs propose do not have a basis in the violation of any constitutional right. Like the standards of the *Davis v. Bandemer* plurality, they require that there be both the intent to dilute the votes of a group and an actual effect on this group. The "effects prong" of the plaintiff's proposed standard was that voters had been "packed and cracked" in districts and that this prevented a majority of voters from electing a majority of representatives. Justice Scalia argues that, contrary to the assertions of the plaintiffs, the right of a majority of voters to elect a majority of representatives necessarily rests on a right to proportional representation (2004, 288). No such right exists in the U.S. Constitution – equal protection is guaranteed only for persons, not equally sized groups. Thus Justice Scalia argues that the majority rule principle cannot be derived from any constitutionally protected right:

> ... we question whether it is judicially discernible in the sense of being relevant to some constitutional violation. Deny it as appellants may (and do), this standard rests upon the principle that groups (or at least political-action groups) have a right to proportional representation. But the Constitution contains no such principle. It guarantees equal protection of the law to persons, not equal representation in government to equivalently sized groups. It nowhere says that farmers or urban dwellers, Christian fundamentalists or Jews, Republicans or Democrats, must be accorded political strength proportionate to their numbers. (2004, 288)

Even if the plaintiffs' standards were judicially discoverable, Justice Scalia argued that they would not be manageable (2004, 288). This is because there is no way of establishing that a group of partisans is a majority in a state. Justice Scalia rejected using the results of elections to statewide offices on grounds that these results vary. In Pennsylvania in the last election period, some offices were won by Democrats and some by Republicans. He cited a law review article arguing, "There is no statewide vote in the country for the House of Representatives or the state legislature. Rather, there are separate elections between separate candidates in separate districts, and that is all there is" (Lowenstein and Steinberg 1985, cited in 541 U.S. 289). Furthermore, he argued that even if we could identify a majority party, it would be impossible to ensure that it won a majority of the representatives while retaining a winner-take-all election system. That is to say, however you draw the districts, it is always possible for the party with the majority of the votes to not win a majority of the seats, as was the case with the Pennsylvania congressional delegation in 2000.

In addition to the "effects prong," Justice Scalia also expressed skepticism of the "intent prong" of the plaintiffs' standard, arguing that the use of the "predominant intent" test from racial gerrymandering cases does not necessarily show that there is a judicially discoverable standard for political gerrymandering cases (2004, 285). Given that he finds neither the *Davis v. Bandemer* standard nor the plaintiff's standard to be judicially discoverable or manageable, he concludes that there is no such standard and that partisan gerrymandering cases should be considered nonjusticiable.

In his concurring opinion, Justice Kennedy agreed with the plurality that no workable standard for adjudicating political gerrymandering cases existed but did not want to foreclose the possibility that such a standard might be found. He thus goes beyond simply affirming the district court decision based on *Davis v. Bandemer* (1986a). His position invalidates the standard proposed by the plurality in *Davis v. Bandemer*

(1986a) but does not overrule the finding that political gerrymandering cases are in principle justiciable.

The dissenting opinions of Justice Souter (joined by Justice Ginsberg) and Justice Stevens, while rejecting statewide claims of political gerrymandering, argued that there were workable standards for district-based claims and that the plaintiffs had met those criteria. Only Justice Breyer argued that statewide political gerrymandering could violate the Equal Protection Clause and then only in extreme cases where there was a risk of harm to basic democratic principles.

Reviving the "Political Question" Debate

In terms of judicial doctrine, Justice Scalia's opinion on *Vieth* can also be seen in the context of a controversy going back to the 1960s or further. Justice Scalia revived the "political question" doctrine in the context of districting – that is, the doctrine that such matters are a matter of political choice and should not be adjudicated by the courts. Justice Frankfurter had argued in *Colegrove v. Green* (1946) that districting per se ought to be considered a nonjusticiable political question, because the Constitution delegated responsibility for this to the state legislatures and Congress. Over Justice Frankfurter's dissent, the Court in *Baker v. Carr* (1962) found that districting was not necessarily a political question and that state legislatures had to respect citizen's constitutional rights when drawing districts. Justice Scalia, however, did not argue that districting *per se* was a political question but only that complaints of partisan gerrymandering were. The standards Justice Scalia used to decide whether something was a political question were not those used by Justice Frankfurter; rather, they were taken from *Baker v. Carr* (1962), the case in which the Court found that districting was not necessarily nonjusticiable. In particular, he uses the standard that a question should be considered nonjusticiable if there are no constitutionally discernable and manageable standards for deciding it. Thus *Vieth v. Jubelirer* (2004) returns to state legislatures much of the power to manipulate districts and engineer political outcomes that they had before *Baker v. Carr* (1962). The argument presented by Justice Scalia, however, is subtle. It does not overrule the finding in *Wesberry v. Sanders* (1964a) and *Reynolds v. Sims* (1964b) that malapportionment violates constitutional rights. It simply limits the argument presented in these cases so it cannot be applied to partisan gerrymandering, which allows state legislatures ample room to bias outcomes as they wish.

Thus Justice Scalia's opinion reestablishes the political question doctrine as a bulwark against claims of equal protection in cases of partisan gerrymandering. However, it does not overrule *Baker v. Carr* (1962) in this (*Vieth v. Jubelirer* 2004, 281). Indeed, it relies on the definition of "political question" from the Court's ruling on that case. In this he follows Justice O'Connor's concurring opinion on *Bandemer*. Indeed, like Justice O'Connor, he relies on the definition of a nonjusticiable political question given in the Court's opinion in *Baker*. In his opinion on *Vieth v. Jubelirer* (2004, 277), Justice Scalia defines a question as "nonjusticiable" or "a political question" if it is the case that "the law is that the judicial department has no business entertaining the claim of unlawfulness – because the question is entrusted to one of the political branches or involves no judicially enforceable rights." While providing background to the case, Justice Scalia notes that Article 1 §4 of the Constitution provides relief in the case of gerrymandering by allowing congressional intervention and notes various laws that Congress has made placing restriction on how States can draw districts (2004, 275). This seems reminiscent of Frankfurter's position that redistricting is intrinsically a political question because it is assigned by the Constitution to the state legislatures and Congress. However, Justice Scalia does not base the argument for nonjusticiability on the criterion that the Constitution explicitly assigns the issue to another branch. Presumably such an argument would be hard to reconcile with the fact that the Court has intervened in congressional districting in cases of malapportionment and racial gerrymandering. Indeed, if pursued, it would require overturning *Baker v. Carr* (1962).

Instead, Justice Scalia's argument for nonjusticiability is based on the lack of a suitable standard for adjudicating such cases. Justice Scalia cites six criteria laid out in *Baker v. Carr* (2004, 275) for an issue to be a nonjusticiable political question and declares that it is the second that is relevant to this case, that is, "the lack of a judicially discoverable and manageable standard." That is, there needs to be a standard that both can be derived from a constitutionally protected right and provides a workable test for determining whether partisan gerrymandering exists. Justice Scalia argued that both the plurality opinion in *Davis v. Bandemer* (1986a) and the plaintiffs in *Vieth* fail to provide such a standard. Given that it is evidently impossible to provide such a standard, Justice Scalia argues that such cases should be considered nonjusticiable.

Thus Scalia's argument turns the tables in a startling way. The definition of "political question" in the Court's opinion on *Baker v. Carr* restricted the use of the "political question" doctrine in earlier cases such as *Colegrove v. Green* (1946) and paved the way for the Court to consider equal protection claims in districting cases. Justice Scalia, however, is able to take these criteria and use them to reapply the political question doctrine to partisan gerrymandering cases.

Vieth v. Jubelirer (1986a) does not technically establish that political gerrymandering claims are nonjusticiable. Only four Justices joined in Justice Scalia's opinion. Justice Kennedy wrote a concurring opinion. However, he claimed that the current lack of a standard for determining gerrymandering was the current barrier to justiciability. In the future, should better metrics be available, such a claim might be justiciable:

> There are, then, weighty arguments for holding cases like these to be nonjusticiable; and those arguments may prevail in the long run. In my view, however, the arguments are not so compelling that they require us now to bar all future claims of injury from a partisan gerrymander. It is not in our tradition to foreclose the judicial process from the attempt to define standards and remedies where it is alleged that a constitutional right is burdened or denied. (2004, 309–310)

Nevertheless, if *Vieth v. Jubelirer* does not *technically* establish that partisan gerrymandering is a nonjusticiable political question, it does so in practice. Five justices agreed that all of the existing standards were inadequate. In a following case, *LULAC v. Perry* (2006), the Court had the opportunity to consider new standards and methods of measurement, but none was satisfactory to the majority. Therefore the task for plaintiffs is to find a new standard or convince a majority of the Court that an old standard should be rehabilitated. This seems an unlikely task, unless there is a significant change in the balance of opinion on the Court. As a result, complaints of partisan gerrymandering have little chance of success.

Confirming *Vieth*: *LULAC v. Perry*

The Supreme Court confirmed the position it took in *Vieth v. Jubelirer* (2004) two years later in the case *LULAC v. Perry* (2006). This case arose as a challenge to the redistricting plan Texas adopted in 2003. This redistricting followed the Republicans gaining control of the Texas House of Representatives in 2002. The plaintiffs claimed that the new districting plan was a partisan gerrymander, that having an extra redistricting in addition to the one required every ten years after the Census was evidence of partisan intent, and that some of the new districts violated the Voting Rights Act.

The Court rejected the claim that the new districts were an unconstitutional partisan gerrymander (2006, 447). However, writing for the Court in section II(a), Justice Kennedy states that the Court does not reconsider whether complaints of partisan gerrymandering are justiciable or not (2006, 414). Instead, he simply reiterates the position that "a plurality of the Court in *Vieth* would have held such challenges to be nonjusticiable political questions, but a majority declined to do so." Of course, *Vieth* made partisan gerrymandering cases *effectively* nonjusticiable, because Justice Kennedy agreed with the plurality that no adequate standard for judging such cases currently existed, although unlike the plurality, he did not deny the possibility that one might be found. In his *LULAC* opinion (section 2(b), not writing for the Court), he does not indicate that he has changed his mind on this matter.

By far the largest part of the Court's opinion on *LULAC* (section III) deals with the alleged Voting Rights Acts violations. The Court finds that the redrawing of District 23 is indeed a violation of the VRA, in that it took a district that was Latino majority and redrew Latino voters into another district so that District 23 was no longer Latino majority as measured in terms of voting-age population. The Court also found that creating a new Latino majority district (District 25, which was extremely irregularly shaped) in no way compensated for the violation in the case of District 23. The Court, however, found that the districts in the Dallas area did not violate the VRA.

An additional reason *LULAC v. Perry* is interesting to us is that the Court considered the partisan symmetry standard, which was proposed in an amicus brief by a group of professors of political science (King et al. 2006). This is the standard method used in political science to measure bias in electoral systems. As Justice Stevens points out in his *LULAC* opinion (2006, 467), it was used by expert witnesses for both the plaintiff and the defendant to assess the level of partisan bias of the Texas districting plan. It is the method we use in the next chapter to measure the partisan bias of the various states. Some commentators have argued that the positive comments about the partisan symmetry standards are very significant (see, for example, Grofman and King 2007; Stephanopoulos and McGee 2015).

The partisan symmetry standard is not mentioned in the opinion of the Court but only in the opinions of various justices. Thus it is certainly true that the Court has not rejected it, and future plaintiffs are free to try to convince the Court that it is an appropriate standard. Some of the justices are quite positive toward it. Justice Stevens (2006, 468) calls partisan symmetry "...a helpful (though certainly not talismanic) tool in this type of litigation." Justice Souter (joined by Justice Ginsberg) does not "rule out the utility of a criterion of symmetry as a test" and calls for further investigation (2006, 483–484). However, the key justice who needs to be persuaded for partisan symmetry to be accepted as a judicial standard is surely Justice Kennedy, given that four other justices have rejected the possibility of finding any standard and declared the issue a nonjusticiable political question. Justice Kennedy is far more skeptical of the symmetry standard. He states, "Without altogether discounting its utility in redistricting planning and litigation, I would conclude asymmetry alone is not a reliable measure of unconstitutional partisanship" (2006, 420). He also rejects the idea that the symmetry standard proposed in the amicus brief can "compensate for appellants' failure to provide a reliable measure of fairness" (2006, 420). He raises two main objections: the standard is based on conjectures about the geographical distribution of changes in the vote, and it does not provide a standard for deciding how much partisan bias is too much.

It is notable that the amicus brief does not make a case for the symmetry standard being a judicially required standard – it merely argues that it is an appropriate measure of partisan bias (King et al. 2006). Neither do the plaintiffs make a judicial case for the standard, as it is not the standard they are proposing. In Chapter 7, we explore whether such a case can be made – whether the symmetry standard can be logically derived from a constitutionally protected right. For now, however, we simply note that *LULAC v. Perry* (2006) left the position on partisan gerrymandering taken in *Vieth* intact. Partisan gerrymandering may be justiciable in principle, but it is clear that a majority of the Court is not convinced that any standard to adjudicate such cases currently exists.

CONCLUSION

In this chapter, we have considered the Court's position toward redistricting and the treatment of districting cases and the evolution of the political question doctrine. Justice Frankfurter in his opinion on *Colegrove v. Green* (1946) argued that all districting issues ought to be considered nonjusticiable because the Constitution gave authority for this to the state legislatures and Congress. In *Baker v. Carr* (1962), however, the Supreme Court ruled that this grant of authority was not unconditional – districting had to be done in a way that respected constitutionally protected rights. In *Baker*, the Court laid out a far more restricted set of criteria for a matter being a political question. This allowed the development of the one-person, one-vote jurisprudence that followed. In cases such as *Wesberry v. Sanders* (1964a) and *Reynolds v. Sims* (1964b), the Court established not only that malapportionment was unconstitutional but that so was any form of vote dilution. That is to say, the Court found that there was a right to equal treatment of all voters. This would appear to rule out vote dilution by political gerrymandering, and *Davis v. Bandemer* (1986a) confirmed this.

Justice O'Connor and Justice Scalia, however, have revived the political question doctrine to argue that partisan gerrymandering is nonjusticiable while at the same time accepting *Baker v. Carr* and the prohibition of malapportionment. While their arguments have considerable similarity with those of Frankfurter, they use the criteria for political questions from *Baker v. Carr*. That is, they argue that partisan gerrymandering is nonjusticiable because there is not a judicially discoverable and manageable standard for adjudicating these cases. This allows them to prevent the logic of the one-person, one-vote cases from being extended to partisan gerrymandering without having to invalidate the conclusion that malapportionment is unconstitutional. However, as we will see in Chapter 3, allowing partisan gerrymandering is quite enough to negate the egalitarian intentions of the Court in *Wesberry v. Sanders* (1964a) and *Reynolds v. Sims* (1964b).

3

Measuring Partisan Bias

We claimed in Chapter 1 that there was a sharp increase in partisan bias as a result of the redistricting that followed the 2010 Census. In this and the following two chapters, we provide systematic evidence for this and ask why this has happened.

Empirically, we have two main tasks. The first is to measure partisan bias at both the national and state level. This will allow us to test whether there has been a significant increase in partisan bias following the 2010 districting round. This is the task of this chapter. Assuming that there is partisan bias, the second task is to test various explanations of why the level of bias has changed and why bias occurs where it does. We have hypothesized that this is a thoroughly political phenomenon – state governments pursue partisan advantage when they are unconstrained by the courts. However, other explanations are possible. Chapter 4 considers nonpolitical alternative explanations. For example, it has been suggested that bias against the Democratic Party is inevitable because of demographic reasons, such as the fact that Democratic voters are concentrated in urban areas or the fact that it is necessary to draw majority-minority districts to comply with the Voting Rights Act. Chapter 5 considers political explanations for the patterns of bias we see. It asks whether we can explain the bias we observe in terms of the political motivations and capabilities of those in charge of drawing districts.

We make use of the established methodology for measuring partisan bias in districting (see Gelman and King 1994b). This has been widely applied, tested, and peer reviewed. It is based on the idea of symmetry: If the Democrats get 52% of the votes and win 60% of the seats as a result, then if the Republicans were to win 52% of the vote in the next election they should get 60% of the seats. We can measure how much a districting plan violates symmetry by estimating how many seats a party would win in the event of different levels of popular support. While popular support varies from election to election, the pattern of support between districts remains quite stable. Using this assumption, we can model how many seats the Democrats would get if the Democrats won (say) 55% of the vote and how much the Republicans would get if they won 55% of the vote. We can do this quite accurately, and we can also calculate our margin of error.

In this chapter, we are interested in this methodology purely as a means of measuring partisan bias and gerrymandering. In Chapter 6, we argue that this technology should indeed be used as a judicial standard to judge whether a districting plan is an unconstitutional partisan gerrymander. This methodology was in fact presented to the Supreme Court during *LULAC v. Perry* (2006) in an amicus brief by a group of political science professors (King et al. 2006). While it was favorably mentioned in some minority opinions, it was not adopted by the Court as a judicial standard. This, however, is not our concern in this chapter. Whether or not it is a suitable *judicial* standard, it is an appropriate *scientific* measure. We are not interested in this chapter in determining whether the Supreme Court should declare certain kinds of bias unconstitutional; rather, we are concerned with measuring how much partisan bias there is.

Using this methodology, we can determine how much partisan bias there is in the U.S. House in 2012 and how this compares with the level of bias from 2002 to 2010. We can do this both at the national level and at the level of individual states. We can also consider the relationship between partisan bias and the compactness of districts (whether districts are irregularly shaped). It is notable that some people have argued that the effects of partisan gerrymandering are likely to be limited because state legislators have to balance two competing goals–maximizing the number of seats their party wins and giving their incumbents safe seats (Cain 1985). If a party draws districts so that it wins many very close races, it will maximize its seats but will make its incumbents very insecure. Therefore, it will only gerrymander in a moderate way. We dispute this conclusion. There is indeed a trade-off between partisan advantage and incumbent protection. However, if a party is able to concentrate its opponents ruthlessly enough in packed districts (in which they win 80% of the vote or more), it can gain enough advantage to draw a large number of districts that are still relatively safe. We will see that this is precisely what has happened in numerous states.

PARTISAN GERRYMANDERING AND HOW TO MEASURE IT

Before laying out how partisan gerrymandering can be measured, it is necessary to understand how districting can create bias. We can start with a very simple example in which we have a state with ten districts and two parties (Party A and Party B). Let us assume that in a typical election, the state is evenly split between the two parties. We can then see how different ways of dividing the voters into districts can lead to very different results, even if the voters vote in exactly the same way.

Of course, there are constraints on how we can draw districts – we cannot simply assign any voter to any district. However, these constraints are less binding than we might think. Indeed, for every hypothetical example produced here, it is possible to find a real world example with the same pattern. The most basic constraint is that we cannot assign individual voters to districts. In practice, the smallest unit is the census block (about 300 homes). Laws passed by Congress require that districts must elect only one representative and be contiguous (it must be possible to get from any part of the district to any other part without leaving the district). The Supreme Court has declared that all districts must have approximately the same population (*Wesberry v. Sanders* 1964). Districting plans may also be struck down if they dilute the influence of a racial minority and thus violate either the Fourteenth Amendment or the Voting Rights Act. It is possible to challenge a districting plan on the grounds that it is partisan gerrymander, but since the Supreme Court's decision in *Vieth v. Jubelirer* (2004) such a challenge would be extremely unlikely to succeed. As a result, the drawers of districts (usually state legislatures) have a great deal of discretion.

A simple starting point is to consider a districting plan in which every district is a microcosm (politically speaking) of the entire state. Given that 50% of the state typically supports Party A, 50% of the voters in each district typically support Party A. What happens as the support for Party A in the state in a given election increases beyond 50% or falls below 50%? We will assume that Party A's increase or decrease in support is spread evenly across all districts. If Party A wins 1% more of the vote statewide, then Party A will win 1% more of the vote in every district (the technical name for this assumption is "uniform partisan swing"). Using this assumption, we can calculate how many seats Party A would win if it won 51% of the statewide vote or 52% or 53% and so on. Of course, if every district is a microcosm of the state and Party A won 51% of the statewide vote, this would mean it would win every district 51–49. If it

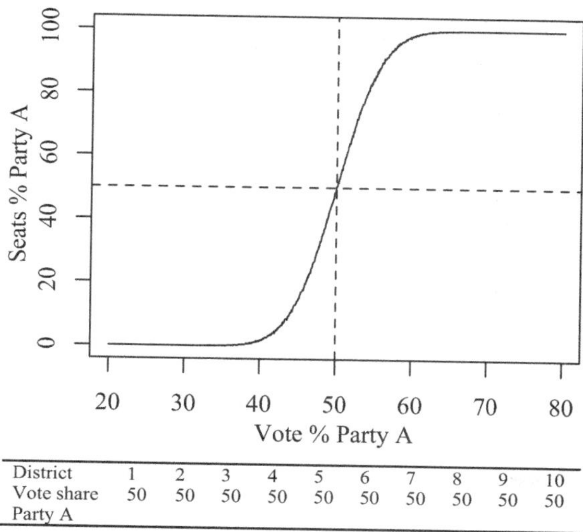

District	1	2	3	4	5	6	7	8	9	10
Vote share Party A	50	50	50	50	50	50	50	50	50	50

FIGURE 3.1. Seats/votes function with "winner take all" districting plan.

got 49% of the statewide vote, it would lose every district. This is clearly unrealistic.

To make things more realistic, we can relax the assumption of uniform partisan swing to approximately uniform partisan swing (Gelman and King 1994b). We continue to assume that if Party A gains an extra 1% of the statewide vote, it gets an extra 1% in every district. However, we also assume that in every district in every election, there is some random variation. We can think of this as reflecting local conditions, the effect of the campaign and candidates, or anything else that is not a result of the statewide swing in support. These local variations turn out to be quite large in the United States – we estimate the average of these variations to be about 5%. To take account of these random variations, we use computer simulation. We simulate 1,000 elections, each time adding a different random variation to each district.[1] For each simulated election, we see how many seats Party A would win if it had 50% or 51% or 52% and so on of the statewide vote. We then take the average seats won for each level of support. This "seats/votes function" is plotted in Figure 3.1. As can be seen, as statewide support for Party A grows beyond 50%, the number of seats it expects to win increases smoothly. If Party A wins 52% of the vote, it does expect to win all of the seats. It has a

[1] Technically, we add an independent normally distributed random term with mean 0 and a standard deviation of 5.

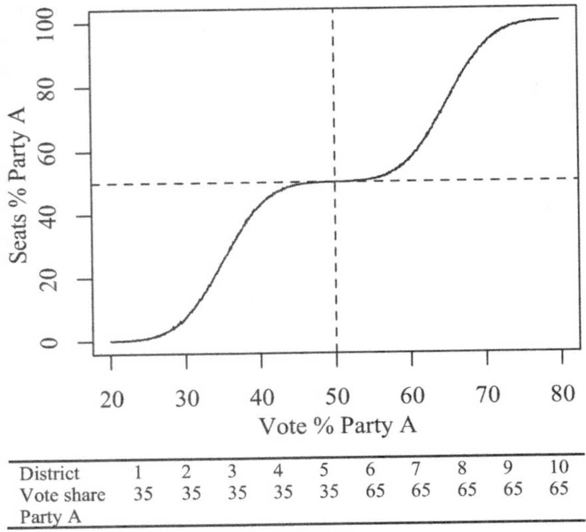

District	1	2	3	4	5	6	7	8	9	10
Vote share Party A	35	35	35	35	35	65	65	65	65	65

FIGURE 3.2. Seats/votes function with "incumbent protection program" districting plan.

52–48 advantage in expected vote in every district, but in some districts, the random variation is in favor of Party B and overwhelms Party A's advantage. Hence Party A will usually only win six seats out of ten for 52% of the vote.

The pattern we see in Figure 3.1 is very typical in first-past-the-post elections in countries and states with two parties. It is what we observe in U.S. House of Representatives elections in many states and also in countries such as the United Kingdom (see Taagepera and Shugart 1989). It has a very strong winner-take-all character. That is to say, it is very responsive to changes in support. If the parties are roughly equal in votes, then a swing of 1% in votes produces a swing in seats of between 3% and 4%. In this example, if Party A gets 60% of the vote, it probably wins all ten seats.

Figure 3.2 illustrates a very different way of drawing districts – an "incumbent protection plan." As before, half the votes in the state typically support Party A and half Party B. However, we have drawn the districts so that in five districts, 65% of the voters support Party A, and in the other five districts, 65% of the voters support Party B. Using the same computer simulation techniques as before, we can calculate how many seats Party A would expect to win with different levels of statewide support.

The pattern is very different from the "winner take all" plan. It is very unresponsive to changes in support. If Party A gets 45% of the vote, it

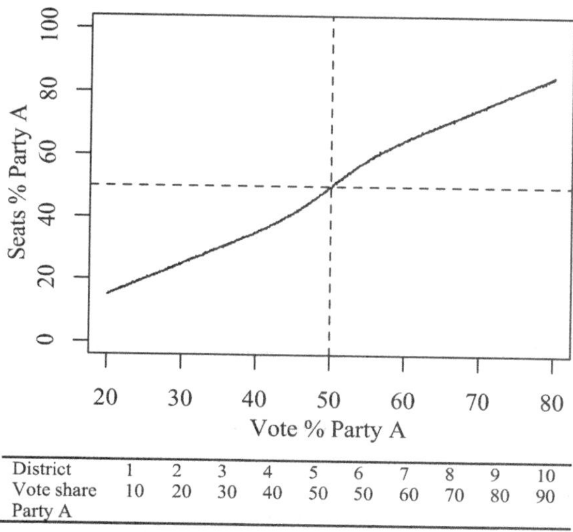

District	1	2	3	4	5	6	7	8	9	10
Vote share Party A	10	20	30	40	50	50	60	70	80	90

FIGURE 3.3. Seats/votes function with "proportional" districting plan.

expects to win five seats out of ten. If it wins 55% of the vote, it still only wins five seats out of ten. Whereas in the graph in Figure 3.1 around 50% of the vote is nearly vertical, in Figure 3.2, it is almost horizontal. This essentially represents a truce between the two parties – they give up the opportunity to win all or most of the seats in a good year in order to make sure they retain most of their seats in a bad year. This kind of plan is likely to be popular with the incumbents from both parties (who get very safe seats) but will probably find less favor from their national parties, who want to win a national majority in the House. This pattern has also been seen in many U.S. states, although we will see that in the last redistricting round, it became less common.

It is possible to draw districts to produce something between a "winner-take-all" and an "incumbent protection plan" districting scheme. If you draw the districts so that there is an even mixture of all different levels of support for Party A, you get a "proportional" districting plan. Such a plan is illustrated in Figure 3.3. Once again, 50% of the state typically supports Party A and 50% typically supports Party B. However, if Party A's support increases 1% in an election, it would expect its seat share to increase 1%. If it wins 60% of the vote, it would expect to win six seats out of ten. This districting plan effectively mimics proportional representation elections – except for the fact that proportional representation elections would encourage the entry and success of more than two parties (see Rae 1967; Taagepera and Shugart 1989).

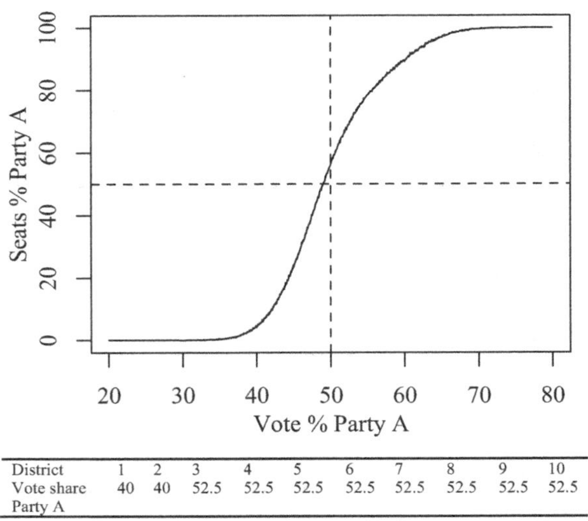

District	1	2	3	4	5	6	7	8	9	10
Vote share Party A	40	40	52.5	52.5	52.5	52.5	52.5	52.5	52.5	52.5

FIGURE 3.4. Gerrymandered districts with 60% "packed" districts.

All the plans we have considered so far have been symmetric and thus unbiased. If there is one district favoring Party A 60/40, then there is another district favoring Party B 60/40. If we wish to create a plan that gives a partisan advantage, we have to abandon this symmetry. The basic method for creating a partisan advantage combines elements of the "winner-take-all" and "incumbent protection plan" districting schemes. Essentially you create a few safe seats for the party you wish to disadvantage. This uses up the votes of this party. You are then able to create a greater number of more marginal seats that lean toward the party you wish to advantage. This is sometimes known as "cracking an packing" – you "pack" many of your opponents into as few districts as possible and "crack" the remainder among the larger number of the remaining districts so they are never a large enough concentration to win. Figure 3.4 illustrates a moderate example of this strategy.

In Figure 3.4, we have two districts in which Party A expects to win 40% of the vote. This allows the creation of eight districts in which it wins 52.5% of the vote. Thus it concedes two safe seats for an advantage in eight seats. This seems like a good deal. However, the random variation (which averages 5%) means that it does not win all of these eight seats. In fact, the bias in its favor is quite slight, and in a bad year may do very badly indeed. We will see that in order to effectively gerrymander, you need to pack more than 60% of your opponents into a district.

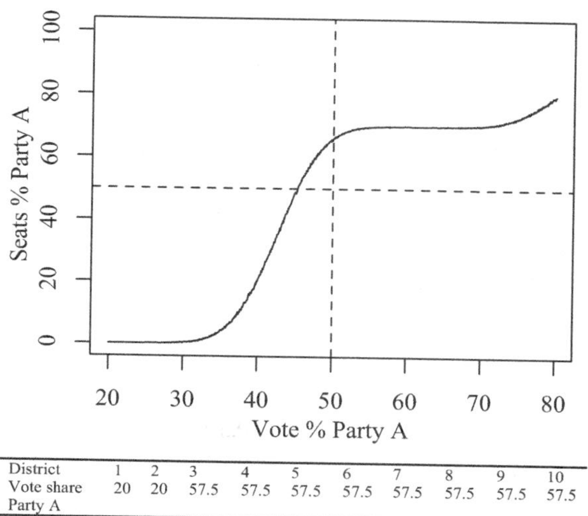

District	1	2	3	4	5	6	7	8	9	10
Vote share Party A	20	20	57.5	57.5	57.5	57.5	57.5	57.5	57.5	57.5

FIGURE 3.5. "Seats maximizing" gerrymandered districts with 80% "packed" districts.

Figure 3.5 shows a far more successful partisan gerrymander. This time we create two districts in which Party A wins 20% of the vote and Party B 80%. This is a very inefficient use of Party B's support – there is virtually no benefit in having an 80% seat as opposed to a 60% one in terms of security. This allows the creation of eight more marginal – but still quite safe – districts for Party A. Party A expects to win 57.5% in each of these districts. By giving Party B two seats that are far safer than it needs, Party A can get eight seats that are just safe enough. When we look at Figure 3.5, the bias is obvious from the lack of symmetry. If Party A wins 44%, it expects to get a majority of the seats. If it gets 50% of the vote, it expects to get between six and seven seats out of ten. This is the kind of partisan gerrymander we would want if our goal was to maximize the seats that Party A wins on average and thus make the greatest possible contribution to Party A's national majority in Congress.

However, we could also use the two "packed" 80% seats for Party B to create a different kind of partisan gerrymander. Instead of Party A trying to maximize its seats share on average, it could try to lock in a narrower majority with safer seats. We would call this an "incumbent protection" gerrymander. Figure 3.6 illustrates this. Party B gets four seats where it has an 80/20 advantage. In return, Party A gets six seats with a 70/30 margin. The results are spectacularly unresponsive to public support. Party A wins six votes out of ten, even though the statewide

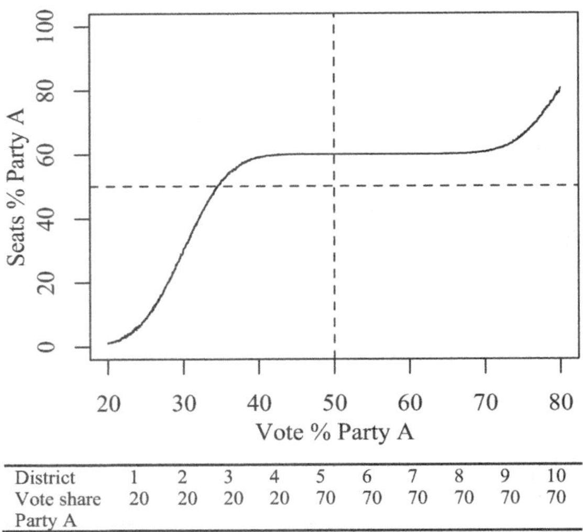

District	1	2	3	4	5	6	7	8	9	10
Vote share Party A	20	20	20	20	70	70	70	70	70	70

FIGURE 3.6. "Incumbent protection" gerrymandered districts with 80% "packed" districts.

public is evenly divided. In fact, any result from 60/40 in favor of Party A to 70/30 in favor of Party B gives this same result. The advantage of this arrangement for Party A is that its six incumbents are safe even in extremely bad years. The disadvantage compared to the plan in Figure 3.5 is that Party A will almost certainly never win more than six seats. With the seat-maximizing gerrymander in Figure 3.5, it will average 6.5 seats. This may seem like a small difference, but half a seat per state could easily mean the difference between majority and minority status for Party A nationally.

Of course, these two examples rely on the assumption that we can draw districts in which 80% of the voters support one party or the other. It is reasonable to ask whether this is possible in the real world. The answer to this question is that it is indeed possible. It is, of course, easiest to draw such districts where there are large concentrations of (politically) like-minded people. There are large urban areas where there is this kind of support for Democratic candidates and rural areas with similar levels of Republican support. There is also a considerable literature debating whether the need to draw minority-majority districts has created districts with these concentrations. However, it is also possible to create such concentrated districts by careful drawing. With current geographical information system technology, it is possible to have partisan data at the level of the census block (around 300 homes) and draw boundaries accordingly.

Measuring Gerrymandering

Given the framework we have established, we can define measures of districting plans. There are two qualities that we wish to measure. First, we wish to measure the bias of a districting plan – whether the districting plan advantages one party over another. Second, we wish to know how responsive the districting plan is. That is to say, if one party increases its vote total by a certain amount, how many extra seats does it win? These two qualities are independent – an unbiased districting plan can be "winner-take-all" or an "incumbent protection program," as can a plan with a strong partisan bias.

The measures that we use are taken from Gelman and King (1994b) (see also King and Browning 1987; King 1989; Gelman and King 1990, 1994a). We start by calculating seats/votes functions similar to those in the last section, only using actual election results. We then use these seats/votes functions to calculate the Gelman/King measures. (Full details of the calculations are given in the appendix to this chapter.) Briefly, we use computer simulation to generate a large number of hypothetical elections, each with a different random component. For each of these, we calculate the seats/votes functions and then use this to calculate our measures of bias and responsiveness. This allows us to calculate not only the expected values of our measures but also the standard deviation and 5% confidence limits. This allows us to estimate how uncertain we are about the accuracy of our measures.

We have two measures of bias and one of responsiveness. The first measure of bias is simply the bias when each party wins 50% of the two-party vote. If a party that wins 50% of the vote gets 50% of the seats, there is no bias by this measure. Graphically, the seats/votes function passes through the intersection of the 50% lines on the graph. This is an intuitively appealing measure – if there is this kind of bias, then the larger party will sometimes get fewer seats than the smaller one. However, it has the shortcoming that it only considers bias at 50%. Suppose we had a districting plan that did give 50% of the seats to a party if it won 50% of the vote; however, suppose Party A gets 80% of the seats for winning 52% of the vote, but Party B only gets 60% if it wins 52% of the vote. Such a districting plan certainly appears biased, but this is not picked up if we only consider bias at 50% of the vote.

To address this, Gelman and King (1994b) introduce the concept of partisan symmetry. This is the principle that if Party A gets 60% of the seats by winning 55% of the vote, then Party B should also get 60% of the seats if it wins 55% of the vote. Note that this does not require proportionality but only that the disproportionality be the same for both parties. It is fine by this standard to give all the seats to Party A if it gets 60% of the vote provided that Party B would also get all the seats if it were to win 60% of the vote. The measure of symmetry at a certain level of vote is defined as the difference between the seat share Party A gets for that level of vote (say 55%) and the seats share Party B would get if it were to win that level (again 55% in our example) of the vote. Following Gelman and King (1994b), we take the average of this symmetry measure at all levels of vote between 45% and 55%. The symmetry measure has the advantage of measuring the degree to which the parties are treated equally over a wide range of vote totals. We use the symmetry measure as our main indicator of partisan bias.[2]

The final measure we calculate is responsiveness. Once again, this is calculated from the seats/votes function. For a given level of support for Party A, we can calculate how much its seat share would increase if it won an additional percentage point of the vote. Thus, graphically, responsiveness is the slope of the seats/votes function. As before, we average responsiveness at all levels of support for Party A between 45% and 55%. If responsiveness is 1, then the districting system behaves in a proportional manner (at least when the vote split is between 45/55 and 55/45). If responsiveness is less than 1, then a party gaining or losing votes has little effect on how many seats it gets, and thus incumbents are protected. If we have high responsiveness, the districting plan is highly "winner-take-all," in that a small change in the vote share will result in many seats changing hands.

It is very important to distinguish between partisan bias and responsiveness. If there is partisan bias, then one party is advantaged over the other – if the Democrats get 55% of the vote, they do not get the same number of seats that the Republicans would get for 55% of the vote. If a districting system has high responsiveness, then it gives an advantage to the larger party, *whichever party that happens to be*. However, even if a districting system is unbiased, the level of responsiveness may still be controversial and have distributional consequence. If a party expects to usually be the larger party, then it will probably favor a districting scheme that is highly responsive, because rewarding the larger party will normally be to its benefit. On the other hand, if a party expects to be the minority most of the time, it will probably prefer a plan that is less responsive and guarantees it many safe seats. Furthermore, if a state changes the responsiveness of its districting scheme, it may well be accused of

[2] See King (2006) and Grofman and King (2007) for an argument that the symmetry measure ought to be used by the courts to determine the presence of partisan gerrymandering.

gerrymandering by those who expect to lose by the changes, especially if the new districting scheme involves some oddly shaped districts.

The problem with accusing a state of gerrymandering on the grounds that its districting plan is too responsive or not responsive enough is that we do not have a clear standard of what level of responsiveness is appropriate. With partisan bias, there is a clear standard – if the districting plan is fair, then it should treat both parties equally and there should be zero bias. With responsiveness, one possible standard would be proportionality – every change in vote share has the same effect. However, this is not a standard that is generally accepted in the United States. The United States has a first-past-the-post electoral system, and there is widespread acceptance that it is appropriate that the larger party should receive a bonus in seats over its share of the vote.[3] The problem is, what level of bonus is appropriate? Furthermore, there are perfectly good reasons responsiveness should vary between states. If a state is politically extremely homogenous, then most districts will probably look like a microcosm of the state. This lends itself to districting plans that are highly responsive and give most (or even all) of the seats to the larger party. However, if the state has many areas where supporters of each party are very concentrated, then there will be a tendency toward districting plans with many safe seats and low responsiveness.

For this reason, this book concentrates on partisan bias rather than responsiveness. We provide responsiveness figures for each districting plan, because this is necessary to understand the effects of the districting plan – does it allow one party to maximize its seat share, or does it protect incumbents? However, we do not make normative judgments about what an appropriate level of responsiveness is. It is possible to make a reasonable case for different levels of responsiveness. However, this is not the case with partisan bias. If the level of partisan bias is not zero (or close enough, given the margin of error), then we can say that the districting plan favors one party over the other. For this reason, it is partisan bias that gives us prima facie evidence that there may be political gerrymandering.

Other Measures of Partisan Bias

In this chapter, we estimate the partisan bias and responsiveness of different districting schemes by modeling the behavior of each individual

[3] It should be noted, however, that it is possible to draw "incumbent protection" districting plans that are so unresponsive that the larger party may sometimes receive fewer seats than its vote share would suggest – a negative bonus.

district using the assumption of uniform partisan swing, using the methodology of Gelman and King (1994a). An alternative method would be to estimate the aggregate seats/votes function parametrically using a function such as a logistic and data from several years. Tufte (1973) does this using a logistic function, while King and Browning (1987) use a bilogit form. The advantage of this is that it is computationally cheaper. The disadvantage is that it forces a certain functional form on the seats/votes function with certain symmetry properties (though not partisan symmetry), which may not reflect the actual shape of the seats/vote function. Given that computation is no longer really a constraint, we see no reason to not estimate the seat/votes function by modeling the individual districts.

Far more problematic are estimates of bias that are based on distance from a predefined seats/votes function. These seem similar to the parametric method described in the previous paragraph. However, they conflate partisan bias and responsiveness and are thus highly misleading. One example of this is found in Goedert (2014). Goedert estimates an average seats/votes function for U.S. states between 1972 and 2010. He then calculates a predicted seat percentage for each state using this function and the vote share the party received. Finally, he takes the difference between this and the seat share it actually received and calls this bias. Thus if Goedert's function says that if the Republicans should get 55% of the seats in a state if they win 52% of the vote in a state, and instead they get 60% of the seats, then there is a 5% bias in favor of the Republicans.

This approach, however, is fundamentally flawed. Just because the Republicans get 60% of the seats when Goedert's function says they should get 52% does not prove that there is any bias. It might be that if the districting plan is completely unbiased and that if the Democrats had won 52% of the vote, they also would have gotten 60% of the seats. In this case, Goedert's measure is misinterpreting the high responsiveness of the districting plan (the fact that many districts are very competitive) as bias. Goedert's measure will also misinterpret low responsiveness as bias. Of course, it is also possible that the Republicans did win 60% of the seats from 52% of the vote because of bias. Perhaps if the Democrats had won 52% of the vote, they would only have won 48% of the seats. The problem is that Goedert's measure does not distinguish between these two very different situations. In fact, it is not possible to distinguish between them without estimating the seats/votes function for the particular state (not just the average seats/votes function for all states). Goedert's measure will flag egregious cases of bias, but it will also find bias where none actually exists.

Another measure with a similar problem is the "efficiency gap" measure proposed by Stephanopoulos and McGee (2015). This is framed as making the number of wasted votes equal between both parties. However, in a two-party system, this amounts to requiring a linear seats/votes function that has a slope of 2. Thus if the efficiency gap is 0 and the plan is unbiased, then if a party wins 50% of the vote, it must get 50% of the seats; and if it wins 55% of the vote, it must get 60% of the seats (and if it gets 60% of the vote, 70% of the seats and so on). Anything that deviates from this seats/votes function is interpreted as bias, even if it results from a seats/votes function that is symmetrical. Indeed, if the seats/votes function were strictly proportional (a party gets seat share proportional to its vote share), this would be interpreted as being biased according to the efficiency gap measure. If a party got 60% of the seats for 60% of the vote (and the other party would have gotten the same for 60% of the vote), the efficiency gap measure would be −10%!

Any measure that measures bias in terms of the distance of a single election result from a given seats/votes function has two problems. First, it conflates difference in responsiveness and bias. Second, it sets a certain level of responsiveness as the norm. The problem here is that we do not have a good normative reason for saying that any particular level of responsiveness is correct. There are perfectly legitimate reasons for different states to have different levels of responsiveness. If a state is geographically homogeneous with regard to political preferences (each district is very similar in terms of political preferences), then we would expect the districting plan of that state to be highly responsive. If, however, people in different areas of the state have very different preferences, we would expect much lower responsiveness. Each party would have safe districts in the areas of the state in which it was popular.

Stephanopoulos and McGee (2015) do provide a justification for their chosen normative seats/votes function. It is a logical consequence of the requirement that the number of wasted votes for each party is the same (wasted votes are defined as votes more than 50% when a party wins a seat and all votes in districts the party loses). The problem is, it is not obvious that both parties should have the same absolute number of wasted votes when the parties have different numbers of voters. It seems just as intuitive to argue that the parties should have the same number of wasted votes per district won. That way, each party would pay the same cost in wasted votes per seat. This would logically imply a proportional seats/votes function. You could also make a case for each party having the same percentage of wasted votes compared to its total vote. In spite of its seemingly intuitive normative justification in terms of wasted votes, Stephanopoulos and McGee (2015) are in fact imposing an arbitrary seats/vote function as a norm. As we have argued, there is no way to estimate the bias of state districting plans without estimating the seats/votes function for each state.

PARTISAN BIAS AT THE NATIONAL LEVEL

We now apply these measures of bias and responsiveness to actual data. First, we consider the degree to which the House of Representatives as a whole displays partisan bias and the degree to which it is responsive to changes in the balance of support of the two parties. We are obviously interested in how biased the House of Representatives is for its own sake. However, we can also use the change in bias between the 2002 and 2012 districting cycles to investigate the causes of partisan bias. We have suggested that the Supreme Court's decision in *Vieth v. Jubelirer* (2004) has had an effect. If the Supreme Court's decision has removed constraints on the ability of state legislatures to gerrymander, then we would expect to see an increase in bias between 2002 and 2012. Others, however, have suggested that partisan bias is the result of demographic factors (for example, Democratic supporters being highly concentrated in urban areas, which form "naturally occurring" gerrymanders) or the need to create minority-majority districts to satisfy the Voting Rights Act. However, these demographic and legal factors did not significantly change between the 2002 and 2012 districting cycles, and thus they cannot explain any change in bias we observe (see Chapter 4).

The measures of bias and responsiveness are calculated from the seats/votes function, as explained earlier. The way the seats/votes function is calculated is laid out in detail in the appendix to this chapter. Essentially, the calculation relies on the assumption of uniform partisan swing – if a party gains 5% nationally, it gains 5% in every district, give or take an allowance for local factors. In the case of the 2002–2010 districts, for which we have data for five elections, we use linear regression to estimate what level of support the Democrats expect to win in each district if they win 50% of the national vote, given the national level of support for the party in each year. We also estimate the magnitude of the random local effects from this data (this was on average 5.05% for the national election data). We then generate a thousand simulated elections

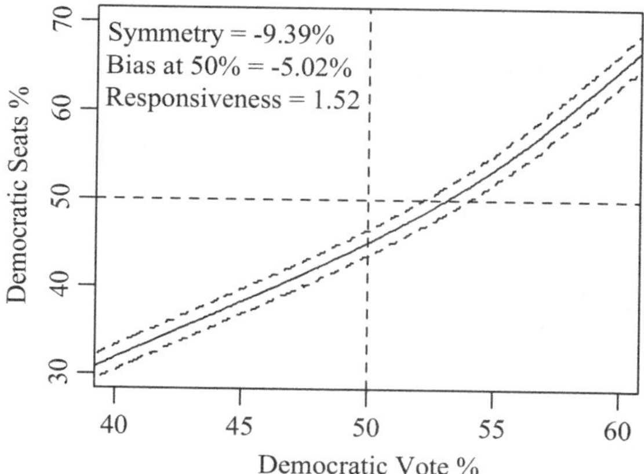

FIGURE 3.7. National seats/votes function 2012 (dotted lines +/−2 standard deviation).

with different random local effects for each district and use this to create the seats/votes function. Finally, we calculate the bias and responsiveness measures from this. In the case of the 2012 districts, the only data we have are the 2012 results. We use these results to calculate the vote each party would win in a district if it were to win 50% overall and then calculate the seats/votes function and measures the same way as with the 2002–2010 data. We assume that the magnitude of the random local effects is the same as for the 2002–2010 period. It should be noted that the inclusion of the random local effects has a conservative effect – it reduces the estimates of bias. Intuitively speaking, a well-designed gerrymander will be partially undermined by random effects that perturb the districts.

Figure 3.7 shows the national seats/votes function for the 2012 districts and gives the bias and responsiveness measures. We can see that there is considerable asymmetry and bias toward the Republican Party – the graph does not pass through the 50% votes/50% seats point. Instead, if the Democrats win 50% of the vote, they only win about 45% of the seats. The level of asymmetry is 9.38% in favor of the Republicans. This means that for a given level of support between 45% and 55%, the Republicans get 9.38% more seats than the Democrats get for that level of support. (The symmetry measure will typically be around twice the bias at 50% measure. If there is a 5% bias to the Republicans at 50% of the vote, then the Republicans get 55% of the seats to the Democrats' 45%, a 10% symmetry difference.) This asymmetry is statistically significant at the 5% level. More importantly, it represents an increase in the Republican

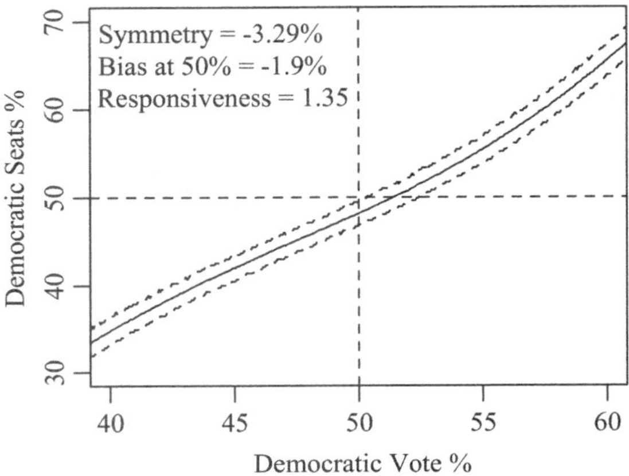

FIGURE 3.8. National seats/votes function 2002–2010 (dotted lines +/−2 standard deviation).

majority of forty-one seats – enough to change control of the House in most years. For the Democrats to expect to win 50% of the seats, they would need to win 53.12% of the vote. However, this figure includes a correction for uncontested seats (see Appendix) that amounted to 0.8% in 2012. Without this correction, the raw share of the two-party vote the Democrats would need to have a 50/50 chance of a House majority is 53.92%.

The responsiveness score for the 2012 districts is 1.52. This means that if the Democrats or Republicans win an extra percentage point of the vote, they get an additional 1.52% of the seats. This responsiveness is considerably less than is observed in many countries with first-past-the-post elections, such as the United Kingdom. However, it is somewhat more than proportionality (a score of 1). Although there has been a great deal of concern about lack of competitiveness in House elections and overprotected incumbents, what we observe certainly does not appear to be an incumbent-protection program. While there are undoubtedly many safe seats, the overall distribution of seats between the parties mirrors the results under proportional representation quite closely, except that there is a very significant bias toward the Republicans, and third-party entry is very difficult.

We can compare these results to the results for the 2002–2010 districts. These are shown in Figure 3.8. There is a 3.4% asymmetry in favor of the Republicans. This is still statistically significant but is only 35% of the bias we observe in 2012. When we consider bias at 50% vote, we see a similar picture. The bias is less than 2%, compared to 5% in 2012. Graphically, the seats/votes function comes far closer to the 50% votes/50% seats point, although this is still just outside the 5% error bounds. The 2002–2010 districts are also somewhat less responsive than the 2012 districts.

Thus we can confirm that partisan bias at the national level increased sharply with the redistricting that followed the 2010 Census. This is compatible with our claim that, following *Vieth v. Jubelirer* (2004), state governments redistricted for partisan advantage to a far greater level than they had previously. Redistricting decisions, however, are made at the state level, not the national. Therefore, to explain the bias we observe, we need to look at the bias of individual state districting plans. It is to this that we now turn.

PARTISAN BIAS AT THE STATE LEVEL

So far, we have considered partisan bias at the national level. However, districting is not done on the national level but state by state. Therefore, we have to consider the bias and responsiveness of individual state districting plans. This allows us to ask which states have districting plans that have partisan bias and to ask how significant this partisan gerrymandering is. In fact, we can classify all state plans according to how biased and how responsive they are. It also allows us to test different explanations of this bias.

We can calculate our measures of bias and responsiveness from the seats/votes function for each state. These are calculated the same way as for the national data. That is to say, we calculate the expected vote share in each district for a year in which the statewide vote for each party is 50% then generate simulated elections by adding a random term to each district to account for random local effects. Using the 2002–2010 data, we estimate the size of the random local effect (this is 4.68% for the statewide data, as opposed to 5.05% for the national data). As with the national data, full details are given in the appendix.

The measures for every state (including standard deviations and 5% confidence limits) are given in the appendix. Table 3.1 gives the symmetry and bias at 50% scores for the ten most biased states. The first thing to note is just how extreme the bias is in these cases. Most have a symmetry score of between −30 and −40%. This means that if the Republicans get a certain vote share (say 52%) and get a certain seat share (say 70%), then the Democrats would get a seat share of 30% to 40% less than that if they won the same vote share. That is, in our example if the Democrats won 52% of the vote, they would only get between 30% and 40% of the seats. To put it another way, 0% asymmetry means that there is no bias, while

TABLE 3.1. *Top Ten States by Partisan Bias*

State	Symmetry		Bias at 50% Vote	
	Mean	SD	Mean	SD
1. Alabama	−43.1	12.4	−25.3	9.91
2. Mississippi	−41.2	11.2	−22.6	7.3
3. Missouri	−41.2	7.97	−22.5	5.1
4. Pennsylvania	−36.4	5.01	−19.7	3.42
5. North Carolina	−36.3	7.47	−19.9	5.82
6. Louisiana	−35.7	13.4	−19	10.8
7. Ohio	−35.5	6.59	−19	4.91
8. Virginia	−30.7	7.97	−17.6	5.85
9. South Carolina	−30.3	11.6	−16.2	9.92
10. Tennessee	−27.8	8.48	−14.3	6.05

100% asymmetry means that one party gets all the seats if it wins 45% or more. This can also be seen in the bias at 50% scores, which are typically around 20%, meaning a 70/30 seat split when the vote split is 50/50.

It has been suggested that for a variety of reasons, partisan gerrymandering is self-limiting. For example, it has been suggested that parties are limited in how far they can gerrymander by the fact that trying to maximize their seat total will make their incumbents very vulnerable (Butler and Cain 1992). However, it is clear that the state legislatures in these states have managed to produce fairly extreme partisan bias. Of course, there is a trade-off between seat maximization and incumbent protections, as we saw in the hypothetical examples in the first section of this chapter. However, as we also saw, if it is possible to pack your opponents into districts where they win 80% or more of the vote, you have plenty of leeway to create a large number of safe-enough seats. Furthermore, the geographical constraints on drawing districts are very weak – essentially only that districts be contiguous. Provided state legislatures are not afraid to draw some very odd-looking districts (and it seems that many are not embarrassed by doing this), it does not appear that difficult to pack your opponents into very one-sided districts.

We can classify states according to the degree of partisan bias and the degree of responsiveness. This allows us to say which of the patterns in the graphs in the first section of this chapter each state most resembles. First, we classify a state as biased if the bias is sufficiently large that we can be confident that it is not by chance (technically, the degree of asymmetry is statistically significant to the 5% level – that is to say, at least 95% of our simulations come out biased in the same direction). Second, we can

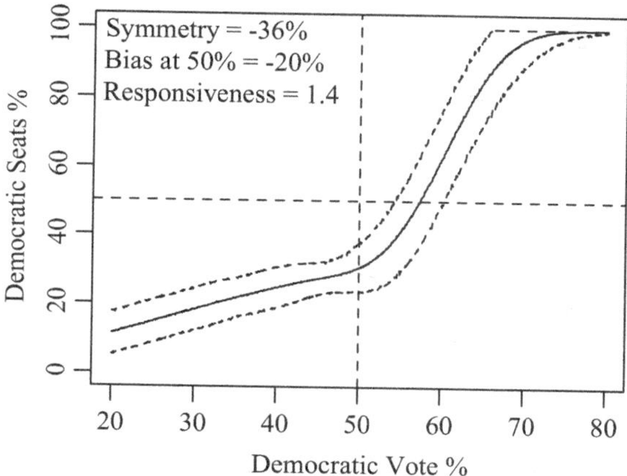

FIGURE 3.9. Seats/votes function Pennsylvania 2012 (dotted line +/−2 standard deviations).

classify the states in terms of their responsiveness score. If a state has a score of less than 1, we consider it an "incumbent protection program" (if a party gets an extra 1% of the vote, it gets less than an extra 1% of the seats). If the responsiveness is between 1 and 2, then we consider the districting plan "proportional". If the responsiveness is greater than 2, we consider it "winner-take-all" (an extra 1% of the vote gets a party at least 2% more of the seats). The cut points between the various responsiveness categories are somewhat arbitrary, but the raw scores are provided in the appendix. Thus we can classify states as biased or unbiased in terms of symmetry; and incumbent protection, proportional or winner-take-all in terms of responsiveness. This gives us a total of six categories.

These different kinds of districting plans can be best illustrated by looking at a few examples. Figure 3.9 gives the seats/votes function for Pennsylvania in 2012, which we classify as a "proportional-biased" plan. As is apparent, it is far from symmetric. In fact, the graph misses the 50% votes/50% seats point by 20 percentage points! The symmetry score is actually 36% in favor of the Republicans. It is moderately responsive between 45% and 55% of the vote – the score of 1.4 is within the range we classify as "proportional." At 50% of the vote, the Democrats expect to win about 30% of the seats. The slope of the curve does increase sharply a bit past 50%. However, the Democrats would need to win between 57% and 58% of the vote to win half the seats.

Figure 3.10 illustrates the seats/votes function from Georgia, an incumbent-protection gerrymander. This looks quite similar to the graph

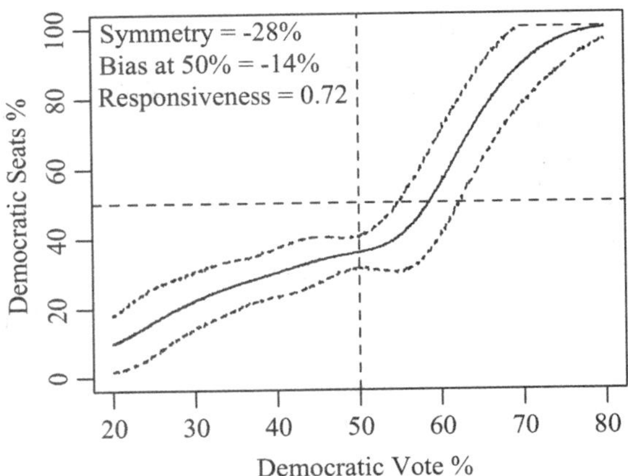

FIGURE 3.10. Seats/votes function Georgia 2012 (dotted line +/−2 standard deviations).

for Pennsylvania. However, the graph is very flat around the 50% vote mark. As a result, winning extra votes makes little difference to the result, and the incumbents of both parties have safe seats. A consequence of this is that Georgia's districting plan is not as efficient in producing Republican seats as Pennsylvania's is. In 2012, the Democrats won five out of fourteen seats in Georgia but only five out of eighteen in Pennsylvania. This is in spite of the fact that the Democrats won a narrow majority of the vote in Pennsylvania, while the Republicans won 60% of the U.S. House of Representatives vote in Georgia. Thus indeed there is a trade-off between maximizing party seats and protecting incumbents when you design a gerrymander. However, as Pennsylvania and Georgia illustrate, you can do either and at the same time give your party an overwhelming advantage.

When we consider a "winner-take-all" partisan gerrymander in Figure 3.11, this also looks quite similar. The difference is that the slope of the line is very steep at 50% of the vote. It should be noted that the average slope of the seats/votes curve must be 1; if a party wins 0% of the vote, it gets no seats, and if it gets 100% of the vote, it gets all the seats. The question is, at what level of vote is the responsiveness concentrated? In Alabama, the seats/votes function becomes highly responsive just below 50%. It should be noted that the Democratic candidates in Alabama won about 36% of the U.S. House vote in 2012, so they did not get close to the level of vote at which this responsiveness would have made a difference.

We can also consider examples of unbiased districting plans. Massachusetts in Figure 3.12 is an "unbiased winner-take-all" plan. It is

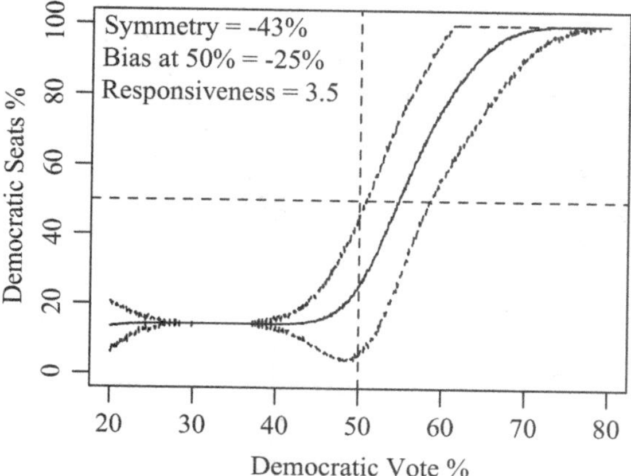

FIGURE 3.11. Seats/votes function Alabama 2012 (dotted line +/−2 standard deviations).

approximately unbiased, as can be seen from the symmetry of the graph. (There is actually a small bias toward the Republicans, but this is not statistically significant and makes no difference given that the Democrats typically win 65% to 70% of the vote.) It is extremely responsive between 40% and 60% of the vote: 1% more in vote share means 3.6% more in seat share. This responsiveness is, of course, advantageous to the Democrats. They are able to win all ten of the Massachusetts seats. However, the plan is not biased. If the Republicans were to win 65% to 70% of the vote in Massachusetts, they would also win all ten seats.

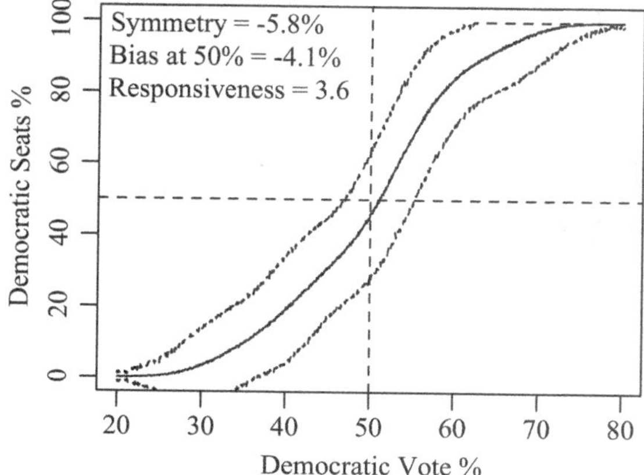

FIGURE 3.12. Seats/votes function Massachusetts 2012 (dotted line +/−2 standard deviations).

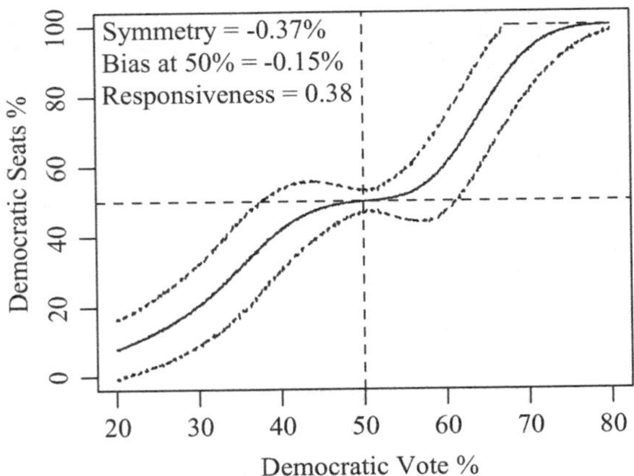

FIGURE 3.13. Seats/votes function New Jersey 2012 (dotted line +/−2 standard deviations).

New Jersey in Figure 3.13 is an example of an "unbiased incumbent protection" plan. The graph is extremely flat around 50% of the vote, with a responsiveness of only 0.38. Essentially, most seats have been divided up between the two parties and are safe for one or the other of them. A party has to win considerably more than 50% before it has any chance of challenging in any of the other party's seats. It is, however, virtually symmetric and unbiased. It is a fair deal between the parties, even if it may not be considered so fair to the voters.

Figure 3.14 shows the seats/votes graph for California. This is an example of an "unbiased proportional" plan. It is more or less unbiased

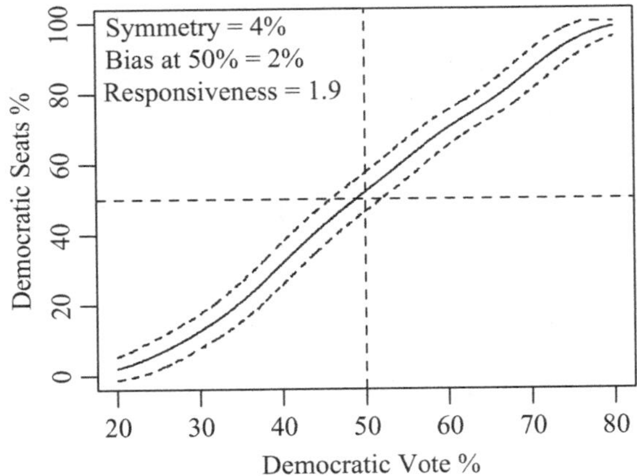

FIGURE 3.14. Seats/votes function California 2012 (dotted line +/−2 standard deviations).

TABLE 3.2. *Classification of States by Partisan Bias and Responsiveness, 2012*

	Responsiveness		
	Incumbent Protection	**Proportional**	**Winner Take All**
Unbiased	New Jersey	Arizona California New York	Arkansas Colorado Connecticut Illinois Iowa Kansas Massachusetts Minnesota Nebraska Nevada New Mexico Oklahoma Oregon Utah Washington West Virginia
Partisan bias	Republican: Georgia	Republican: Michigan Mississippi Missouri Ohio Pennsylvania Tennessee Wisconsin	Republican: Alabama Florida Indiana Kentucky Louisiana North Carolina South Carolina Texas Virginia Democratic: Maryland

(the very slight bias toward the Democrats is well within the bounds of error). It is moderately responsive, with its responsiveness score of 1.9 – just within the limits of what we consider proportional. The graph is linear and passes very close to the 50% votes/50% seats mark. The linear shape is a result of there being a roughly even distribution of seats of different degrees of competitiveness. It is notable that these 2012 California districts were drawn by a citizens' commission as a result of Proposition 11, which was passed by the voters in 2008.

We can now classify all states in terms of the partisan bias and responsiveness of their districting plans. This is done for 2012 in Table 3.2. A

TABLE 3.3. *Classification of States by Partisan Bias and Responsiveness, 2002–2010*

	Responsiveness		
	Incumbent Protection	**Proportional**	**Winner Take All**
Unbiased	Illinois Mississippi Wisconsin	Connecticut Indiana Minnesota North Carolina	Arizona Arkansas Colorado Iowa Kansas Kentucky Louisiana Massachusetts Nebraska Nevada New Mexico Washington West Virginia
Partisan bias	Republican: Michigan Missouri Utah Democratic: California New Jersey Tennessee	Republican: Georgia Ohio Democratic: Maryland New York	Republican: Alabama Florida Oklahoma Pennsylvania South Carolina Texas Virginia Democratic: Oregon

few things are notable. The states are divided roughly equally between biased and unbiased. However, of the biased states, all of them are biased toward the Republicans, with the exception of Maryland. (Connecticut, New Mexico, and Oregon also have biases toward the Democrats of more than 10%, but none of these biases are large enough to be statistically significant.) Among the biased states, most are from the South, although there are also some notable non-Southern states such as Missouri, Michigan, Ohio, Pennsylvania, and Wisconsin. In terms of responsiveness, there are only two incumbent protection plans, one biased (Georgia) and one unbiased (New Jersey). In fact, the majority of states have a "winner-take-all" level of responsiveness.

We can classify the states and their 2002–2010 districts in exactly the same way. This is done in Table 3.3. Many of the states are classified in exactly the same way as in 2012. However, there are some notable differences. There are slightly fewer cases of bias toward the Republicans. There are more cases of partisan bias toward the Democrats (California, New Jersey, Tennessee, New York, Oregon, as well as Maryland). There are also considerably more incumbent-protection plans.

Thus the patterns we see are compatible with bias toward the Republicans increasing in the post-2010 districting round. There are more states in which there is pro-Republican bias and fewer states with bias toward the Democrats. Furthermore, when we consider the full bias figures in the appendix, we will find that pro-Republican bias increased in many states that were already somewhat biased in 2002 (this will be considered in more depth in Chapter 5). The real significance of the state bias and responsiveness measurement, however, is that they will allow us to assess alternative explanations of partisan bias in Chapters 4 and 5.

PARTISAN BIAS AND COMPACTNESS

We have seen that partisan bias increased sharply in the districting round following the 2010 Census. We have also identified the states in which this increase in bias occurred. Although it is not essential to our argument, it is interesting to ask whether these states are the same states in which we find oddly shaped districts. We noted in Chapter 1 that as the districts in Pennsylvania became more biased, they also became more oddly shaped – that is, less compact. Newspaper articles graphically demonstrate gerrymandering by displaying the contorted shapes of some congressional districts (see Ingraham 2014). Compactness in districts has a strong intuitive appeal – if districts appear oddly shaped, people naturally seem to believe that someone is manipulating something. Furthermore, we have mathematical tools by which we can measure the compactness of districts.

However, there is no logical link between compactness and partisan bias. There is no reason districts that are biased should not be compact and vice versa. It is quite possible to create partisan bias in compact districts. As we have seen, the way you create partisan bias is to "pack" your opponents' supporters into a few districts, allowing you to win the rest. Ideally, you would like your opponents to win districts with 80% of the vote or more. If there are large areas where you opponent is very strong, it may be possible to achieve this goal without needing to draw oddly shaped, noncompact districts. (We would resist calling these "naturally occurring gerrymanders," because as we will see, they only seem to occur where the political incentives and opportunities align correctly.) Conversely, it is possible to have very odd-shaped, noncompact districts without partisan bias. Indeed, this has frequently occurred when state legislatures have drawn districts to create "incumbent protection" gerrymanders. Here there are violations of compactness, but there is no partisan bias.

Furthermore, there is no legal reason, either constitutional or statutory, that congressional districts should be compact. There was a requirement from the Apportionment Act of 1841 that House districts needed to be contiguous and compact. However, as we have seen, the Supreme Court in *Wood v. Broom* (1932b) found that Congress had repealed this in 1929 when the new Apportionment Act failed to explicitly renew it. Since then, district compactness has not been a legal requirement. However, compactness has at times been used as an indicator or as evidence of gerrymandering. For example, Justice Stevens in his concurring opinion on *Karcher v. Daggett* (1983, 755) argued that "substantial divergences from a mathematical standard of compactness may be symptoms of illegitimate gerrymandering"; and that "drastic departures from compactness are a signal that something may be amiss" (1983, 758).

Nevertheless, we would expect to find in general that where partisan bias increases, district compactness falls. We argue that after *Vieth v. Jubelirer* (2004), state legislatures were free to pursue partisan advantage in districting. In seeking to optimize partisan advantage, we would expect some of them to resort to drawing oddly shaped districts. Where it was possible to create partisan advantage and retain compactness, state legislatures would presumably do this. But where there was a partisan advantage to be gained by drawing oddly shaped districts, we would expect state legislatures to take advantage of this.

We turn now to how we can measure compactness. Compactness is a property that refers to the geographic shape of a district and the manner in which the area of a district is dispersed within its boundaries. Quantification of compactness involves, at a minimum, a consideration of irregularities in the perimeter of a district (deviations from straight or circular lines that would maximize compactness) as well the dispersal, or spread, of either land or people within a district (Niemi et al. 1990). More sophisticated treatments that draw on the capacity of geographic information systems (GIS) to identify roads, rivers, and uninhabitable land have been used to "control" for such features counting against compactness, but our concern with change across time, as opposed to absolute levels of compactness, reduces the need for such refined treatment.

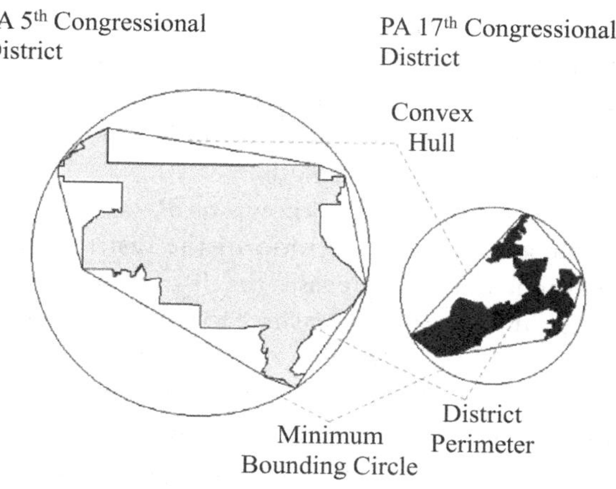

FIGURE 3.15. Comparing measures of compactness.[4]

Because different measures of compactness capture distinct geographic properties, the selection of any single measure is somewhat arbitrary. Most compactness measures reflect the deviation of an actual district trait relative to a constant such as a circle. We employ GIS software from ESRI to calculate both perimeter and dispersal compactness measures on 2002 and 2012 districting plans for the thirty-eight states with three or more congressional districts. In Figure 3.15, four of the most frequently used compactness measures in election research are compared using the 5th and 17th congressional districts in Pennsylvania's 2012 districting plan.

First, we list a standardized (to range in value from 0 to 1) Schwartzberg measure, which is the ratio of the district perimeter to the perimeter of a circle with the same area. Next, the Polsby/Popper measure is similar to Schwartzberg but divides district area with the area of a circle with the same perimeter length. Both of these measures are very sensitive to changes in perimeter, with compactness maximized as district shape approaches a smooth circle. Note that while both measures indicate that the 17th District is less compact, the Polsby/Popper compactness measure is more sensitive to the differences between the 5th District and the 17th, which has greater perimeter irregularities relative to its area. Because compactness measures based on perimeter length are so sensitive to boundary

[4] Source: Shapefiles provided by the U.S. Census: http://www.census.gov/geo/maps-data/data/cbf/cbf_cds.html.

changes, they may not be ideal for evaluating GIS-based changes in districting plans across time. When the U.S. Census releases the shape files for districting maps, care must be taken to match the quality of resolution between plans, as more detailed coastlines and other natural boundaries are reflected in greater perimeter length.

The next measure, commonly known as Reock (after the political scientist E.C. Reock), reflects the ratio of the district area to the area of the smallest circle that encompasses the district (minimum bounding). This compactness measure is less sensitive to perimeter change, but it also reflects a rather narrow construction of compactness, with long, skinny districts consistently receiving the lowest scores.

Finally, we calculate a compactness measure based on the ratio of district area over the convex hull (minimum bounding polygon) of the district. Unlike a minimum-bounding circle, the shape of the convex hull conforms to the particular boundaries of a district (like a rubber band), reflecting the extent to which a district bypasses some geographic areas for others. As a result, a skinny I-shaped district may reflect high compactness, while C- or S-shaped districts will receive much lower scores as a result of their concave shapes. Figure 3.15 demonstrates these measures using two districts in Pennsylvania.

In this example, the 17th District is less compact than the 5th according to all measures, but there is substantial variation in the magnitude of difference between measures. Whereas the Schwartzberg measure indicates that the 17th District is 74% as compact as the 5th, the Polsby/Popper measure indicates that the 17th is only 33% as compact. Therefore, we will rely on multiple compactness measures when analyzing the linkage between the average compactness of statewide districting plans and the level of partisan symmetry that those plans produce.

Table 3.4 gives the change in the average compactness of each state's districts, as measured by the Polsby/Popper perimeter measure and the ratio of district area to the area of their compact hulls. It also gives the change in the absolute value of partisan bias as measured by the symmetry measure for each state. (If a state goes from having a 10% bias in favor of the Democrats to having a 20% Republican bias, the absolute value change is 10%. Here we are interested in how much bias there is, not in who benefits.) As we have already stated, we would expect to see a drop in district compactness as a byproduct of state legislatures trying to maximize partisan advantage. Therefore, in those states where there is increased partisan bias, we would also expect to see a loss of compactness. However, we would not expect this relationship to be perfect, as there is no necessary link between partisan bias and compactness.

TABLE 3.4. *Change in Average Compactness and Absolute Value of Partisan Symmetry (states with statistically significant asymmetry in bold)*

	No Change or Increased Symmetry				Reduced Symmetry (> 2% reduction)			
		Δ Compactness		Δ Symmetry		Δ Compactness		Δ Symmetry
		Polsby-Popper	Convex Hull			Polsby-Popper	Convex Hull	
No Change or Increased Compactness	CA	.04	.08	15.92	**AL**	**.01**	**−.02**	**−22.20**
	CT	.00	.00	−.60	**GA (+1)**	**.12**	**.14**	**−12.60**
	FL (+2)	**.09**	**.09**	**8.10**	**IN**	**.13**	**.06**	**−11.66**
	IA (−1)	.04	.06	3.85	**MO (−1)**	**−.01**	**.03**	**−31.59**
	KS	.03	.02	.56	NE	.00	.01	−11.60
	MA (−1)	.01	.02	5.60	**SC (+1)**	**−.03**	**.05**	**−10.40**
	MN	.01	.00	2.50	**TN**	**.02**	**.03**	**−18.32**
	NJ (−1)	.00	.01	7.32				
	NM	−.02	.00	2.20				
	NV (+1)	.22	.14	−1.88				
	NY (−2)	.09	.10	10.27				
	OK	.00	.00	31.85				
	OR	.02	.02	10.30				
Reduced Compactness	AR	−.06	−.08	20.76	AZ (+1)	−.04	−.04	−5.01
	IL (−1)	−.05	−.03	2.56	CO (+1)	−.05	−.05	−6.74
	MD	**−.04**	**−.08**	**13.60**	**KY**	**−.09**	**−.07**	**−14.69**
	UT	−.08	−.06	15.60	**LA (−1)**	**−.09**	**−.13**	**−30.35**
	WA (+1)	−.05	−.03	10.01	**MI (−1)**	**−.07**	**−.05**	**−6.40**
	WV	−.03	−.03	−1.00	**MS**	**−.01**	**−.01**	**−41.03**
					NC	**−.04**	**−.04**	**−26.20**
					OH (−2)	**−.07**	**−.05**	**−15.20**
					PA (−1)	**−.03**	**−.05**	**−18.30**
					TX (+4)	**−.06**	**−.03**	**−4.80**
					VA	**−.03**	**−.03**	**−13.60**
					WI	**−.07**	**−.03**	**−16.99**

In general, we find the patterns we would expect. The states that have become less compact tend to be those in which there was an increase in bias (i.e., a decrease in symmetry) and vice versa. In most of the states where bias has increased, districts have on average become less compact. This includes many of the states in which bias increased the most – for example, Kentucky, Louisiana, Michigan, North Carolina, Ohio, Pennsylvania, Texas, Virginia, and Wisconsin. This is consistent with our story that state governments resort to drawing irregularly shaped districts in their pursuit of maximum partisan advantage. In most states where districts have not become less compact, there is no increase in bias.

However, there are quite a number of cases that do not fit the anticipated pattern. In particular, there are seven cases where an increase in compactness was accompanied by an increase in bias. In all of these cases (Alabama, Georgia, Indiana, Missouri, Nebraska, South Carolina, and Tennessee), the increase in bias was quite considerable. In some of these cases, this can be explained by incumbent-protection gerrymandering in the previous districting round. If a state had drawn oddly shaped boundaries in the 2000 districting round to protect incumbents, it would already have low compactness. If in 2010 it adopted a partisan gerrymander, the new districts might not be any less compact. Indeed, they might even be more compact. This appears to have been the case in Tennessee, Georgia, and, to some degree, Indiana. Tennessee was certainly an "incumbent protection" gerrymander after 2000, with a responsiveness score (see Chapter 3) of 0.41 – that is, a 1% change in a party's vote only produced a 0.41% change in its expected seat share. Georgia and Indiana also had low responsiveness in the 2000 districting round (1.32 and 1.64, respectively). In these states, there were already oddly shaped districts designed to reduce responsiveness and protect incumbents.

However, we should not push this explanation of unexpected cases too far. It is true that the districts in Indiana drawn after the 2000 Census were somewhat oddly shaped, presumably in order to protect incumbents. However, the districts adopted in 2010 – which exhibit a very high level of partisan bias – are admirably compact. In fact, considering the district map of Indiana in the 2012 election, it is hard to imagine how the districts could have been made much more compact. As a result, compactness increased very considerably. A similar argument can be made about Georgia. What this demonstrates is that it is sometimes possible to draw districts that have a high level of partisan bias but nevertheless are still quite compact. The relationship between partisan bias and compactness is not a simple one.

It should be emphasized that compactness is not really the story here – partisan bias is. However, when arguing about gerrymandering, pointing to ill-shaped districts has a really strong intuitive appeal. It is possible to see that something is clearly being manipulated. Indeed, we appealed to this in Chapter 1 when we pointed to some of the more wildly shaped districts in Pennsylvania after 2010. Empirically, there does seem to be a link between compactness and bias – many of the states in which there has been a large increase in partisan bias are those in which compactness has fallen. If a state legislature is seeking maximum partisan advantage, it will often have to resort to drawing irregularly shaped districts, which will in turn result in decreased compactness. However, it is sometimes possible to draw compact districts that are extremely biased, just as it is possible for improbably shaped districts to be unbiased. *Vieth v. Jubelirer* (2004) did not remove a constraint on states drawing oddly shaped districts; it removed a constraint on them engaging in partisan gerrymandering.

CONCLUSION

We started this chapter by asking whether partisan bias in U.S. House elections had increased significantly between the 2000 and 2010 districting rounds. It is clear that partisan bias did increase very noticeably over this period. At the national level, the partisan asymmetry in 2012 was 9.38%, whereas for the 2002 districts, it was 3.4%. In terms of the bias, if the parties split the national vote 50/50, there is now a 5% bias toward the Republicans, as opposed to a 2% bias in 2002. Of course, the national picture is the result of a collection of state-level districting plans. When we look at the state level, we see a great deal of diversity. Many states are approximately unbiased, but a significant number display a very high level of partisan bias. Indeed, nine states have an asymmetry score of more than 30%. This indicates an extreme level of partisan gerrymandering, where one party gets 30% more than what the other party would have gotten if it had done equally well at the polls. There is also far more bias than we typically saw in 2002.

We can thus completely reject the idea that partisan gerrymandering is held in check by the need to balance seat maximization and incumbent protection. It is true that there is a trade-off between these goals. However, armed with modern geographical information system software and an absence of judicial constraints, it is possible to engineer so much advantage that it is possible to satisfy both of these goals. Put bluntly, if you can pack your opponents into a single district where they win 80% of the vote, you can create four districts where you have a 7.5% advantage. It is notable that the number of "incumbent protection" districting plans declined sharply between 2002 and 2012. It seems that more states are districting for national partisan advantage, even though it makes their incumbents slightly more vulnerable.

Of the states that have high levels of partisan bias in 2012, nearly all of them are biased toward the Republicans. A majority of these are in the South, although there are also some very significant mid-sized non-Southern states such as Pennsylvania, Ohio, and Michigan. However, it is possible to create pro-Democratic gerrymanders, as Maryland shows. There were also rather more pro-Democratic gerrymanders in 2002.

Thus we see an increase in partisan bias at both the national and state levels. This is exactly what we would expect given our story that the *Vieth v. Jubelirer* decision removed the threat of judicial challenge and effectively gave a green light to partisan gerrymandering. However, it has been argued by some that this bias is not the result of deliberate gerrymandering, but rather the inevitable result of various demographic factors, such as the fact that Democratic voters are concentrated in urban areas or the fact that the Voting Rights Act requires the drawing of majority-minority districts. Given that we now have a measure of partisan bias at the state level, we can turn to these explanations in the next chapter.

APPENDIX 3A – RESULTS

TABLE 3.A1. *Symmetry Measure by State 2012 (positive numbers indicate bias in favor of Democrats; bold indicates asymmetry significant at 5% level)*

Symmetry State	Mean	SD	5%	95%
Alabama	−43.1	12.4	−62.1	−21.4
Arizona	6.3	6.48	−5.83	14.3
Arkansas	0.045	9.67	−16.3	16.5
California	3.98	3.74	−2.15	10
Colorado	−7.67	10.2	−24.4	9.3
Connecticut	11.6	12.2	−10.2	29.9
Florida	−16.8	5.45	−25.7	−8.05
Georgia	−27.6	3.89	−33.9	−20.7
Illinois	2.89	7.26	−8.31	15
Indiana	−17.3	10.3	−33.4	−.0489

Symmetry State	Mean	SD	5%	95%
Iowa	−0.527	10.9	−19.6	17.7
Kansas	3.19	15	−21	29.9
Kentucky	−24	10.5	−36.1	−4.72
Louisiana	−35.7	13.4	−57.7	−12.6
Maryland	25.3	11.4	5.9	43.1
Massachusetts	−5.8	10.9	−24.1	12.7
Michigan	−20.1	5.99	−28.6	−9.42
Minnesota	−0.864	10.8	−19	17.1
Mississippi	−41.2	11.2	−50	−17.7
Missouri	−41.2	7.97	−50	−25
Nebraska	−19.6	15.9	−33.4	12.8
Nevada	1.89	13.9	−22.4	26.9
New Jersey	−0.37	2.98	−6.42	3.88
New Mexico	16.7	15.1	−10.9	33.4
New York	1.63	4.63	−5.64	9.19
North Carolina	−36.3	7.47	−48.4	−23.4
Ohio	−35.5	6.59	−45.5	−24.3
Oklahoma	7.35	13.7	−16	29.2
Oregon	16.1	14.9	−8.5	40.6
Pennsylvania	−36.4	5.01	−43.7	−27.6
South Carolina	−30.3	11.6	−48.9	−12
Tennessee	−27.8	8.48	−42.3	−12.6
Texas	−14.8	4.37	−21.8	−7.62
Utah	−15.3	15.5	−44.4	2.6
Virginia	−30.7	7.97	−42.8	−16.9
Washington	−0.887	9.14	−16.9	13.7
West Virginia	−12.7	18.3	−33.4	21.6
Wisconsin	−18	7.33	−25	−3.54

TABLE 3.A2. *Bias at 50% Vote Measure by State 2012 (positive numbers indicate bias in favor of Democrats)*

Bias at 50% State	Mean	SD	5%	95%
Alabama	−25.3	9.91	−35.7	−7.14
Arizona	4	4.56	−5.56	5.56
Arkansas	−1.1	15.1	−25	25
California	1.98	2.75	−2.83	6.6
Colorado	−3.56	7.96	−21.4	7.14
Connecticut	7	9.42	−10	10
Florida	−9.11	4.27	−16.7	−1.85
Georgia	−14.3	2.52	−21.4	−7.14
Illinois	0.856	5.29	−5.56	11.1
Indiana	−9.41	8.51	−27.8	5.56
Iowa	0.1	10.8	−25	25
Kansas	2.8	13.1	−25	25
Kentucky	−13.4	7.5	−16.7	0
Louisiana	−19	10.8	−33.3	0
Maryland	14	9.61	0	25
Massachusetts	−4.1	9.17	−16.7	5.56
Michigan	−11.3	4.18	−14.3	−7.14
Minnesota	−0.8	8.75	−12.5	12.5
Mississippi	−22.6	7.3	−25	0
Missouri	−22.5	5.1	−25	−12.5
Nebraska	−11.5	12	−16.7	16.7
Nevada	0.225	10.8	−25	25
New Jersey	−0.15	1.53	0	0
New Mexico	12.3	11.3	−16.7	16.7
New York	0.856	3.47	−5.56	5.56
North Carolina	−19.9	5.82	−26.9	−11.5
Ohio	−19	4.91	−25	−12.5
Oklahoma	4.52	11.9	−10	30
Oregon	9.02	12.3	−10	30
Pennsylvania	−19.7	3.42	−22.2	−16.7
South Carolina	−16.2	9.92	−35.7	−7.14
Tennessee	−14.3	6.05	−27.8	−5.56
Texas	−8.5	3.33	−13.9	−2.78
Utah	−7.52	12.3	−25	0
Virginia	−17.6	5.85	−22.7	−4.55
Washington	0.86	7.05	−10	10
West Virginia	−7.9	14.7	−16.7	16.7
Wisconsin	−10.7	4.51	−12.5	0

TABLE 3.A3. *Responsiveness by State 2012*

Responsiveness State	Mean	SD	5%	95%
Alabama	3.5	1.09	1.54	5.46
Arizona	1.57	1.05	0	3.33
Arkansas	7.26	2.25	3.67	10
California	1.86	0.388	1.21	2.49
Colorado	2.43	1.33	0.0411	4.51
Connecticut	3.09	1.82	0	6
Florida	2.37	0.573	1.41	3.33
Georgia	0.716	0.581	0	1.84
Illinois	2.21	0.646	1.11	3.31
Indiana	3.09	1.07	1.34	4.68
Iowa	4.21	2.54	0	8.86
Kansas	3.88	2.09	0	7.38
Kentucky	2.11	1.38	0	4.93
Louisiana	2.88	1.14	0.875	5
Maryland	3.77	1.22	1.57	5.69
Massachusetts	3.64	1.23	1.7	5.63
Michigan	1.32	0.617	0.403	2.36
Minnesota	2.92	1.18	1.25	5
Mississippi	1.76	1.36	0	4.29
Missouri	1.54	0.893	0	2.97
Nebraska	2.32	1.58	0	3.33
Nevada	2.99	1.86	0	5
New Jersey	0.382	0.487	0	1.37
New Mexico	2.69	1.55	0	4.95
New York	1.36	0.451	0.679	2.13
North Carolina	2.34	0.767	1.01	3.67
Ohio	1.96	0.653	0.834	3.12
Oklahoma	4.17	1.76	1.4	6.77
Oregon	3.73	1.46	1.41	6
Pennsylvania	1.4	0.578	0.55	2.34
South Carolina	3.66	1.29	1.43	5.71
Tennessee	1.59	0.858	0	3.23
Texas	2	0.435	1.33	2.73
Utah	2.78	1.59	0	5
Virginia	2.22	0.823	0.909	3.64
Washington	2.28	0.861	1	3.94
West Virginia	2.79	1.4	0	3.87
Wisconsin	1.35	0.864	0	2.55

TABLE 3.A4. *Symmetry Measure by State 2002–2010 (positive numbers indicate bias in favor of Democrats; bold indicates asymmetry significant at 5% level)*

Symmetry State	Mean	SD	5%	95%
Alabama	−20.9	11.5	−39.2	−1.29
Arizona	−1.29	10.3	−17.9	16.4
Arkansas	20.8	15.8	−1.55	47.1
California	19.9	2.5	15.5	23.6
Colorado	0.927	12.5	−19.4	20.4
Connecticut	−11	10.1	−20	9.54
Florida	−24.9	5.56	−33.9	−15.4
Georgia	−15	6.14	−23.1	−4.38
Illinois	−5.45	4.64	−13.3	2.37
Indiana	5.64	7.25	−7.93	14.8
Iowa	4.38	11.2	−16.3	20
Kansas	−3.75	16.9	−32.6	25.2
Kentucky	−9.31	12.1	−30.2	10.5
Louisiana	−5.35	13	−26.1	16.2
Maryland	38.9	9.13	21.9	50
Massachusetts	−11.4	8.31	−25.3	2.75
Michigan	−13.7	5.06	−20	−4.44
Minnesota	3.36	6.2	−3.98	16.3
Mississippi	−0.173	2.9	−0.255	0
Missouri	−9.61	3.58	−11.1	−1.34
Nebraska	8	16.8	−20.8	33.4
Nevada	0.0118	20.3	−33.4	33.4
New Jersey	7.69	3.14	1.85	13.1
New Mexico	−18.9	14.2	−33.4	8.86
New York	11.9	5.25	3.25	20.1
North Carolina	10.1	7.04	−2.97	21.6
Ohio	−20.3	5.91	−29.4	−9.98
Oklahoma	−39.2	13.8	−59.8	−14.1
Oregon	26.4	14.6	2.92	50.6
Pennsylvania	−18.1	6.02	−27.9	−7.99
South Carolina	−19.9	10.6	−33.4	−0.783
Tennessee	9.48	3.58	1.32	11.1
Texas	−10	4.64	−17.5	−2.05
Utah	−30.9	7.07	−33.4	−16.4
Virginia	−17.1	9.2	−32	−1.53
Washington	10.9	10.1	−6.19	26.4
West Virginia	11.7	19.7	−25.8	33.4
Wisconsin	−1.01	5.2	−11.7	6.55

TABLE 3.A5. *Bias at 50% Vote Measure by State 2002–10 (positive numbers indicate bias in favor of Democrats)*

Bias at 50% State	Mean	SD	5%	95%
Alabama	−12.1	9	−21.4	7.14
Arizona	−0.838	9.23	−12.5	12.5
Arkansas	12.6	12.9	0	25
California	10.6	1.61	8.49	12.3
Colorado	0.729	10.3	−21.4	21.4
Connecticut	−7.38	6.87	−10	10
Florida	−14.3	4.3	−22	−6
Georgia	−8.12	4.51	−11.5	−3.85
Illinois	−2.98	3.41	−7.89	2.63
Indiana	3.54	4.87	−5.56	5.56
Iowa	3.94	10.3	−10	10
Kansas	−2.28	12.4	−25	25
Kentucky	−5.37	9.84	−16.7	16.7
Louisiana	−4.63	11.1	−21.4	7.14
Maryland	21.3	6.22	12.5	25
Massachusetts	−7.02	9.25	−20	10
Michigan	−7.63	3.48	−10	−3.33
Minnesota	1.08	4.27	0	12.5
Mississippi	−0.075	1.77	0	0
Missouri	−5.36	1.64	−5.56	−5.56
Nebraska	5.77	15.6	−16.7	16.7
Nevada	0.0667	16.7	−16.7	16.7
New Jersey	3.82	1.84	3.85	3.85
New Mexico	−12.6	11	−16.7	16.7
New York	6.28	3.86	1.72	12.1
North Carolina	5.45	5.18	−3.85	11.5
Ohio	−11	4.45	−16.7	−5.56
Oklahoma	−23.1	10.2	−30	−10
Oregon	14.9	11.8	−10	30
Pennsylvania	−9.69	4.7	−18.4	−2.63
South Carolina	−12.2	7.92	−16.7	0
Tennessee	5.06	2.41	5.56	5.56
Texas	−6.04	3.69	−12.5	0
Utah	−16.4	2.78	−16.7	−16.7
Virginia	−9.43	7.66	−22.7	4.55
Washington	7.62	7.89	−5.56	16.7
West Virginia	7.7	14.8	−16.7	16.7
Wisconsin	−0.512	3.15	−12.5	0

TABLE 3.A6. *Responsiveness by State 2002–2010*

Responsiveness State	Mean	SD	5%	95%
Alabama	2.44	1.01	0.736	4.29
Arizona	3.75	1.19	1.58	5.53
Arkansas	3.15	1.52	0.0119	5
California	0.76	0.269	0.36	1.22
Colorado	2.97	1.09	1.32	4.29
Connecticut	1.8	1.3	0	4
Florida	2.45	0.578	1.5	3.44
Georgia	1.32	0.685	0.0846	2.33
Illinois	0.899	0.431	0.0812	1.58
Indiana	1.64	1.03	0	3.33
Iowa	3.71	1.96	0.31	6.91
Kansas	3.04	1.73	0	5
Kentucky	3.23	1.57	0.641	6.28
Louisiana	4.39	1.32	2.26	6.84
Maryland	1.72	0.906	0	3.3
Massachusetts	5.55	1.28	3.35	7.66
Michigan	0.996	0.515	0.013	2
Minnesota	1.12	0.968	0	2.59
Mississippi	0.255	0.753	0	2.5
Missouri	0.376	0.563	0	1.11
Nebraska	3.97	2.16	0.597	9.5
Nevada	2.89	1.1	0	3.33
New Jersey	0.472	0.498	0	1.54
New Mexico	2.96	1.97	0	6.67
New York	1.92	0.484	1.14	2.73
North Carolina	1.34	0.574	0.296	2.31
Ohio	1.73	0.592	0.73	2.77
Oklahoma	3.07	1.28	0.93	5.14
Oregon	3.4	1.46	0.51	6
Pennsylvania	2.43	0.801	1.13	3.82
South Carolina	2.32	1.31	0	4.87
Tennessee	0.41	0.559	0	1.12
Texas	2.13	0.509	1.3	2.99
Utah	0.662	1.21	0	3.33
Virginia	3.26	1.08	1.45	5.17
Washington	2.81	0.949	1.18	4.44
West Virginia	2.61	1.38	0	3.33
Wisconsin	0.782	0.858	0	2.5

APPENDIX 3B – METHODOLOGY

The fact that some congressional elections are uncontested creates some complications in calculating the seats/votes function and thus the symmetry measure. In 2012, forty-five congressional seats were uncontested by one of the two main parties. Furthermore, the practices for reporting the results in uncontested races vary from state to state. Although it is safe to assume that most seats are uncontested because the result would be lopsided in favor of one party, we cannot simply take the votes cast (where state law records them) at face value. Instead, we have to ask what the two-party share of the vote would have been if voters had been given the choice between two parties.

Fortunately, all voters are given a choice between the two parties in presidential elections. We can take the vote shares of the two main parties in recent presidential elections and use this to estimate the relative support for each party in each district. Data is available for the vote for presidential candidates apportioned over each congressional district (Nir 2008, 2012).[5] Using this data, we can model the relationship between presidential and congressional vote in congressional districts and use this to estimate the two-party vote share in the uncontested races. The simplest way to do this would be to simply regress the party's vote share at the presidential election on that at the congressional election and use this to estimate the missing values. However, we also estimate the party's share of support in uncontested seats in years when there is a presidential election. Therefore, we use the following procedure.

First, we estimate the overall level of Democratic support in a district, using all the presidential election years for which we have data apportioned over the district (2008 and 2012 for the 2012 districts, 2000, 2004, and 2008 for the 2002–2010 districts). Formally, the model we estimate is:

$$\text{DemPresidentialVote}[\text{district } i, \text{year } y] \sim \text{dnorm}(\text{muDemPresidentialVote}[i, y], \text{sigma}[y])$$

$$\text{muDemPresidentialVote}[i, y] <\!- \text{alphaP}[y] + \text{betaP}[y]^{*}\text{DemVoteShare}[i]$$

where i is the district, y is the year, and *dnorm* is the normal distribution. DemPresidentialVote[i,y] is the Democratic share of the two-party vote in

[5] Nir (2008) provides the results of the 2000, 2004, and 2008 presidential elections apportioned over the 2002–2010 congressional districts. Nir (2012) provides results for the 2008 and 2012 presidential elections apportioned over the 2012 congressional districts.

congressional district *i* in year *y*, while DemVoteShare[*i*] is the estimated level of Democratic support over the whole districting period in district *i*. The model was estimated using JAGS. The DemVoteShare[*i*] variable was then used to estimate the share of the two party vote the Democrats would have received in uncontested congressional races. To do this, we simply regress DemVoteShare on the actual two-party Democratic congressional vote share for the years in question and use the fitted alpha and beta coefficients to estimate the values of Democratic House Vote Share for uncontested races. Formally, the model is:

$$\begin{aligned}&\text{DemHouseVoteShare}[\text{district } i, \text{ year } y]\\&\quad = \text{alpha}[y] + \beta[y]^{*}\text{DemVoteShare}[i]\end{aligned}$$

where DemHouseVoteShare[i,y] is the Democratic share of the two-party House vote in district *i* and year *y*.

The measures of bias and responsiveness rely on a stochastic term to model variation in district vote share that cannot be accounted for by national- or state-level changes in party support. We estimate the size of this stochastic term at the national level by regressing the national democratic vote share on democratic vote share in each district for the five elections fought under the 2002–2010 districts. The model is as follows:

$$\text{DemocraticVoteShare}[\text{district } i, \text{ year } y] \sim \text{dnorm}(\text{mu}[i, y], \sigma)$$

$$\begin{aligned}\text{mu}[i, y] &< -\text{DistrictIntercept}[i, y] + \text{Dem\_Incumbent}[i, y]^{*}\text{incumbent}\\&\quad - \text{Rep\_Incumbent}[i, y]^{*}\text{incumbent}\\&\quad + \text{NationalDemocraticVoteShare}[y]\end{aligned}$$

where *i* is the district, *y* is the year, and *dnorm* is the normal distribution. Dem_Incumbent and Rep_Incumbent are dummy variables for the presence of an incumbent from the two parties. The point of this procedure is to estimate sigma, the standard deviation of the normal distribution. This is then used in the simulations to generate bias and responsiveness scores. This procedure was repeated with statewide Democratic vote share as the independent variable instead on national Democratic vote share. Unsurprisingly, the standard deviation estimates are quite high – 5.05% for national vote share and 4.68% for statewide vote share. Local and idiosyncratic factors are indeed important, and our estimates of bias take this into account.

4

Geographic Explanations for Partisan Bias

In the previous chapter, we found considerable evidence of partisan bias in the districting plans in many states that, when aggregated over the entire nation, gave the Republican Party a considerable advantage. Furthermore, we found that the level of bias in the 2010 districting round was approximately three times that in the 2000 round. However, it could be argued that this bias is not the result of deliberate partisan gerrymandering, but rather the inevitable results of geographical or demographic factors. For example, it could be argued that the observed bias is a result of the fact that Democratic voters tend to be concentrated in urban areas. This leads to Democratic votes being inefficiently distributed without the need for conscious gerrymandering. In this chapter, we consider the plausibility of such explanations.

There are a number of ways partisan bias could be explained without the need for deliberate gerrymandering. First, as we just noted, it could result from the fact that Democratic voters tend to be concentrated in urban areas. As a result, the Democrats win districts in these areas by far greater margins than they need, leaving the Republicans to win a greater number of nonurban districts by smaller margins. Thus the kind of bias we described in the previous chapter comes about as a result of where people live and would be hard to avoid regardless of who drew the boundaries. Alternatively, it has been suggested that the desire to provide descriptive representation for minorities and the need to draw majority-minority districts to comply with the Voting Rights Act might reinforce the concentration of Democratic voters in overwhelmingly Democratic districts. Finally, increased bias might result from the fact that the technology for districting (in particular geographic information systems) has improved. This explanation is slightly different in that it does not claim that bias is not the result of partisan motives. However, it argues that the increased bias we observe is not the result of a change in the motives of districting authorities or the constraints they face, but rather a result of the fact that they are more able to gerrymander accurately. That is, the motives have not changed, but the tools available to fulfill those motives have improved.

All these explanations sound initially plausible. This is because all these factors can be observed and almost certainly do constrain the districting process to some degree. For example, there are indeed many urban areas in which Democrats win with extremely lopsided margins, and this may well make it easier to produce a pro-Republican gerrymander than a pro-Democratic one. Similarly, the number of majority-minority districts has risen. In terms of majority-minority districts, minority voters (and, in particular, African Americans) tend to vote Democratic and be geographically concentrated. Finally, there is no doubt that our computing capabilities have made continuous progress.

None of this, however, shows that these factors can explain the increase in partisan bias we have observed. In fact, we have to carefully distinguish between two senses of the word "explanation." On the one hand, there is explanation in the strong sense. Here when we say that some factor (say the urban concentration of Democratic voters) explains partisan bias, we mean that this factor *forces* states to adopt biased districting plans, whether they want to or not. If we want to argue that partisan bias is not a matter of political choice, but rather the result of, say, demographic factors, we need an explanation in this sense. We need to argue that demographic factors make it impossible not to draw biased districts, given other constraints. That is to say, we have to argue that even if the other party had drawn the districts, they would have been forced to draw districts just as biased. Districting is not a random process in which bias emerges at the end as a result of a variety of factors. Rather, districting plans are chosen by the districting authorities (most commonly state legislatures with the approval of the governor). Furthermore, with modern geographical information systems, districting authorities will be quite aware of the partisan implications of their choices. Therefore, if we wish to absolve districting authorities from responsibility for biased districts – or even argue that the bias was unintentional – we need to argue that the partisan bias was unavoidable and thus that the districting authorities had no choice but to create biased districts.

There is one clear way to show when demographic or geographic factors cannot explain away partisan bias in this (strong) sense. We simply have to show that unbiased districting was, in fact, possible. Suppose we can show that it is relatively straightforward to produce a districting plan that is unbiased, in spite of geographical concentration and other constraints. Then the districting authorities cannot argue that they were forced by these constraints to produce a biased plan – unbiased plans were available, but they chose not to adopt them. In such cases, adopting a biased plan was a choice the districting authorities made – and quite possibly a choice made for political motives. There are at least two ways we can show that unbiased districting plans were possible. We can demonstrate that there are states that manage to avoid partisan bias in spite of the presence of, say, large urban concentrations of Democratic voters. In states where biased plans were adopted, we can use alternative districting plans to demonstrate that unbiased districting was possible.

On the other hand, there is a second, weaker sense in which demographic factors may serve as an explanation for partisan bias. Here when we say that (for instance) urban concentration explains partisan bias, we mean that urban concentration was a contributing factor that made it easier for districting authorities to district in a biased way. That is to say, if districting authorities wish to create partisan bias, urban concentration may increase the opportunity for them to do this. Suppose we have a state in which the party controlling the districting process wishes to district for partisan advantage in both the 2000 and 2010 districting cycles. We might explain the increase in partisan bias between 2000 and 2010 in terms of the growing urban concentration of Democrats. The reason, we might claim, that partisan bias has increased is that increasing urban concentration has increased the potential for drawing biased districts. This kind of explanation does not absolve the districting authorities from responsibility – there is a biased plan because the districting authorities chose to adopt it. Rather, what has increased is the ability of the districting authorities to get the districting outcomes they want.

Testing this weaker kind of explanation is more difficult and often involves statistical evidence. For example, if the urban concentration explanation were true, we would expect to find partisan bias in those states where the Democratic vote is extremely concentrated in urban areas. We would also want to consider the increase in partisan bias between 2000 and 2010. After all, the urban concentration of Democrats is not exactly new – it has been remarked on at least since Erikson (1972, 1241) – but the level of partisan bias nationally increased almost threefold between 2002 and 2012. If we want to explain this in terms of the urban concentration of Democrats, then we would need to find increasing concentration of Democratic voters relative to Republican voters. Furthermore, we would need to find this increased concentration in the states where partisan bias increased. Other explanations can be approached in the same way.

In the rest of this chapter, we consider the three alternative explanations we have outlined: the urban concentration of Democratic voters, the Voting Rights Act and majority-minority districts, and improvements in districting technology. In each case, we first ask whether it can serve as an explanation of partisan bias in the first, strong sense – that is, whether it forces states to draw biased districts. Our strategy is to show that drawing unbiased districts is in fact possible. Second, we ask whether each factor can serve as an explanation in the second, weaker sense – that is, whether it makes it easier or increases the potential for partisan bias. We explore this using patterns of change in bias across states and across time.

THE URBAN CONCENTRATION HYPOTHESIS

The first alternative explanation we consider is that the bias we observe is not due to gerrymandering, but rather due to the geographic distribution of Democratic voters. In particular, it is argued that Democrats are concentrated in urban areas and that this leads to a bias in favor of the Republicans without the need for active gerrymandering. The most recent – and most rigorous – version of this argument is that presented by Chen and Rodden (2013b) in a recent article in the *Quarterly Journal of Political Science*. Democratic voters tend to be concentrated in urban areas, particularly members of ethnic minorities. As a result, there are districts where the Democrats win 80% or more of the vote. This distribution of support is very inefficient, as only 50% of the two-party vote is required to win the seat. The Republican vote, however, is more evenly dispersed in suburban and rural areas. This allows the Republicans to win many districts comfortably enough but without wasting votes. The result is – to use Chen and Rodden's phrase – an "unintentional gerrymander." The bias happens due to geographic and demographic factors even in the absence of conscious partisan gerrymandering.

This explanation initially sounds plausible because many of the premises it is based on are, as a matter of fact, true. It is undoubtedly true that Democratic support – particularly from ethnic minorities – is concentrated in urban areas and that Republican support is more evenly

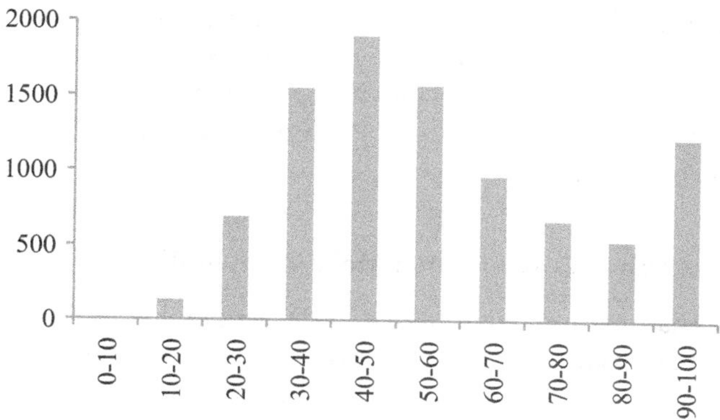

FIGURE 4.1. Number of precincts in Pennsylvania by Democratic percentage of two-party presidential vote 2012.

distributed. As Chen and Rodden (2013b) argue, when you look at support at the precinct level, the distribution of support is heavily skewed. Consider Figure 4.1. In Pennsylvania in 2012, the Democrats won 90% or more of the two-party vote in 1,219 of the 9,235 precincts; the Republicans won 90% or more in four precincts. If we consider precincts where one party wins 80% of the vote or more, the balance is 1,757 to the Democrats against 134 to the Republicans. There are even fifty-seven precincts where the Republicans won no votes at all. In Pennsylvania, the Democratic vote is definitely more concentrated than the Republican vote, even if we go down to the precinct level. Chen and Rodden (2013b, 243) consider the twenty states for which they can obtain precinct-level data and find a similar pattern of the Democratic vote being more concentrated, particularly in the more urbanized states. They also show (2013b, 245–246) that, at least in Florida, Democratic precincts are far more clustered around other Democratic districts than is the case with Republican precincts.

There seems to be little reason to doubt that the geographical concentration of Democratic support makes it easier to draw maps that have a partisan bias toward the Republican Party while making it more difficult to draw maps with a pro-Democratic bias. It has been argued for some time that these factors make it easier to produce Republican gerrymanders (Erikson 1972, 1241; Hirsch 2003, 194). However, this does not mean that such gerrymanders are "natural," "unintentional," or not a matter of political choice. It merely shows that the *opportunity* to produce pro-Republican gerrymanders exists. For urban concentration to explain partisan bias in the *strong* sense – that is, it forces states to adopt bias plans whether they want to or not – it is necessary that a state have no choice but to draw biased plans. We can refute this by showing that it was indeed possible to produce unbiased plans. It is to this task that we turn in the next section.

Does Urban Concentration Make Partisan Bias Inevitable?

To show that partisan bias results from geography and not political choice, it is necessary to show that those creating districting plans had no choice but to create plans with partisan bias. The authors of the districting plan may have had no choice but to create bias because it was simply impossible to draw unbiased districts. Alternatively, they may have had to draw biased districts because of the need to satisfy some other goals, such as having compact districts. (Of course, they would then have to justify giving this goal over unbiasedness.) If we can show that it was indeed possible to draw unbiased districting plans and state legislatures (or other districting authorities) chose not to, then the argument that bias is a result of geography rather than political choice collapses.

We can indeed show that drawing unbiased plans is possible and thus reject the explanation that electoral geography made partisan bias inevitable. This is true even in the states with the most extreme concentrations of urban Democratic voters. Indeed, in these states (New York, California, Illinois, New Jersey), there is a remarkable lack of partisan bias. In several states where severely biased plans were adopted, we can show that there existed other plans that were either unbiased, biased toward the Democratic Party, or only had a minor Republican bias. Some of these plans were even available to the districting authorities at the time of their deliberations, such as the student-generated districting plans generated for the Independent Bipartisan Redistricting Commission in Virginia (Altman and McDonald 2013, 792–795).[1] A further problem with the argument that geography produced partisan bias is the need to explain why partisan bias increased between 2002 and 2012. We consider demographic changes and find that these cannot explain the changes in bias over the last decade.

[1] Note that the Independent Bipartisan Redistricting Commission in Virginia was only advisory. The state legislature and the governor had authority over congressional districting.

TABLE 4.1. *Democratic Vote Shares in Major Metropolitan Areas*

Metropolitan Area	2010 Population	2012 Democratic Share of Two-Party Vote
New York:		
Bronx, Kings, New York, Queen, Richmond counties	8,175,133	81.7
California:		
Los Angeles County	9,818,605	68.9
Alameda, Contra Costa, Marin, Santa Clara, Santa Cruz, San Francisco, San Mateo counties	6,379,415	76.1
Illinois: Cook County	5,194,675	75.0
New Jersey:		
Essex, Hudson, Mercer, Middlesex, Union	3,131,105	71.0

New York, Los Angeles, Chicago

If partisan bias were the result of the geographic concentration of Democratic voters in urban centers, then we would expect to see evidence of bias in the state with the largest urban centers. These, as McDonald (2013) argues, are the places where it is simply not possible to draw maps that blend urban areas with suburban and rural precincts to prevent heavy (and electorally inefficient) concentrations of Democratic voters. The problem is when we look at the states that contain the largest metropolitan areas, we do not find evidence of partisan bias toward the Republicans.

Let us consider the three largest metropolitan areas in the United States according to the 2010 Census, New York, Los Angeles, and Chicago, and the states of which they are part. In all of them, there are contiguous areas comprising millions of people who vote overwhelmingly Democratic. Table 4.1 gives the 2010 population of various contiguous counties that are part of the major urban area and also the Democratic share of the two-party vote in 2012. Given that a congressional district typically has a population of 710,000, it is hard to see how it would be possible to avoid drawing multiple districts with high concentrations of Democratic voters. It is in these places that the "packing" of Democratic voters for geographical rather than political reasons is to some degree inevitable.

However, we do not find evidence of partisan bias toward the Republican Party in these states, in spite of the fact that the urban areas listed account for at least 35% of the population of each state. If we turn to the symmetry measures calculated in the last chapter, we find that the districting plans in New Jersey and New York are virtually unbiased (symmetry scores of −0.37% and 1.63%, respectively, where positive scores are bias toward the Democrats). In California and Illinois, there is very minor bias toward the Democrats, but this is not statistically significant (3.98% and 2.89%, respectively). It is also notable that we find that the 2002 districts in California, New Jersey, and New York were significantly biased in favor of the Democrats.

The question is, how are unbiased districting plans in these states possible when drawing "packed" Democratic districts seems unavoidable? We might note who controlled the 2010 districting process in these states. In Illinois, the districts were drawn by the state legislature, which was Democratic controlled. In California and New Jersey, there were districting commissions, on which there were representatives of both parties. In New York, the districts were determined by the courts. However, if partisan bias is a result of inevitable demographic factors, such as the urban concentration of Democratic voters, this should not matter.

In the case of New York and California, one explanation for the lack of bias is the fact that these are overwhelmingly Democratic states. The urban concentration of Democratic voters in New York City, Los Angeles, and the Bay Area may be electorally inefficient from the point of view of the Democratic Party. However, there is still considerable Democratic support in other parts of these states. The fact that the Democrats won 82% of the House vote in New York City in 2012 has to be balanced against the fact that they won 69% in the state as a whole. Similarly, the Democrats won 62% of the House vote in California in 2012, which puts the 69% they won in Los Angeles County into perspective. Thus while Democratic voters are "packed" in urban area, this packing is not that great relative to the support for the Democratic party in other parts of the state. The packing of Democrats into urban areas would pose a far greater problem for the Democrats in states that were more competitive, especially in those where it is difficult for them to win districts outside the urban concentrations.

This is why the examples of Illinois and New Jersey are so interesting. These are states where the urban concentration of Democratic voters should work most to the disadvantage of the Democratic Party. In both states, the urban counties in Table 4.1 account for at least 35% of the population and have Democratic support in 2012 of more than 70%. However, these are both competitive states, with strong Republican support in suburban and rural areas. In Illinois, the Democrats won 55% of the two-party congressional vote in 2012 and only 52% in 2010. In New Jersey, the Democrats won 56% in 2012 but actually narrowly lost the popular vote in 2010. By combining extreme urban concentration of the Democratic support with strong (but more dispersed) Republican support in the rest of the state, these states should be the hardest cases in which to avoid demographically generated Republican bias. And yet their districting plans are approximately unbiased.

This poses the question of how it is possible for Illinois and New Jersey to produce unbiased districting plans. In the case of Illinois, the answer seems to be with a great deal of effort. Illinois's plan was passed by a Democratic-controlled state legislature and approved by a Democratic governor. It was challenged in federal court by state Republicans (*Radogno v. Illinois State Board of Elections* 2011; *Committee for a Fair and Balanced Map v. Illinois State Board of Elections* 2011). A casual inspection of the maps reveals a great deal of cartographical creativity – District 4 and District 13 are among the least compact districts in the United States. Of course, the challenge in the courts failed – following *Vieth v. Jubelirer* (2004), the court found that the plaintiffs failed to produce a workable standard for adjudicating such cases (*Committee for a Fair and Balanced Map v. Illinois State Board of Elections* 2011). However, the plaintiffs did produce emails that they argued demonstrated that the map drawers had deliberately sought to maximize partisan advantage (*Committee for a Fair and Balanced Map v. Illinois State Board of Elections*, December 15, 2011, p.12). Indeed, the court agreed with the plaintiffs that "the crafting of the Adopted Map was a blatant political move to increase the number of Democratic congressional seats" (*Committee for a Fair and Balanced Map v. Illinois State Board of Elections,* December 15, 2011, p.2).

This demonstrates the limits that geography places on the drafters of congressional maps. As we have argued, it was indeed possible for the state legislature in Illinois to draw an unbiased map. However, it is notable that they were not able to do more than this – they were not able to produce a map that was strongly biased to the Democrats. If we accept the contention of the plaintiffs and the finding of the court that the map drawers were clearly seeking partisan advantage, this is notable. This suggests that it is difficult to produce a map biased toward the Democrats, even if the drafters are willing (as they certainly were in

Illinois) to draw very oddly shaped districts. Thus what we see in Illinois is certainly consistent with the idea that geographical concentration of Democratic support in very large urban areas can make drawing biased districts easier for Republicans than Democrats.

The alternative plan proposed by the *Committee for a Fair and Balanced Plan* (a group made up largely of Illinois Republicans) during litigation is interesting. It seems to be biased toward the Republicans but only to a modest degree. This shows that it is possible to achieve a plan that is not severely biased without the severely noncompact districts of the Adopted Plan. The political analysis presented by the plaintiffs suggests that eight districts would favor the Democrats and eight would favor the Republicans, while two would be balanced by the Cook Partisan Voter Index (*Committee for a Fair and Balanced Map v. Illinois State Board of Elections*, December 15, 2011, p. 13). Thus the plan would make a 10–8 split to the Democrats equally likely to a 10–8 split in favor of the Republicans. Given that Illinois very definitely leans toward the Democrats in terms of votes, this equality in districts represents a bias toward the Republicans. However, it represents a modest bias compared to some other states. The Republicans might win ten seats out of eighteen while Democrats win a majority of the vote. In Pennsylvania in 2012, the Republicans won thirteen seats out of eighteen in spite of a Democratic majority in the popular vote.

In New Jersey, it was also possible to produce an unbiased redistricting plan. However, in New Jersey's case, this came at the cost of very low responsiveness – in other words, the plan was an incumbent-protection gerrymander. As calculated in Chapter 3, the responsiveness of New Jersey's plan is 0.382 – a 1% increase in a party's vote share gets it a 0.382% increase in its seat share. This is by far the lowest in the United States. New Jersey's districting plan was produced by an independent commission made up of six Democrats, six Republicans, and one nonpartisan tiebreaker. Under the New Jersey districts, the Democrats and Republicans have won six seats each in both 2012 and 2014.

Thus we can reject the theory that the urban concentration of Democratic voters makes it impossible to draw unbiased districting plans. If we look at the states with the largest urban concentrations, we find that these actually have unbiased plans. This is true even of states such as Illinois and New Jersey that are electorally quite competitive. It is in these states that it should be hardest to avoid bias against the Democratic Party – urban concentrations are simply too large to blend away into mixed urban/suburban districts, while the Republican Party has enough strength in suburban and rural areas to take advantage of the inefficient distribution of the Democratic vote. Having said that, it is clear that geography constrains what the drafters of congressional maps can do. In order to produce a relatively unbiased map in Illinois, for example, the state legislature needed to draw some very noncompact districts. It seems unlikely that it would be possible to draw a map that is much more favorable to the Democrats, whereas drawing a plan that is biased to the Republicans in Illinois would be far easier. However, even in Illinois, it is possible to produce a compact plan that is only mildly biased toward the Republicans, as the alternate plan produced by the Committee for a Fair and Balanced Plan shows. The urban concentration of the Democratic vote may make the drawing of pro-Republican partisan gerrymanders easier, but they certainly do not make them inevitable. The bias of district plans, even in the most urbanized states, is a matter of political choice.

Other States and Alternative Districting Plans

As we have seen, the states with the largest urban concentration draw congressional districting plans with little partisan bias. We can now consider the states where we do find considerable partisan bias. Some of these do contain large metropolitan areas, such as Pennsylvania and Florida. However, we would not expect it to be so hard to avoid partisan bias from the urban concentration of Democratic voters in these cases. As McDonald (2013) argues:

> Upon some reflection by anyone who has drawn a redistricting plan – and I've been a redistricting consultant in 14 states – geography is not really constraining on congressional redistricting. Congressional districts are very large. In moderate- to large-sized states they consist of over 700,000 persons. It is easy in all but the most densely-urban areas to combine urban, suburban, and rural voters within a compact district. And again, the plans implemented in the states with the largest urban centers are not responsible for the current partisan imbalance among the congressional plans.

What evidence is there that partisan bias was not geographically inevitable in these states? The definitive way to show that it was possible to draw districts that were relatively unbiased is to produce such districting plans. Altman and McDonald (2013, 2014, 2015) have done this for three states with considerable partisan bias (Virginia, Ohio, and Florida). There is also an alternative districting plan for Pennsylvania that produces an approximately unbiased result (Perkins 2014). Wolf (2012) has also produced alternative, relatively unbiased districting plans for a considerable number of states. Furthermore, in the case of several Southern states in the 2000 districting round, Democratic-controlled state legislatures drew plans that were notably biased toward the Democrats (North Carolina, Tennessee, Texas).[2]

Altman and McDonald (2013, 2014, 2015) analyze citizen-drawn districting plans in Virginia, Ohio, and Florida. In the case of Virginia, they administered a competition to draw plans under the auspices of the Independent Bipartisan Redistricting Commission, while in Ohio they ran a competition hosted by various good-government groups. In the case of Florida, the state made the required district-drawing tools available online. The plans submitted by citizens do not represent all the alternatives or even a representative sample of them. Indeed, as Altman and McDonald (2014) argue, this would be an impossible task, as the number of potential plans is incommutably high. Nevertheless, the citizen plans do explore a wide range of possibilities, and all we need to show is that it is possible to draw plans that are relatively unbiased. It is untenable to argue that geographical concentration makes drawing unbiased districting impossible if a citizen can in fact draw such a plan that conforms to all legal requirements. Indeed, if various groups of citizens can independently come up with unbiased plans, it becomes difficult to argue that drawing an unbiased plan is even that difficult. Altman and McDonald find that in the cases of Florida and Ohio, there are legal citizen plans that are unbiased or even biased toward the Democrats. In the case of Virginia, they find citizen plans that slightly favor the Republicans (a one-seat advantage instead of the three-seat-advantage plan the state legislature adopted).

In the case of Virginia, Altman and McDonald (2013, 819–820) compare the adopted districting plan with plans drawn by the Independent Bipartisan Redistricting Commission and by teams of college students engaged in a competition using Web-based redistricting tools. The Commission's and many of the student plans are far less biased than the adopted plan – they give the Republicans a 6–5 split of Virginia's eleven districts when the vote is 50–50, as opposed to the adopted plan's eight seats out of eleven. Furthermore, they find that the lack of partisan bias in the Commission's and some of the student plans did not come at the expense of other desirable criteria. Indeed, they find that it is possible to draw a plan that has a 6–5 partisan balance that is more compact, retains the majority-minority district, and splits no more local political boundaries than the adopted plan. They do note that no submitted plan created a partisan advantage for the Democrats. Thus they accept that "there may

[2] Texas redistricted in 2003, replacing a plan that was strongly biased toward the Democrats with a plan more favorable to the Republicans.

be some modest truth to the claim that urban Democrats are inefficiently concentrated within their urban communities from a redistricting standpoint" (2013, 820). Although the fact that no one proposed a plan does not prove that it is impossible to draw one, they suggest that the need to keep District 3 as a majority-minority district makes it difficult to district for maximum Democratic advantage. Nevertheless, they state, "The numerous congressional plans demonstrate that the Republican legislature had a choice to create a Republican-favored congressional plan and was not mechanically following administrative criteria that resulted in a Republican-favored plan created as a byproduct of Democrats' inefficient concentration in urban areas" (2013, 819).

In Ohio, the picture is even clearer. Altman and McDonald (2014) analyze redistricting plans submitted to a competition organized by good-government groups from 2009 to 2011. They find that some of the plans submitted both satisfy the required criteria (population equality, a majority-minority district) and do as well or better on every other criterion (not splitting jurisdictions, compactness, partisan balance, and competitiveness). There are viable plans that are unbiased and balanced – indeed, there are even plans that are biased toward the Democrats by two seats (the adopted plan gave the Republicans a four-seat advantage at a 50–50 split of the vote). As a result, they conclude, "that had the legislature desired to improve any good-government criterion – it could have done so, simply by sacrificing some partisan advantage" (2014, 16).

Another state with evidence of partisan bias that Altman and McDonald consider is Florida (2015). Here they consider districting plans that were submitted to the state by the public using the state's online redistricting software. Of the 179 plans submitted by the public, forty-two met all legal requirements. There were plans submitted that were unbiased between the two parties. Indeed, there were biased toward the Democrats, giving them sixteen or seventeen seats out of twenty-seven with 50% of the vote (the adopted plan gives the Republicans seventeen seats with a 50–50 vote split). This, Altman and McDonald (2015, 16) argue, provides "strong counterfactual evidence to claims that Democrats must suffer a pro-Republican bias in Florida's congressional redistricting because they are inefficiently concentrated in urban areas of the state." However, they do note that there may be a trade-off between the number of majority-minority seats and the number of Democratic-leaning seats (we will consider this in detail later in the chapter).

Altman and McDonald's (2015) analysis of Florida's districts is interesting because the conclusions contradict those in the article by Chen and Rodden (2013b) in the *Quarterly Journal of Political Science* (*QJPS*), although not the expert report by the same authors for the plaintiffs in *Romo v. Detzner* (2014d). In the 2013 *QJPS* article, Chen and Rodden use a computer algorithm to generate a large number of simulated districting plans from 2000 election data. They find that the level of bias found in the actual districting plan adopted in the 2000 round is just within the 95% confidence limits of the bias found in their computer-generated plans. Thus they conclude that the bias found in the Florida districts may have been unintentional – generated by the geographical concentration of Democratic voters rather than by deliberate manipulation. The expert report for the plaintiffs in *Romo v. Detzner* (2014d), however, uses a similar methodology with 2010 data and the 2010 districts but reaches very different conclusions. They find that the adopted plan in the 2012 round was outside the confidence bounds of the plans produced by their simulations, which in this report seem to be only mildly biased toward the Republicans (61% of simulations gave the Republicans an advantage in fourteen or fifteen districts out of twenty-seven, while less than 1% gave the Republicans the advantage in seventeen districts, which is what the adopted plan gave them).

Why are the results of the two exercises by Chen and Rodden so different, and what does this mean for the possibility of drawing unbiased districts in Florida? The difference in the conclusions cannot be due to the 2010 districts being more biased than the 2000 districts. Indeed, according to our analysis in Chapter 3, asymmetry was 16.8% in 2010 districts, as opposed to 24.9% in 2000. This corresponds to the Republicans having an advantage in seventeen districts out of twenty-seven in 2010 but an advantage in seventeen out of twenty-five in the 2000 districts. Instead, what is different between the two exercises is the amount of bias generated on average by Chen and Rodden's districting simulations. The *QJPS* paper simulations produced gave the Republicans an average of 61% of the districts with a 50% vote, while the most biased expert report simulations (those with the three African-American majority districts taken as given) gave the Republicans only 52.7% of the districts on average. It is hard to say what accounts for this difference. However, as Altman and McDonald (2014, 6) argue, districting is mathematically a very, very difficult problem – there are more ways to assign census blocks to districts than there are quarks in the universe. It is impossible to enumerate all the possibilities and also impossible to know whether some algorithm that samples from the space of alternatives (as Chen and Rodden's does) gives a representative sample. Any algorithm may be unintentionally biased toward some outcomes rather than others, and there is no way to check this. As a result, we should be skeptical of results based on the distribution of simulation results.

The importance of Chen and Rodden's (2013a) expert report to us is that it provides additional evidence that drawing unbiased districts in Florida is possible, even if the three current African-American-majority districts are retained. We should be skeptical about any conclusions based on the distribution of simulations because we have no way of knowing whether the simulations generated are a representative sample. Furthermore, there are other reasons to be skeptical of conclusions based on the distribution of simulated plans. Districts are not generated by a random process by computers that are blind to political considerations. Instead, they are chosen by state legislators that are very aware of the political consequences of their choices. If the state legislature is presented with an unbiased plan but instead chooses a heavily biased plan, then it has made a political choice; it really does not matter that there are more ways to draw biased plans than unbiased ones. What the Chen and Rodden report demonstrates is that it is possible – indeed, not that difficult – to generate plans that are unbiased while retaining the current majority-minority districts.

We also have two alternative plans for Pennsylvania, another state with a very high level of partisan bias (an asymmetry score of 36.4%). Alec Perkins (2014) produced a plan using a computer algorithm for fairvote.us based on demographic and geographic considerations but blind to political considerations. This plan produced a partisan split of nine districts to each party given the 2012 vote (the adopted plan produced a 13–5 split in favor of the Republicans from 49% of the two-party vote). Perkins argues that computer-generated plans have the advantage that they are not susceptible to political manipulation. We do not necessarily accept that a computer-generated plan is unbiased or objectively correct for the reasons given earlier – any algorithm can have implicit biases. However, the alternative plan does have the value that it shows that a relatively unbiased plan is possible. Using political and demographic data, Stephen Wolf at Daily Kos also produced a plan using Dave's Redistricting App (Bradlee 2014) that results in three fairly safe seats for Democrats and three to five seats that lean Democratic (Wolf 2012).

Wolf's exploration of alternative plans also demonstrates the possibility of drawing fair plans in which a single party dominates a state geographically. In Tennessee, Indiana, and Missouri, Democratic voters are heavily concentrated in the urban centers. The 2002 Tennessee plan that was biased in favor of Democrats was essentially reversed in 2012, with Republicans insulating the seven-seat victory they won in 2010 but preserving two safe seats for Democratic incumbents. Similarly, under Wolf's alternative, the 5th Congressional District of Nashville looks much the same as it did under Democratic gerrymanders of the past, and the 9th District continues to encompass all of Memphis, home of the only nonblack representative of a majority-African-American district (Steve Cohen). However, the 4th and 7th districts become increasingly more competitive, balancing out the state's partisan distribution but still favoring Republicans in six of nine districts.

As previously noted, GOP-controlled redistricting in Indiana produced quite a compact plan, but in the process, it moved a number of Republican counties into the northern 2nd district, narrowly won by Democrats in 2010. The legislature also strengthened GOP control in the southern region by moving conservative suburban counties around Indianapolis into the 9th district, won by Republican Todd Young in 2010. In 2012, with 53% of the statewide vote, Republicans took seven of nine seats, but it was far from inevitable. The alternative plan drawn by Wolf puts at least three additional seats into play while maintaining a high level of compactness, even with Democrats remaining concentrated in the 1st (Chicago suburbs) and 7th (Indianapolis) districts.

Missouri is an interesting case for a number of reasons. First, the state lost a seat as a result of population shifts. Second, the GOP-controlled legislature took that opportunity break up one of two Democratic districts encompassing St. Louis, which also had the result of improving compactness. Third, over the Democratic governor's veto, the GOP plan was passed with the help of a handful of state Democratic incumbents. As a result, the two remaining Democratic congressional incumbents, both members of the Congressional Black Caucus, were also fairly well protected. With a single district representing St. Louis proper, even Wolf's alternative plan is moderately biased in favor of Republicans, but two additional districts, the 2nd and the 3rd, are made considerably more competitive. This yields a less biased plan overall while maintaining a high level of community cohesion and compactness.

Although our interest in alternative plans has mainly been to show that it is usually possible to draw unbiased districts, we do not mean to imply that it is never possible to draw districts strongly gerrymandered in favor of the Democrats. We have noted that there are some states, such as Illinois, where geography would probably make it extremely difficult to draw a strongly pro-Democratic gerrymander. However, there are other states where this is not the case. For example, a recent hypothetical districting plan (Daily Kos 2015) shows that it would be possible to redistrict California to create forty-seven safe Democratic seats out of fifty-three while still retaining plausibly compact districts. This would mean that the Democrats would win 89% of the seats from 58% of the vote they received in 2014. Of course, California now has an independent redistricting commission, and previously the Democratic-controlled state legislature seems to have drawn districts for incumbent protection rather than maximizing partisan advantage. Nevertheless, the hypothetical plan shows that it is quite possible to draw districts that massively advantage the Democrats, at least in one very large state.

Furthermore we can show that in several Southern states where there is now significant pro-Republican bias, pro-Democratic gerrymanders existed in the previous districting round. In these cases, it is clear that demographic and geographic factors did not make a bias toward the Republican Party inevitable. In the 2000 districting round, North Carolina and Tennessee both had asymmetry scores of around 10%, and in the case of Tennessee, this was statistically significant. Additionally, the districts in Texas prior to the mid-decade redistricting in 2003 were heavily biased toward the Democrats. Democratic support rapidly declined in the 1980s and 1990s, from 60% of the two-party congressional vote in 1988 to less than 43% in 1994. However, as a result of the districting plan passed by the Democratic-controlled legislature, the Republicans did not have a majority of the Texas congressional delegation until 2004. Evidently pro-Democratic gerrymanders are possible in some places.

Thus when we consider states where there is now considerable partisan bias toward the Republican Party, we can show that there are alternative plans that are either unbiased or only marginally biased. Indeed, in many cases it is possible to gerrymander in favor of the Democratic Party. Furthermore, it is possible to create unbiased plans while satisfying other requirements, such as drawing majority-minority districts. This is not to say the geography does not have an impact. The urban concentration of Democratic voters and the need to preserve majority-minority districts almost certainly make it harder to draw plans that favor the Democrats in some states. However, the fact that it is possible to draw unbiased plans shows that the decision to select heavily biased districts is a political choice.

Did Demographic Change Make Biased Districting Easier?

We have shown that it is quite possible to draw districting plans that are unbiased or almost unbiased, even in states where there are very large concentrations of urban Democratic voters. Therefore, we conclude that the urban concentration of Democrats cannot explain partisan bias in the *strong* sense – state governments were not forced to draw biased plans whether they wanted to or not. However, it is also clear that demographic concentration can constrain what kinds of districts a state can draw. In this section, we will consider whether the urban concentration of Democratic voters can serve as an explanation of partisan bias in the second, weaker sense – does it make drawing biased districts easier or make it possible to create more bias? In particular, can the increase in partisan bias we observe between 2002 and 2012 be explained in terms of an increase in the urban concentration of Democrats? Has demographic change made it easier to district against the Democrats?

We can measure the disproportionate concentration of Democratic voters using county-level data for the 2012 presidential election. The measure we use is Pearson's moment coefficient of skewness. This allows us to assess whether Democrats are concentrated in counties that are more extreme with regard to the mean than the Republicans. The definition of Pearson's coefficient of skewness is:

$$\text{Skewness} = M_3/\sigma_{vi}{}^3, \text{ where } M_3 = \Sigma\,(v_i - \mu_{vi})^3/n$$

while v_i is the Democratic share of the two-party vote in county i, μ_{vi} is the mean of the Democratic vote share, σ_{vi} is the standard deviation of the Democratic vote share, and n is the number of votes cast. If we weight this by the total votes per county, we get:

$$\begin{aligned}\text{Skewness} &= M_3/\sigma_{vi}^3\\ \text{where } M_3 &= (\Sigma\, p_i(v_i - \mu_{vi})^3)/\Sigma\, p_i\\ \mu_{vi} &= (\Sigma\, p_i v_i)/\Sigma\, p_i\\ \sigma_{vi} &= ((\Sigma\, p_i(v_i - \mu_{vi})^2)/\Sigma\, p_i)^{0.5}\end{aligned}$$

and p_i is the total number of votes cast in county i. A skewness score of zero indicates a symmetric distribution where the Democratic concentrations and Republican concentrations of voters mirror each other. A positive skewness score indicates a situation in which Democratic voters are more concentrated in extremely Democratic counties, while the Republican voters are more spread out in more balanced counties. A negative score indicates that the statewide distribution is skewed toward the Republicans – that is, Republicans are more concentrated in extreme counties.

TABLE 4.2. *Disproportionate Concentration of Democratic Vote and Partisan Bias 2012*

Skewness	No Significant Republican Bias in 2012			Significant Republican Bias in 2012		
		Skew	Symm		Skew	Symm
Distribution not skewed toward Democrats (Democrats not more concentrated)	CA	−.03	3.98	FL	−.42	−16.8
	CT	−.89	11.6	KY	.06	−24
	IL	−.07	2.86	NC	.03	−36.3
	IA	−1.36	−.53	OH	−.13	−35.5
	MN	−.11	.86	TX	.02	−14.8
	NE	−.47	−19.6	VA	.01	−30.7
	NV	−2.24	1.89	WI	−.08	−18
	NJ	.07	−.37			
	NM	−.17	16.7			
	OK	−.52	7.35			
	UT	.04	−15.3			
	WA	−.29	−.89			
	WV	−.34	−12.7			
Distribution skewed toward Democrats > 0.1 (Democrats more concentrated than Republicans)	AZ	.48	6.3	AL	.43	−43.1
	AK	.70	.05	GA	.28	−27.6
	CO	.14	−7.67	IN	.36	−17.3
	KS	.53	3.19	LA	.94	−35.7
	MD	.21	25.3	MI	.36	−20.1
	MA	1.08	−5.8	MS	.60	−41.2
	NY	.64	1.63	MO	.80	−41.2
	OR	.17	16.1	PA	.86	−36.4
				SC	.77	−30.3
				TN	.67	−27.8

We can now ask whether the states with biased boundaries are those where the Democratic voters are disproportionately concentrated compared to Republican voters. Table 4.2 gives the skewness of the distribution of county-level support and the level of partisan bias for the thirty-eight states with more than two House districts. As expected, the majority (25 out of 38) states have a distribution of counties skewed toward the Democrats – it is indeed the case that Democratic support is generally more concentrated in fewer counties than that of the Republican Party. There are, nevertheless, thirteen states where this relationship is reversed.

In terms of the relationship between skewness and partisan bias, we do not find a clear pattern. It is true that many of the states that have the most partisan bias also have a disproportionate concentration of Democratic voters. For example, Pennsylvania has one of the highest skewness scores (0.86) and partisan bias of 36.4% toward the Republicans. On the other hand, numerous states that have also managed to create biased districts with distributions that are hardly skewed at all, or even skewed toward the Republicans. For example, Ohio manages a pro-Republican bias of 35.5% even though there is a skewness coefficient of −0.13 (the Republicans are slightly more concentrated). Similarly, of the states where there is skewness of more than 0.1, there are eight cases of no significant bias as opposed to ten cases with significant bias. It is notable that states such as New York and Massachusetts are highly skewed toward the Democrats (not surprising when you consider the urban concentrations) but do not have significantly biased districts. As we have said before, we do not doubt that having heavy concentrations of Democratic voters makes it easy to draw districts that favor the Republicans. If these concentrations are there, it is easy to create inefficient one-sided districts without having to draw oddly shaped boundaries or even split counties. However, it is clear that it is possible to create very high levels of partisan bias without disproportionate concentration of Democratic voters, as states such as North Carolina and Ohio demonstrate. It is equally clear that it is possible to draw unbiased districts even when the distribution of counties is heavily skewed.

Of course, we should not conclude from these mixed results that geographical concentration does not make it easier to produce partisan bias. While it is true that North Carolina was able to produce a highly biased plan without the benefit of a skewed distribution of counties, to achieve this, it had to draw some extremely oddly shaped districts (Districts 4, 9, 12, and 13 are particularly noncompact). If the Democratic vote were concentrated in large urban areas, it would presumably have been possible to achieve the same result while drawing relatively compact districts. Furthermore, where we would really expect the geographical concentration of Democratic voters to have an effect is where states try to draw districting plans that are biased toward the Democrats. We have already commented on Illinois, where the Democratic-controlled state legislature drew some extremely noncompact districts but still only managed to produce a plan that was approximately unbiased between the parties. If there are large urban concentrations of Democratic voters that cannot be broken up, then even if the state legislature draws districts that pack Republican voters, the two sets of packed districts will approximately balance out. Of course, there are only five states where the Democrats controlled the entire redistricting process (Arkansas, Illinois, Maryland,

Massachusetts, and West Virginia – see next chapter). Of these, only Maryland produced a plan with significant bias toward the Democrats. The case of Maryland is instructive. The distribution of counties is only slightly skewed toward the Democrats, with a skewness coefficient of 0.21. The Democratic concentrations in Baltimore and the Washington, DC, suburbs are to some degree balanced by Republican concentrations in the East Bay and the west of the state. Furthermore, the state legislature had to draw some extremely noncompact districts to spread the main concentrations of Democratic voters among as many districts as possible. Thus it appears that while the urban concentration of Democratic voters makes producing districting plans biased toward the Republicans only slightly easier, it makes producing pro-Democratic gerrymanders very hard.

We turn now to whether the disproportionate concentration of Democratic voters can explain the almost threefold increase in partisan bias that took place between the 2000 and 2010 districting rounds. If this increase is to be explained by the disproportionate concentration of Democrats, then there must have been an increase in the relative concentration of Democrats compared to Republicans over the time period. Given that the disproportionate concentration of Democrats in urban areas has been documented for a long time, we might be tempted to assume that the relative concentration of Democrats has not changed much over the last ten years. However, we cannot assume this. While it is clear that Democrats did not suddenly start congregating in urban areas in 2010, there is a considerable literature that argues that the concentration of voters of both parties has changed considerably over the last ten years.

There is considerable evidence that the supporters of both parties have become more concentrated in areas inhabited by copartisans, although there is considerable debate as to why this is the case. Bishop and Cushing in their book *The Big Sort* (2008) argue that both liberals and conservatives have migrated to areas dominated by people with similar views. Furthermore, they argue, the fact that people are living in communities of like-minded people leads to increased ideological polarization. As a result, the percentage of people who live in "landslide" counties, where one presidential candidate received at least 60% of the vote, has nearly doubled since 1976 (Bishop and Cushing 2008). Analyzing survey and county data in more recent presidential elections (2000 and 2004), McKee and Teigen (2009) find increased geographic sorting across both regional sections of the United States, as well as urban-suburban-rural sorting. However, the fact that Democrats and Republicans are becoming geographically more sorted could be the result either of migration or of realignment (for example, people who already live in Republican areas become Republicans). Tam Cho et al. (2012) analyze registered voter migration across zip codes in two- and four-year intervals and find that across seven states, both Democrats and Republicans have relocated to areas populated with copartisans but that there has also been a more general pattern of relocation into predominantly Republican suburbs among registrants of both parties. Others have argued that there has not been ideological polarization at the mass level, but rather that the observed partisan sorting is a result of the parties at an elite level offering more distinct ideological alternatives (Fiorina et al. 2006, 2008; Abrams and Fiorina 2012; Jacobson 2013). In his book *The Partisan Sort* (2009), Levendusky argues that partisan polarization has taken place because liberals increasingly identify themselves as Democrats, while conservatives increasingly become Republicans. With the previously cited work, this is the result of the parties becoming more polarized at the elite level, as the liberal wing of the Republican Party and the conservative wing of the Democratic Party wither away.

Given that we are concerned with partisan bias and redistricting, what interests us here is the geographical concentration of party voters, regardless of what process causes it. Considering county-level data for the 2004 and 2012 presidential elections, we find that there is some evidence for increased partisan sorting over the period in which we are interested. (The first presidential election year after the 2002 congressional redistricting is 2004.) As a measure of geographical sorting, we simply use the standard deviation of the Democratic percentage of the two-party county vote, weighted by the total votes cast in each county. The more polarized the state, the more the Democratic vote in each county will be either above or below the statewide mean. Table 4.3 gives the results for the various states. What is apparent is that the level of dispersion increases in most states. It falls in only three and stays level in five. The increase is particularly marked in the southern states – most of the states with an increase of 0.02 or greater are in the South.

However, there is absolutely no reason increased partisan sorting should lead to partisan bias. The claim is that partisan bias is the result of the Democratic being *more* concentrated than the Republican vote. Because the Democratic vote is highly concentrated in urban areas, it is argued, Democrats use up votes inefficiently winning urban districts by far more votes than is necessary, leaving the more dispersed Republicans to win more districts by lower margins. However, symmetric sorting, in which both parties become more concentrated in their heartlands, does

TABLE 4.3. *Change in Standard Deviation of Democratic Vote Share 2004–2012 for U.S. President by County*

	SD	ΔSD		SD	ΔSD
Vermont	0.04	−0.01	Massachusetts	0.07	0.01
California	0.12	−0.01	South Dakota	0.10	0.01
New York	0.13	−0.01	Wisconsin	0.12	0.01
West Virginia	0.07	0.00	Kansas	0.11	0.01
Colorado	0.13	0.00	Pennsylvania	0.15	0.01
Delaware	0.10	0.00	Oklahoma	0.07	0.01
Michigan	0.11	0.00	Maine	0.04	0.02
Ohio	0.12	0.00	Nebraska	0.11	0.02
Iowa	0.08	0.01	Montana	0.11	0.02
Connecticut	0.04	0.01	New Jersey	0.12	0.02
Washington	0.11	0.01	Kentucky	0.11	0.02
Minnesota	0.10	0.01	Virginia	0.13	0.02
Oregon	0.13	0.01	North Carolina	0.12	0.02
Arizona	0.06	0.01	South Carolina	0.12	0.02
Idaho	0.11	0.01	Mississippi	0.17	0.02
New Mexico	0.14	0.01	Missouri	0.15	0.03
New Hampshire	0.05	0.01	Georgia	0.19	0.03
Utah	0.12	0.01	Louisiana	0.17	0.03
Florida	0.11	0.01	North Dakota	0.10	0.03
Indiana	0.12	0.01	Arkansas	0.12	0.03
Nevada	0.08	0.01	Alabama	0.15	0.04
Illinois	0.14	0.01	Texas	0.15	0.04
Maryland	0.19	0.01	Tennessee	0.14	0.04

not affect the relative concentration of Republicans and Democrats. In fact if the partisan sorting we observe is disproportionately the result of Republicans becoming more concentrated, it might even help the Democrats.

The question we need to consider is whether the concentration of Democratic voters has changed *relative* to that of Republican voters. In particular, if it is the case that urban concentration causes partisan bias, then we would expect to find relative Democratic concentration increasing in those states where partisan bias increases. As before, we measure the concentration of Democratic voters relative to that of Republicans using the Pearson moment coefficient of skewness, which we have defined above. Table 4.4 gives the change in the relative concentration of Democratic voters for the various states and the change in partisan bias.

The first thing that is apparent from Table 4.4 is that in most states, the level of skewness toward the Democrats *decreases*. This happens in

TABLE 4.4. *Change in Concentration of Democratic Voters Relative to Republicans and Partisan Bias*

Partisan Symmetry	*Static/Decreased Skewness* (Democrats *not* becoming more concentrated relative to Republicans)			*Increased Skewness* (Democrats becoming more concentrated relative to Republicans)		
Improved Partisan Symmetry (significant bias in 2012)	CA	−.21	15.92	AR	.39	20.76
	UT	.00	15.60	OK	.20	31.85
	MD	−.07	13.60	NY (−2)	.10	10.27
	OR	−.01	10.30	WA (+1)	.09	10.01
	FL (+2)	−.24	8.10	IA (−1)	.05	3.85
	NJ (−1)	−.04	7.32			
	MA (−1)	−.21	5.60			
	IL (−1)	−.17	2.56			
	MN	−.05	2.50			
	NM	−.08	2.20			
	KS	−.36	.56			
Reduced Partisan Symmetry (significant bias in 2012)	MS	−.30	−41.03	TN	.34	−18.32
	MO (−1)	−.33	−31.59	PA (−1)	.15	−18.30
	LA (−1)	−.34	−30.4	OH (−2)	.01	−15.20
	NC	−.22	−26.20	MI (−1)	.05	−6.40
	AL	−.12	−22.20	TX (+4)	.06	−4.80
	WI	−.01	−16.99	NV (+1)	.20	−1.88
	KY	.00	−14.69			
	VA	−.52	−13.60			
	GA (+1)	−.32	−12.60			
	IN	−.01	−11.66			
	NE	−.09	−11.60			
	SC (+1)	.00	−10.40			
	CO (+1)	−.20	−6.74			
	AZ (+1)	−.70	−5.01			
	WV	−.10	−1.00			
	CT	−.42	−.60			

twenty-seven out of the thirty-eight states with at least three districts. That is to say, the relative concentration of Democratic voters compared to Republican voters actually falls in these states. Rather than explaining partisan bias against the Democrats, this kind of change should actually benefit the Democratic Party. The more geographical concentrations of Democratic voters are balanced by similar concentrations of Republican voters, the easier it should be to draw unbiased districting plans or even pro-Democratic gerrymanders. Of course, the fall in the relative skewness might not be so surprising when we consider that the Democratic vote was already extremely concentrated in urban areas. If the Democratic vote is already highly concentrated and there is nevertheless further partisan sorting, we may speculate that this is disproportionately the consequence of the previously more dispersed Republican voters becoming more concentrated in heavily Republican areas.

Second, if the concentration of the Democratic vote is going to explain partisan bias, then we should expect to see an increase in Democratic concentration in those states where partisan bias increases. But this is not what we observe. Of those states where partisan bias increased between the 2000 and 2010 districting rounds, those with an increase in skewness are outnumbered by those where there was no increase in skewness by more than two to one. We also find that there was reduced skewness in most of the states where there was statistically significant partisan bias in 2012. Furthermore, when we consider those states where there was increased skewness, we find that they are almost balanced between those where partisan bias increases and those where it decreases (six increases versus five decreases). The results we observe are simply not consistent with the increase in partisan bias being the result of the increased concentration of Democratic voters.

We can now summarize our results with regard to the urban concentration hypothesis. We can certainly refute the urban concentration hypothesis as an explanation of the *strong* type. The urban concentration of Democrats does not force states to draw biased districting plans. We can show, using both the adopted plans of highly urbanized states and alternative plans, that it is quite possible to draw unbiased districting plans in spite of the urban concentration of Democrats. In terms of urban concentration as an explanation of the second *weak* type, the urban concentration of Democratic voters may make districting in favor of the Republican Party slightly easier, but not as much as we might have thought. If there are large concentrations of Democratic voters, it is easy to pack them into a few compact districts. However, if these concentrations do not exist, it is still possible to produce bias, but it will require drawing some very noncompact districts, as in the case of North Carolina. What is notable, however, is that the almost threefold increase in partisan bias that we saw between 2002 and 2012 cannot be explained in terms of the urban concentration of Democrats. This is because the geographical concentration of Democrats relative to Republicans actually moved the opposite way expected – the Democrats actually became less concentrated relative to the Republicans in most states.

MAJORITY-MINORITY DISTRICTS AND THE VOTING RIGHTS ACT

We have seen that the urban concentration of Democratic voters cannot explain the rise in partisan bias we observe after 2010, although this concentration certainly does constrain what outcomes are possible. However, even if it is theoretically possible to draw unbiased districts in spite of the urban concentration of Democrats, it might be suggested that the need to draw majority-minority districts might make biased outcomes inevitable. As with the urban concentration hypothesis, this sounds initially plausible. Given very strong minority (particularly African-American) support for the Democratic Party, we would expect drawing majority-minority districts would lead to "packed" Democratic districts, similar to those we would draw if we were trying to gerrymander against the Democrats. Furthermore, the number of majority-minority districts has indeed increased in the last districting round. However, we will see that this cannot explain the increase in partisan bias. Most of the new majority-minority seats are not in the states where partisan bias has increased. Furthermore, many of the alternative districting plans we have already considered include as many majority-minority districts as the districting plans the state adopted. The need to draw majority-minority districts clearly does not make drawing highly biased plans inevitable.

We need to consider exactly what constraints the Voting Rights Act places on states drawing congressional districts. Section 2 of the 1965 Act states, "No voting qualifications or prerequisite to voting, or standard, practice, or procedure shall be imposed or applied by any State or political subdivision to deny or abridge the right of any citizen of the United States to vote on account of race or color." In 1975, this was amended to include language minorities. In 1982, the Act was amended to make clear that a violation could be established if, considering "the totality of circumstances," it could be shown that "the political processes leading to nomination or election in the State or political subdivision are not equally open to participation by members of a class of citizens" protected by the Act. That is to say, it was not necessary to prove intent. Interpreting this in *Thornburg v. Gingles* (1986b), the Supreme Court laid out a three-part test – to show vote dilution, it was necessary to show that (1) there is a minority community geographically compact enough to make a majority-minority district; (2) this community is politically cohesive; (3) there is bloc voting by the majority community that will generally prevent the minority from electing candidates of its choice. Thus, if there is a large, compact minority community that could easily make a congressional district, but the district drawers nevertheless choose to split it and prevent minority voters being in the majority in any district, then this would violate the Voting Rights Act.

It is important to recognize what the Voting Rights Act does not require. It does not require that majority-minority districts must be drawn whenever possible, nor does it require that a certain proportion of districts be majority-minority. It is not enough to show that a majority-minority district could be drawn – it is necessary to show that there is a reasonably compact majority-minority district. Although the Supreme Court has not given a precise definition of compactness, it has stated emphatically in *Abrams v. Johnson* (1997, 91–92) and *LULAC v. Perry* (2006, 433–434) that oddly shaped districts that reach out to combine more than one community do not meet the criteria. Furthermore, in *Johnson v. DeGrandy* (1994), the Supreme Court found that the Voting Rights Act does not require that the number of majority-minority districts be maximized, nor that the number must be proportional to the minority population of the state. Indeed, such proportionality is not only not required, but it does not even prove that a violation has *not* taken place (see Levitt 2014 for recent attempts by states to argue this). It is notable that the 1982 amendment to the Voting Rights Act explicitly states that it does not provide a right to proportional representation of minorities.

Although it is possible to exaggerate what the Voting Rights Act requires, it is clear that it does constrain those drawing districts to some degree. If there is a clear, compact minority community that could form a majority-minority district, and a state chooses to split the community to prevent a majority-minority district, then there may well be a violation. Furthermore, even without the Voting Rights Act, ensuring descriptive representation for minority voters may be considered a valid goal for districting authorities. The question that concerns us is what effect this has on partisan bias. It has been argued that the need to draw majority-minority districts disadvantages the Democrats because it forces the inefficient concentration of overwhelmingly Democratic minority voters. Indeed, there were numerous studies arguing that this was the case in the 1990s (Cameron et al. 1996; Lublin 1997; Epstein and O'Halloran 1999), although this finding was disputed by other studies (Engstrom 1995; Shotts 2001; Grigg and Katz 2005). We would also expect other factors to influence the degree to which majority-minority districts disadvantage the Democratic Party, such as whether the district is substantially more than 50% minority and on whether the nonminority voters in the districts are heavily Democratic (see Shotts 2001). It is also possible, as Shotts (2001) argued, that in some states, the requirement to draw minority-majority districts may help the Democrats. For example, if the Republicans regularly win 65% of the vote in state and control districting, they can win every district in the state simply by drawing every district to be a microcosm of the state. However, the requirement to draw majority-minority districts may force them to create one or two safe Democratic districts that they would not have drawn otherwise. Indeed, there are a number of states where the only Democratic Congress members represent majority-minority districts.

We can now consider whether the Voting Rights Act and the need to draw majority-minority districts can explain partisan bias in the two senses laid out at the beginning of the chapter. For the Voting Rights Act to explain partisan bias in the first *strong* sense, it must force states to draw biased districts. That is to say, it must make it impossible to draw districts that are unbiased. If it is possible to draw unbiased districts, and districting authorities choose to draw biased districts instead, then this is a choice that the districting authorities have made. They cannot claim to have been forced by the Voting Rights Act or anything else. For the Voting Rights Act to explain partisan bias in the second *weak* sense, it is only necessary for it to contribute to partisan bias by making it easier to produce biased districts. We will be particularly interested to see whether the creation of additional majority-minority districts in certain states can explain the increase in partisan bias between 2002 and 2010.

Does the Voting Rights Act Make Partisan Bias Inevitable?

For the Voting Rights Act to be an explanation of partisan bias of the first *strong* type, it is necessary for it to force states to district in a biased manner. That is to say, it must make it impossible to draw unbiased districts. To refute this claim, we have to show that it is possible to draw districts that are unbiased while at the same time providing minority representation and compliance with the Voting Rights Act. We can do this by pointing to states that adopted such districts and, in the case of states with strongly biased districting plans, by showing that alternative plans were available that treated both parties symmetrically while still providing majority-minority districts. Much of the evidence we present here is the same as that related to the "urban concentration" hypothesis. This is not surprising, of course, given minority populations tend to vote Democratic and be concentrated in urban areas.

As we have already noted, some states with very large urban concentrations (such as New York, New Jersey, California, and Illinois) also have unbiased districting plans. These states also have considerable minority populations and multiple majority-minority districts. Indeed, California has the highest number of majority-minority districts in the nation. Currently, in thirty-five out of the fifty-three California districts, minorities form a majority in the sense that non-Hispanic whites are not a majority. Even if we consider majority-minority districts in the sense relevant to the Voting Rights Act – a particular minority group is a majority in the district – there are thirteen such districts. New York and Illinois both have four majority-minority districts (three African American, one Hispanic), while New Jersey has two. All these states conform to the Voting Rights Act. It is true that some states with multiple majority-minority districts do have biased districting plans (for example, Texas, Florida, and Georgia). Nevertheless, it is clear that it is possible for some states with large minority populations to draw unbiased maps.

In the case of states with biased district plans, we can consider alternative plans that have been proposed. A number of the studies of alternative plans that we have already considered explicitly take minority representation into account. The work of Altman and McDonald (2013, 2014, 2015) is notable in this respect. In the case of the alternative plans they consider for Ohio (Altman and McDonald 2014), they find that it is possible to find unbiased plans that provide equal minority representation to the adopted plan and meet all other constraints. Indeed, they even find such plans that are biased in favor of the Democrats. In the case of Virginia (Altman and McDonald 2013), they find that all of the proposed alternative plans have a slight bias toward the Republicans. However, this bias (6–5 to the Republicans when the statewide vote is evenly split) is far less than the 8–3 advantage the adopted plan gives the Republicans. Of course, as Altman and McDonald point out, the fact that none of the plans submitted in the competition gave the Democrats an advantage does not mean that it is impossible to draw such a plan. Nevertheless, they conclude that an independent commission "would likely produce a plan that modestly benefited Republicans, although nowhere near as much as the plan adopted by the Republican controlled state legislature" (2013, 830).

In the case of Florida, Altman and McDonald find that there were alternative plans proposed that were unbiased (and some even biased toward the Democrats) while still providing four Hispanic majority districts and two African-American majority districts. However, the plan adopted by Florida created three African-American majority districts. The additional African-American majority district is District 5. This is one of the least compact districts in the United States, running 200 miles from

Jacksonville south along the James River, inland to Gainesville, and south past the Ocala National Forest before taking in some parts of Orlando. It is hard to argue that this is required by the Voting Rights Act, as it clearly does not represent a geographically compact African-American community. Indeed, in 2014, a Florida court ruled that the district violated Florida's Fair District Amendment, which was passed by initiative in 2010. (District 5 was ordered to be redrawn for the 2016 election, but the new district retains essentially the same shape as the old.)[3] Nevertheless, Altman and McDonald argue that while drawing unbiased plans is possible, there may be some trade-off between Democratic seats and majority-minority seats.

However, Chen and Rodden (2013a) show that it is possible to create an unbiased districting plan for Florida while retaining the existing majority-minority districts. In their expert report or the plaintiffs in the case of *Romo v. Detzner* (2014d), Chen and Rodden find that even if we take the three African-American-majority districts (Districts 5, 20, and 24) as given, 64% of the simulated plans their computer algorithm generated gives the Republicans an advantage in either fourteen or fifteen districts out of twenty-seven. This represents a modest pro-Republican bias (the adopted plan gives the Republicans an advantage in seventeen districts). Furthermore, around 25.3% of these simulations produced a modest (in most cases one-seat) pro-Democratic bias, showing that this indeed is possible even with the majority-minority districts. As the number of majority-minority districts required was reduced, the plans on average became more unbiased. This suggests that, while majority-minority districts may make drawing unbiased plans more difficult, they certainly do not make it impossible.

Thus we can conclude that the need to draw majority-minority districts and comply with the Voting Rights Act does not make it impossible to draw unbiased districting plans. Some of the states with the largest minority populations and most majority-minority districts, such as California, have relatively unbiased districting plans. Furthermore, in the case of some states that are notably biased, it is possible to provide alternative plans that are either unbiased or exhibit only a very modest bias toward the Republican Party. This is not to say that there is never a trade-off between minority representation and partisan fairness. It will sometimes

[3] See http://thehill.com/blogs/ballot-box/house-races/211930-judge-strikes-down-florida-congressional-lines; http://www.washingtonpost.com/national/a-new-district-yields-the-same-result-in-florida/2014/08/17/9564479e-2164-11e4-86ca-6f03cbd15c1a_story.html.

be possible to propose a plan that both increases partisan advantage and provides more minority representation. Thus we will see surprising alliances, such as African-American state legislators in Missouri voting with Republicans to override the veto from a Democratic governor and Democratic Congress Member Corrine Brown and Florida Republicans both opposing legal challenges to Florida District 5. Nevertheless, we can reject the argument that requiring minority representation makes partisan bias unavoidable.

Did the Increasing Number of Majority-Minority Districts Contribute to Partisan Bias?

We have seen that it is possible to draw unbiased districts while still complying with the Voting Rights Act. Here we consider whether the Voting Rights Act can serve as an explanation of partisan bias in the second *weak* sense. That is to say, is the Voting Right Act a factor that contributed to partisan bias? In particular, can the increase in the partisan bias between the 2000 and 2010 districting rounds be explained by the increase in the number of majority-minority districts over the same period?

While there are a number of ways to measure the ethnic or racial majority status of populations (absolute majority of a single race or ethnicity, percentage of nonwhite population, etc.), the number of majority-minority congressional districts has grown substantially over the last several decades however measured, largely as a result of the growth of Latino populations in the South and Southwest (Johnson 2003; Bell and Wasserman 2013). Figure 4.2 gives the number of nonwhite majority districts by state in 2002 and 2012, with nonwhite majority district being defined as a district where non-Hispanic whites are not a majority.

Of course, the Voting Rights Act does not require or grant any particular status to nonwhite majority districts. In Voting Rights Act cases, the courts have only recognized majority-minority districts in the sense that a particular minority is a majority. These are required when such a district can be drawn from a geographically compact community and the other conditions laid out in *Thornburg v. Gingles* (1986b) are met. Figure 4.3 charts the distribution and growth of majority Latino and black congressional districts from the 110th Congress to the 113th Congress, with the "new" majority-minority districts from the 113th Congress stacked above those from prior state districting plans. States are sorted along the spectrum of increasing partisan symmetry change. There are also two Asian-American majority districts, one in California and one in Hawaii.

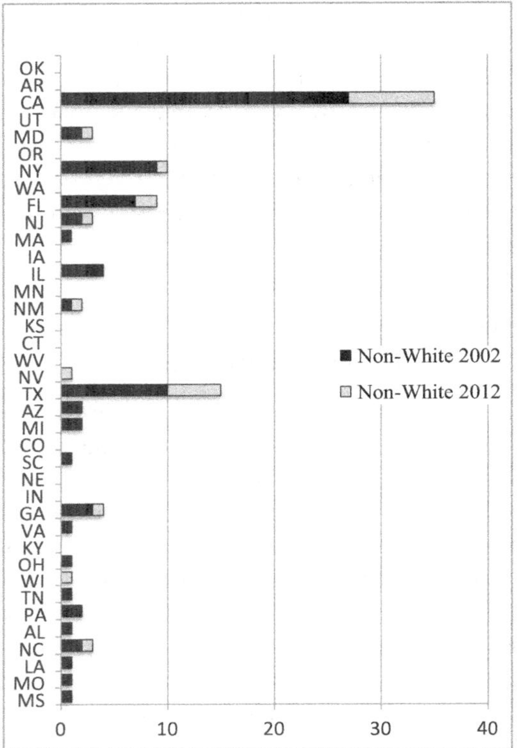

FIGURE 4.2. Majority-nonwhite congressional districts.

These figures reinforce the findings of the previous section that the presence of majority-minority districts does not make biased districting inevitable. There are four states with four or more majority-minority districts – California, Texas, Florida, and New York – and they account for more than 60% of the total number of majority-minority districts. Of these, Texas and Florida have statistically significant partisan bias, but California, Illinois, and New York do not.

It is also clear that the increase in partisan bias that we observed in many states cannot be explained in terms of the increase in the number of majority-minority districts. This is simply because the number of majority-minority districts did not increase in those states. In fact, there were additional majority-minority districts in only six states – there were two additional Latino districts in California, two in Texas, one in Michigan, New Mexico, and New York, and one new African-American district in North Carolina. Of these states, there was an increase in partisan bias in Texas, Michigan, and North Carolina, but not in California, New

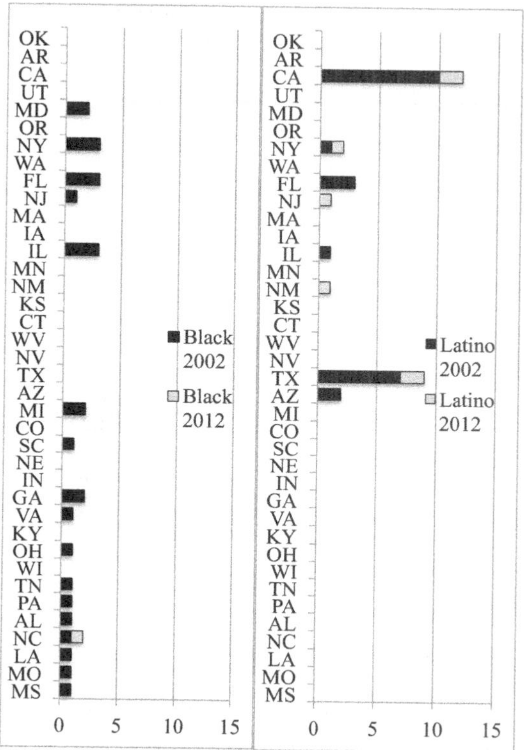

FIGURE 4.3. Majority Black and Latino/a congressional districts.

Mexico, or New York. However, of the sixteen states that had partisan bias in 2012 that was both increased and statistically significant, thirteen of them had no additional majority districts.

However, while the Voting Rights Act and the need to create majority-minority districts cannot explain the increase in bias we observe between 2002 and 2012, majority-minority districts may still have some role in the process. Many of the states that saw partisan bias increase have majority-minority districts – or rather a single majority-minority district in most cases. It is possible that partisan bias is in part created by packing more minority voters into existing majority-minority districts. This is, of course, in no way required by the Voting Rights Act. Rather, it represents a choice by the state legislature or other districting authorities. In order to create partisan bias, it is necessary to pack your opponents into districts that they win by overwhelming margins. Majority-minority districts may often be the most convenient instruments of such a policy.

TABLE 4.5. *Symmetry and Average Minority District Density for Minority-Majority Districts in States with MMDs (sorted by 2012 symmetry)*

State	2012 Sym	Δ Sym	% Black*	Δ	% Latino**	Δ
Alabama	−43.1	−22.2	64.1	1.7		
Mississippi	−41.2	−41.0	65.1	1.2		
Missouri	−41.2	−31.6	51.0	0.3		
Pennsylvania	−36.4	−18.3	61.6	−0.9		
North Carolina	−36.3	−26.2	53.6	2.4		
Louisiana	−35.7	−30.4	62.9	−1.9		
Ohio	−35.5	−15.2	55.9	−1.0		
Virginia	−30.7	−13.6	59.7	2.2		
South Carolina	−30.3	−10.4	58.7	1.3		
Tennessee	−27.8	−18.3	65.4	5.2		
Georgia	−27.6	−12.6	57.2	1.7		
Michigan	−20.1	−6.4	59.2	−2.9		
Florida	−16.8	8.1	55.2	−0.5	69.3	7.0
Texas	−14.8	−4.8			71.7	2.8
New Jersey	−0.4	7.3	55.2	−4.7		
New York	1.6	10.3	56.1	−6.2	55.3	−2.5
Illinois	2.9	2.6	55.3	−8.8	67.9	−3.4
California	4.0	15.9			63.7	3.4
Arizona	6.3	−5.0			59.9	8.2
Maryland	25.3	13.6	56.5	−2.9		

* % black in black MMDs
** % Latino in Latino MMDs

To test this possibility, we subtract the average percentage of African Americans and Latinos in districts where those races that made up a majority of the population in the 110th congressional districts from the 113th Congress averages. That is, we are measuring changes in district racial densities only for majority-majority districts, not changes in racial densities across all districts. There was only a single majority Asian district (Hawaii) in the prior districting, and only two (Hawaii and California) in the 113th Congress, so we focus our attention on black and Latino districts. Table 4.5 gives the change in minority district density and partisan bias for all states that had Black or Latino majority-minority districts.

Figure 4.4 and Figure 4.5 display the results for these states. For majority-Latino districts, we find no evidence that states with increased densities in majority-minority districts have more biased redistricting plans. Only Florida, Texas, New York, Illinois, Arizona, and California

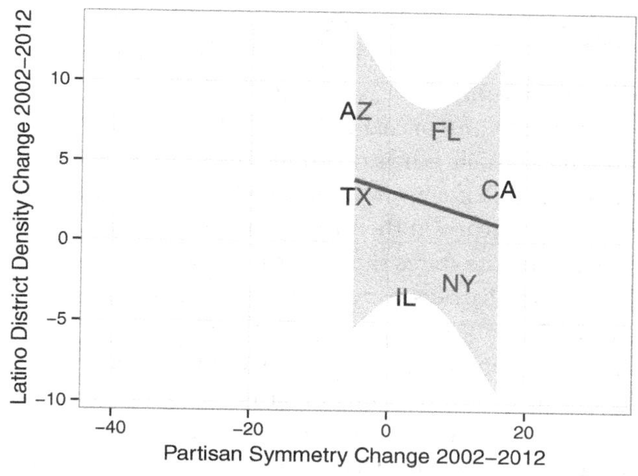

FIGURE 4.4. Majority Latino congressional districts.

had majority-Latino districts in the prior redistricting. Arizona and Florida, the states with the largest average increases in density (8.2% and 7%, respectively), had the same number of majority-Latino seats in the 110th and 113th congressional plans. As already noted, Florida's 2011 plan was an improvement in partisan symmetry, even though the average majority-Latino district density increased from 62.4% to 69.3%. Arizona's districting plan changed very little in terms of partisan bias,

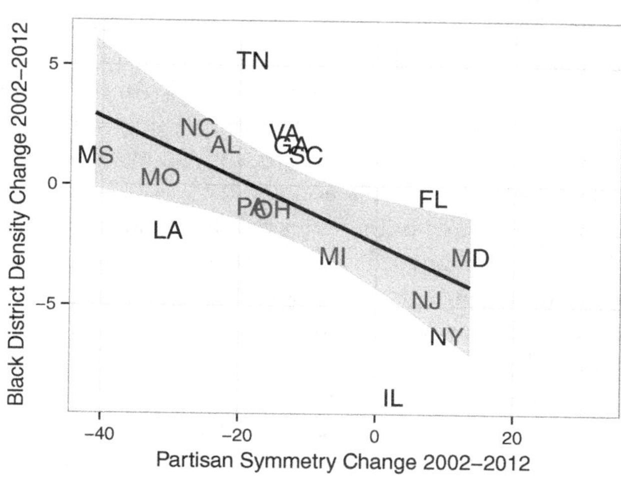

FIGURE 4.5. Changes in majority-Black district density and partisan symmetry change.

even with an additional seat awarded through population growth and a majority-Latino district density increase from 51.7% to 59.9%.

By contrast, states with increased majority-African-American densities have clearly adopted more biased districting plans. Among the states with substantial reductions in partisan symmetry, only Louisiana (−1.9%), Ohio (−1.0%), and Pennsylvania (−0.9%) had lower average percentages of African Americans in their majority-minority districts after redistricting. Conversely, the states that had the largest reduction in density in their Black-majority districts were Illinois (−8.8%), New York (−6.2%), and New Jersey (−4.7%). As previously noted, these states are home to some of the most populous, diverse metropolitan regions in the country. All three states were previously biased in favor of Democrats, but substantial improvement in symmetry has made these states virtually unbiased in 2012. In heavily Democratic New York, the average percentage of African Americans in the state's three majority-Black districts declined from 62.2% to 56.1% in 2012. In more competitive New Jersey (one seat) and Illinois (three seats), average density in African-American majority districts declined from 59.9% and 64.1% to 55.2% and 55.3%, respectively.

The three states with the largest increases in majority-Black district density, Tennessee (5.2%), North Carolina (2.4%), and Virginia (2.2%), include some of the most biased plans in the country. In Tennessee, the single African-American district was already quite safe, but the target population expanded to 65.4% under the new districting plan, for a total nonwhite population of 73.6%. Similarly, Virginia's 3rd District was already a densely packed district, but under the 113th congressional redistricting, the district is now 59.7% African American, two-thirds (67%) nonwhite. North Carolina moved from a single, barely majority-African-American district to two districts with an average population of 53.6% African American (61.6% nonwhite).

Thus we find that many of the states that have increased partisan bias between the 2000 and 2010 districting round have also increased the proportion of African-American voters within existing majority-minority districts. This is not in any way required by the Voting Rights Act – indeed, it reduces the influence of African-American voters by using their votes inefficiently. However, it is consistent with a policy of state legislatures seeking partisan advantage by packing African-American voters, who overwhelmingly vote for the Democratic Party, into districts where the Democratic margin will be far higher than necessary.

Thus the increase in bias between the 2000 and 2010 districting rounds cannot be explained by an increase in the number of majority-minority districts. It is true that the number of such districts increased, but this increase did not happen for the most part in the states where bias increased. Bias did increase in some states where the density of majority-minority districts (the proportion of minority voters in the district) increased. However, this is a result of the districting decisions made by the state, not of the Voting Rights Act. As we have already seen from the adopted and alternative plans for many states, it is possible to draw unbiased (or only slightly biased) districts while still complying with the Voting Rights Act.

We can now summarize our results with regard to the hypothesis that partisan bias can be explained by the Voting Rights Act and the need to draw majority-minority districts. As an explanation of the first *strong* type, we can refute the Voting Rights Act as an explanation. The Voting Rights Act does not force states to adopt biased districting plans, because we can show that it is quite possible to produce unbiased plans that conform to the Voting Rights Act. We can show this by considering both adopted and alternative plans for various states. As an explanation of the second *weak* type, the Voting Rights Act certainly does constrain state districting authorities. The Voting Rights Act, as interpreted by the Supreme Court in *Thornburg v. Gingles* (1986b), requires that a compact minority population that could make a district must be drawn as one, even if this is not convenient for the party that controls the districting process. However, the increase in the number of majority-minority districts cannot explain the increase in partisan bias between 2002 and 2012 – the states where the number of majority-minority districts increased are in general not the states where bias increased.

GEOGRAPHICAL INFORMATION SYSTEMS AND IMPROVED TECHNOLOGY

The third alternative explanation for partisan bias is that bias has increased as a result of the increasingly sophisticated technological tools available to districting authorities. It does not make sense to think of this as an explanation of the first *strong* type – computers do not force state legislatures to make decisions, at least outside the realm of science fiction. So here we are only considering explanations of the second *weak* type. Has the availability of sophisticated geographical information systems made it easier to district for partisan advantage over the last ten years? And can this account for the increase in partisan bias between 2002 and 2012?

Geographic information systems (GIS) and boundary-drawing technology have revolutionized the process of creating district boundaries over the last thirty years. The precision of geographic population data has improved, from census tracts with thousands of people to precincts and blocks with fewer than 100, and the amount of data characteristics available for analysis have grown exponentially (Brace 2004). In addition, as computational and financial costs associated with generating hypothetical redistricting plans have dropped, access to and use of this technology has become widespread (Brace 2004; Altman and McDonald 2011b).

A variety of scholars and political observers have criticized these developments as providing "near-scientific precision" for gerrymandering ("Elections with No Meaning" *New York Times* 2004), as "a powerful tool for political manipulation" (Forest 2005), and a gateway to election rigging ("How to Rig an Election," *Economist* 2002). Geographer Benjamin Forest sums up the technological bias hypothesis nicely when he acknowledges that while GIS has "aided legal enforcement of voting rights laws and opened the process, in principle, to a greater variety of citizen and community groups," political parties and other powerful organizations dominate the use of this technology for "increasingly sophisticated partisan gerrymanders" (Forest 2005). But do technological advancements explain the increased bias in the latest redistricting cycle?

Generally, analyses of the impact of technology on redistricting have not shown a significant impact in terms of changes in district competitiveness, compactness, or partisan advantage (Altman et al. 2005; Altman and McDonald 2010). In their analysis of variation in the intensity of computer and electronic database usage for congressional redistricting in 1991 and 2001, Altman and associates (2005) generally found no difference in either competitiveness or compactness across statewide differences in computer usage. Compared to less computationally intense redistricting, the use of more refined data and software to configure district boundaries may have even aided in the construction of slightly more competitive and compact districts.

The absence of increasingly sophisticated gerrymanders through the use of more sophisticated software is likely a function of both computational and human constraints. It is not yet possible for even the most advanced computer programs to optimize multiple criteria such as contiguity, communities of interest, and equal population simultaneously, except under unrealistically limited conditions (Puppe and Tasnadi 2009; Altman and McDonald 2010). Moreover, because there is no conceptual agreement on the primacy of these criteria or, for that matter, the broader meaning or measurement of representation, computer-redistricting systems necessarily reflect the representational goals of designers.

Dramatic gains in computational speed and precision are important tools that have revolutionized redistricting, but the most important choices are still made by people. Moreover, the use of redistricting technology was already widespread by the 2000 redistricting cycle, with the largest expansion occurring from 1991 to 2001 (Brace 2004; Altman et al. 2005). If technological advances did not result in significantly increased gerrymandering from 1991 to 2001, there is little reason to expect a significant impact in the most recent round of redistricting.

In fact, the biggest change in this cycle regarding advanced redistricting software is public access to it. From browser-based software like Dave's Redistricting App and open-source collaborative software such as Altman and McDonald's DistrictBuilder to commercial programs like Caliper's Maptitude, the capacity to test claims about the "naturalness" or inevitability of biased districting plans with counterexamples has increased tremendously (Bradlee 2014; The Public Mapping Project et al. 2014; Caliper 2014). Furthermore, websites such as Ballotpedia (2015) and those provided by state governments provide far easier access to information on redistricting. That is to say, the technological balance has shifted over the last decade away from the districting authorities and toward the public – the tools to challenge districting plans are now widely available. Thus technological change cannot explain the increase in partisan bias between 2002 and 2012. By 2000, state legislatures already had most of the capabilities they have today. What has changed over the last decade has actually been public access to these tools.

CONCLUSION: DEMOGRAPHY IS NOT DESTINY

Thus we can see that geographic and demographic constraints (such as the urban concentration of Democratic voters, the requirement to draw majority-minority districts, and the geographic sorting of voters) cannot account for the level of partisan bias we observe and certainly cannot account for the increase in bias we observe between the 2000 and 2010 districting rounds. We have distinguished two senses in which demographic factors can be said to "explain" partisan bias. In the first *strong* sense, the demographic factors force the districting authorities to adopt a biased plan, whether they want to or not. This is the kind of explanation we need if we want to absolve state districting authorities of responsibility for partisan bias. Suppose we want to argue that (say) the urban concentration of Democrats is the cause of partisan bias, and deliberate partisan gerrymandering is not. It is not sufficient to show that there is a statistical relationship between geographical concentration and partisan bias. The fact is that the districting plan was chosen by the state districting authorities. If the state could have chosen an unbiased plan but did not, then it has in fact made a choice. A factor like geographical concentration only forces the state to district in a biased manner if it is in fact impossible to adopt an unbiased plan.

There is, of course, a second *weaker* sense in which we can talk about demographic factors explaining partisan bias. A factor such as the urban concentration of Democratic voters may not force states to adopt biased districting plans. However, they may make producing biased districting plans easier. Alternatively, they may make drawing unbiased plans harder. That is to say, demographic factors may change the opportunities to create bias available to districting authorities. Of course, districting authorities are free to take advantage of these opportunities or not. The fact that the geographical concentration of Democrats may make it easier to draw pro-Republican gerrymanders does not mean that state legislatures have to take advantage of this. However, if a state legislature wishes to draw districts for partisan advantage, changes in the opportunities to create bias may explain changes in partisan bias over time.

In terms of the first *strong* sense of explanation, we can decisively reject the hypothesis that the urban concentration of Democratic voters explains partisan bias. It appears to be quite possible to draw unbiased districting plans in spite of these constraints. Some of the states with the largest urban concentrations and most majority-minority districts (California, Illinois, New Jersey, New York) manage to draw approximately unbiased districting plans. In those states where we observe considerable partisan bias, we often find alternatives where either there is no partisan bias or the bias is quite modest. Of course, this should not be surprising, as the overall level of partisan bias in the 2000 districting round was barely statistically significant and around 35% of what we observe after the 2010 redistricting. While there is demographic change between districting rounds, the urban concentration of Democratic voters is a pattern that has been noted for many years, not something that has suddenly occurred in the last few years. What we can conclude from the actual and alternative plans we have considered is that partisan bias was not the inevitable result of geographic factors. Rather, it is a result of a choice by districting authorities: districting authorities could have drawn unbiased (or at least relatively unbiased districts) but chose not to.

Of course, we do not want to push this argument too far. When we consider the second *weak* sense of explanation, demographic and geographic factors most certainly do constrain what districting plans are possible. These factors do have some effect on how easy it is to produce districting plans that favor Republicans and Democrats, although these effects may be less than is sometimes assumed. For example, the fact that Democratic voters are concentrated in urban areas means that it is straightforward to draw districts where Democratic voters are packed. If districting authorities wish to draw a biased districting plan in such states, it will probably be far easier to create a plan that strongly advantages the Republicans, and more difficult (or even impossible) to draw a plan that strongly advantages the Democrats. The case of Illinois demonstrates this point. The districting plan adopted for Illinois by a Democratic-controlled state government is approximately unbiased. However, to achieve this required two extremely oddly shaped districts. When the districting plan was challenged, a panel of federal judges accepted the assertion that the state legislatures had tried to maximize partisan advantage (*Committee for a Fair and Balanced Map v. Illinois State Board of Elections*, December 15, 2011, p.2). However, in spite of this, all the Illinois Democrats were able to achieve was to avoid districts biased against them. In spite of drawing some of the least compact districts in the nation, they did not produce the kind of partisan advantage the Republicans gained in many other states. Of course, as we have argued, Illinois should be one of the states where the Democrats have the most problems because of the urban concentration of its voters. This is because there are extremely large concentrations of Democratic voters in the Chicago area but still enough Republican support in the rest of the state to make the state competitive overall. Thus the geographical concentration of Democratic voters certainly does constrain plans the districting authorities have to choose from, although they are still left with considerable discretion.

However, the explanatory power – even in the *weak* sense – of the urban concentration hypothesis is limited. The urban concentration of Democrats may make districting for partisan advantage easier. However, if states are willing to draw enough oddly shaped districts, it is quite possible to create an extremely biased districting plan in which the Democrats are not particularly concentrated compared to Republicans, as the case of North Carolina shows. In particular, the urban concentration hypothesis cannot account for the almost threefold increase in partisan bias between 2002 and 2012. This is because the demographic change was working in the wrong direction. The concentration of Democratic voters compared to Republicans actually fell in most states over the period in question, including most of those where bias increased. Demographic change should be making it easier to draw unbiased or pro-Democratic districts, not harder.

Similar considerations apply to the effects of the Voting Rights Act and the provision of minority representation. As an explanation in the first *strong* sense, we can for the most part reject the hypothesis that the Voting Rights Act and the need to draw majority-minority districts force states to draw biased districts. Clearly it is quite possible to combine minority representation with unbiased districting – the state with the most majority-minority districts and most minority representatives is California, which has an unbiased districting plan. Furthermore, adopted and alternative districting plans in many other states show that it is possible to draw unbiased districts and conform to the Voting Rights Act. However, there may be some states where drawing majority-minority districts may necessitate districts that are slightly advantageous to the Republicans (Altman and McDonald 2013 argue that Virginia may be an example of this). However, even in Virginia, the bias that may result from this is modest and far less than the bias of the plan adopted by the state legislature (a one-seat advantage to the Republicans as opposed to a three-seat advantage in the adopted plan).

However, it is clear that the Voting Rights Act, as interpreted since *Thornburg v. Gingles* (1986b), does constrain districting authorities. If there is a compact and cohesive minority community that could make up a majority-minority district, there may well be a violation if the state chooses to break it up. Given the fact that minority groups (and African Americans in particular) tend to vote Democratic, this may reinforce the effects of the concentration of Democratic voters in some states. In other states, it may prevent the Republicans from districting in such a way that no Democrats are elected. Furthermore, there will certainly be cases in which it will be possible to come up with a plan that increases both partisan bias and minority representation. We would expect to see cases in which some minority representatives support a Republican redistricting plan, as has occurred in Florida and Missouri.

As with the urban concentration hypothesis, the explanatory power of the Voting Rights Act is limited, even in terms of the second *weak* sense of explanation. The change in bias between 2002 and 2012 cannot be explained in terms of majority-minority districts. The number of majority-minority districts did indeed increase considerably over the period. However, the increase in the number of majority-minority districts was not for the most part in the states where bias increased.

Clearly there have been advances in the technology used to draw districts, which has made it easier to foresee the effect of districting decisions. However, once again, this cannot explain the increase in partisan bias that we observe. Technology may make it possible to more accurately draw biased districts, but it cannot explain the decision to adopt such districts. In fact, the technology available to districting authorities has not changed that much in this districting round. Desktop geographical information systems were already widely used in the 2000 round. If there is a real innovation in this round, it is the ability to crowdsource districting, that is, to create web applications that allow citizens to draw their own districts. This does not make gerrymandering easier; rather, it makes it easier for citizens to hold those who gerrymander to account.

Thus we can conclude that demography is not destiny when considering partisan bias in congressional districting. The bias we observe is not the inevitable effect of factors such as the urban concentration of Democratic voters or the need to draw majority-minority districts. It is for the most part possible to draw unbiased (or nearly unbiased) districting plans in spite of these constraints. Thus if state districting authorities draw districts that give a strong advantage to one party, this is a choice they have made – it was not forced on them by geography. Of course, geographic and demographic factors do constrain which districting plans state authorities can choose from. Nevertheless, the plan actually adopted is a matter of choice, and relatively unbiased plans are among those that can be chosen. We have suggested that the choices states make are very much a matter of politics. In the next chapter, we consider the degree to which we can make sense of the patterns of partisan bias we observe in terms of political motives.

APPENDIX – WHAT, IF ANYTHING, CAN WE LEARN FROM THE UNITED KINGDOM?

The case of the United Kingdom presents something of a paradox. Districting in the UK is sometimes presented in contrast to that in the United States. The UK and the United States have similar single-member-district plurality election systems. However, in the UK districting is not done by interested politicians. Instead, it is administered by nonpartisan Boundary Commissions, who are required to only take into account technical, geographical criteria. Thus in the UK, we should not see the kind of deliberate partisan gerrymandering that allegedly happens in the United States.

However, in recent UK elections, there has been considerable partisan bias toward the Labour Party, although this seems to have disappeared with the 2015 election. In the 2010 UK election, it was calculated that the Labour Party would have won an absolute majority of seats in the House of Commons if it had a 3% lead over the Conservative Party. The Conservative Party, on the other hand, would have required an eleven-point lead to win an absolute majority (Curtice 2010). As it turned out, the seven-point lead the Conservative Party actually obtained was insufficient for an absolute majority. How does this happen with supposedly impartial districting? Does this prove that partisan bias is to be expected, even without deliberate gerrymandering?

At the outset, we should point out various differences between the UK and the United States. The first is that, unlike the United States, the UK no longer has a two-party system. At the last three elections, the two largest parties (Labour and Conservative) between them received around two-thirds of the vote. This forces us to rethink what we mean by partisan bias – in 2010, if we consider three parties, there was bias in favor of both the Conservatives and Labour, although the bias in favor of Labour was far greater (Thrasher et al. 2011). It also means that the mechanics of partisan bias work very differently from those we described in Chapter 3. Second, in the United States, all districts have approximately the same population. In the UK, however, there is required malapportionment for Wales, Northern Ireland, and (to a lesser extent) Scotland, although this is being addressed. Third, the requirement in the UK that districts be drawn for strictly geographical reasons is a double-edged sword. It means that the Boundary Commissions cannot draw districts to advantage one party over another. However, it also means that they cannot replace districts on the grounds that they provide partisan advantage – partisan advantage cannot be considered.

Nevertheless, it is clear that the electoral system did produce considerable bias in favor of the Labour Party before 2015, even when we consider the UK a three-party system (Johnson et al. 2006; Curtice 2010; Borisyuk et al. 2010; Thrasher et al. 2011). Borisyuk and colleagues (2010) provide a method for measuring bias that is similar to that we outlined in Chapter 3 but is extended to three-party systems. Using this method, Thrasher and colleagues (2011) find that the electoral system gave the Labour Party a net bias of sixty-three seats, the Conservative Party a net bias of thirteen seats, but the Liberal Party a net bias of negative seventy-six seats (there are 650 seats in the UK Parliament). It should be noted that the negative bias of seventy-six seats suffered by the Liberal Democrats is not the result of the fact that the third party in first-past-the-post elections suffers a disadvantage – by bias, we mean that the Liberal Democrats would have gotten seventy-six seats less than expected even if they had not been the third party. It appears that the current high levels of bias in favor of the Labour Party date from the 1997 election (Johnson et al. 2007; Curtice 2010). Before that, electoral bias appears to have been modest and if anything favoring the Conservative Party because of the overwhelming (and thus electorally inefficient) strength of the Labour Party in industrial areas.

There are various reasons for the recent electoral bias toward the Labour Party. First, all districts (or constituencies, as they are called in the UK) are not the same size. There are two reasons for this. By statute, Scotland, Wales, and Northern Ireland get more districts per head than England, although the 1998 Scotland Act partially addresses this. As a result, in 2010, the average constituency in Wales had a population of 56,626 and the average constituency in Scotland was 65,234, while the population of the average English constituency was 71,909 (Curtice 2010). As Wales and Scotland vote disproportionately for Labour, this advantages the Labour Party. The second reason Labour constituencies tend to be smaller than average is that population movements tend to be out of (mostly Labour) inner-city areas into (more Conservative-voting) suburbs, so a pro-Labour bias grows up over time. However, this source of bias seems to be relatively modest. Thrasher and colleagues (2011) find that differences in the size of constituencies only account for six seats out of the sixty-three-seat bias toward Labour. Furthermore, this source of bias is addressed by the Parliamentary Voting System and Constituencies Act 2011. This requires uniform constituency sizes (within a 5% range) for the whole UK and requires a review of boundaries every five years, although these reforms were implemented in time for the 2015 General Election.

A second source of bias is differential turnout. Labour tends to win in constituencies where fewer people vote. As a result, Labour wins more seats than its vote share would suggest. Thus the population of the average Labour constituency in 2010 was 3,733 less than that of the average Conservative constituency, but the difference in the number of voters was 7,894. Thrasher and colleagues (2011) find that turnout accounts for thirteen seats out of Labour's sixty-three-seat advantage.

However, the main source of Labour's advantage seems to have been electoral geography. That is to say, Labour's vote has been more efficiently distributed than that of the Conservatives or the Liberal Democrats.

According to Thrasher and colleagues (2011), this accounts for thirty-one seats of Labour's sixty-three-seat advantage in 2010, with the effect of minor parties accounting for two seats and interaction among the various factors accounting for the remaining eleven seats. The fact that Labour's distribution of support accounts for around half of the bias in its favor poses an interesting question: Is there something about the geographical distribution of political support that gives Labour an inevitable advantage? Is there something equivalent to the urban concentration of Democratic voters in the United States, which some people have claimed makes bias against the Democrats inevitable?

If there is something about the geographical distribution of support that has given Labour an advantage, it is not clear what it is. There is nothing as simple as the urban concentration of Democrats in the United States. This is in large part due to Britain no longer having a two-party system. In a two-party system, your party has an advantage if your opponent has its support concentrated in a few districts that it wins by overwhelming margins. For example, in the United States, the Democrats can win 85% of the vote or more in some urban districts. However, in the 2010 UK General Election, the highest vote share obtained was 72%. In only four seats did the winner get 70% or more, and even 60% was reached in only twenty-nine seats (Electoral Reform Society 2010). In the case of two-thirds of all seats, the winning candidate got less than 50% of the vote. The bias in favor of the Labour Party cannot be explained by the fact that the Conservative vote is packed into a few districts.

One explanation of why Labour has an advantage is that it appears extremely successful at winning close races. Thrasher and colleagues (2011) find that Labour was disproportionately successful at winning constituencies where it wins between 30% and 40% of the vote, compared to the other two parties. If Labour wins a constituency with less than 40% of the vote, then this is a "cheap seat" in that Labour has won a seat with close to the minimum number of votes necessary. It also means the other parties have "wasted" a considerable number of votes without winning a seat. Both these things improve Labour's seats/votes ratio compared to the other parties.

It is not clear why Labour was so successful in close races. One reason that has been proposed is tactical voting. It appears that in close races, Labour and Liberal Democrat voters have voted tactically whichever party has the best chance of defeating the Conservative (Fisher and Curtice 2006; Electoral Reform Society 2010). In addition to tactical voting by Liberal Democrats helping Labour win seats, tactical voting by Labour supporters in seats Labour cannot win will reduce Labour's vote share in these seats, which also improves Labour's seats/votes ratio. If tactical voting was at work here, it could be argued that Labour's electoral advantage was not so much the result of geography but of the behavior of voters when presented with a strategic dilemma by the electoral system (see Electoral Reform Society 2010, 53). Tactical voting also makes partisan gerrymandering far more complex – the gerrymander would have to second-guess how voters will react, as the voters could use tactical voting to effectively undo the gerrymander. Of course, none of these issues apply in the United States, where there is still effectively a two-party system.

The results of the 2015 UK General Election demonstrate the fragility of partisan advantage based on such complex multiparty dynamics. The Labour Party increased its vote share from 29% in 2010 to 30.4% in 2015. However, it suffered a net loss of twenty-six seats, falling from 258 to 232. As a result, it took 40,228 votes to elect a Labour MP but only 34,345 to elect a Conservative. The most plausible explanation of this is the effect of the smaller parties. Most obviously, Labour lost forty of its forty-one Scottish seats to the Scottish National Party, which won fifty-six of the fifty-nine Scottish seats. The vote for the Liberal Democratic Party fell from 23% to 7.9%, which principally seems to have benefited the Conservative Party. The anti-EU UK Independence Party (UKIP) won 12.6% of the vote. Although it was commonly supposed before the election that UKIP would primarily take votes from the Conservatives, it now appears that it may have won a considerable number of votes from Labour. Thus it appears that the partisan advantage toward Labour has evaporated not because Labour lost votes but because of changes in the relative strength of the smaller parties.

The remit of the Boundary Commissions also does not assist the pursuit of fairness between the political parties. Since 1986, Boundary Commissions have had to consider population and the geographical size of constituencies. The Parliamentary Voting System and Constituencies Act 2011 makes the population and size targets binding, with some exceptions such as the Shetland and Orkney Islands. In addition, the commissions can consider factors such as special geographical considerations, local government boundaries, existing constituencies, and whether a proposed change will cause inconvenience or break existing local ties (Borisyuk et al. 2010). Fairness between the political parties is not a factor that can be considered. Furthermore, the consultation process may have produced a bias toward the status quo (Borisyuk et al. 2010). For example, the Labour Party might object to a proposed change to a constituency it currently wins. It could argue that the change would break local ties or that existing constituency boundaries should be maintained. However, the counterargument that these boundaries benefit the Labour Party could not be considered – the Boundary Commissions cannot consider partisan advantage.

The idea that the British process is not subject to partisan politics is also becoming harder to defend. Section 6 of the Electoral Registration and Administration Act 2013 postponed the Sixth Periodic Review of constituency boundaries from 2013 to 2018. The postponement of the Sixth Periodic Review required that Liberal Democrat MPs and Lords vote with the Labour Party and against their Conservative coalition partners.

What then can we learn from the case of the United Kingdom? On one hand, it shows that it is certainly possible for a process based solely on geographic and demographic criteria to produce partisan bias. On the other hand, we already knew this. As we argued in the section on compactness in the last chapter, there is no logical link between geographical compactness and the lack of bias. True, some of the most biased districting plans also involve some very oddly shaped districts, with North Carolina arguably the most egregious example. However, it is also possible sometimes to produce highly biased plans with districts that are admirably compact, as in the case of Indiana. Geographic criteria alone cannot guarantee a lack of partisan bias. To guarantee a lack of partisan bias, we need to take partisan fairness into account when we draw the districts – something the UK explicitly does not allow.

We should certainly not take districting in the UK as "best practice" and use this to argue that nonpartisan districting commissions in the United States will also fail to produce unbiased districting plans. We actually have many examples of nonpartisan and bipartisan districting commissions in the United States. We will see in the next chapter that in general, they do produce unbiased districting plans. The British Boundary Commissions have various practices that are not conducive to a lack of political bias. Indeed, their rules may actually empower those who wish to entrench existing bias – for example, it is possible to object to new boundaries on the grounds that they break existing local ties. Most significantly, Boundary Commissions are not allowed to consider political effects. This prevents them from deliberately drawing boundaries to the advantage of a political party, but it also prevents them from undoing partisan bias that may have accumulated over time.

It should also be noted that the partisan bias we have observed in the United Kingdom has different causes from that we see in the United States. This is because the UK no longer has a two-party system like the

United States does. In a two-party system you can create bias through a simple strategy of "cracking and packing" – you ensure your opponents are concentrated in a few districts, leaving your party to win the rest. In the UK, however, there is little evidence of this kind of packing – in two-thirds of constituencies, no one wins even 50% of the vote. Rather, partisan advantage is the result of a complex game among the supporters of three or more parties. Labour apparently has had a partisan advantage, because it narrowly won a lot of close three-way races. These victories may often depend on tactical voting – Labour and Liberal Democratic supporters voting for whoever is most likely to defeat the Conservative. However, the 2015 General Election shows how fragile an advantage based on such strategic interactions can be. It has been suggested by some that the problems with the British electoral system are a result of the fact that first-past-the-post elections are becoming incompatible with a British electorate who are no longer willing to share their support between two main parties (Dunleavy 2005; Electoral Reform Society 2010; see also Colomer 2004). There is no such transition to multiparty politics currently underway in the United States.

Thus we should be skeptical about drawing too many conclusions from the comparison with the United Kingdom. We do find considerable partisan bias in spite of a nonpartisan districting process. However, there are reasons for this, and they are reasons that do not apply to the United States. Most prominently, the two-party system in the UK appears to be in the process of breaking down, with the two largest parties winning only two-thirds of the vote in the last three elections. First-past-the-post elections can produce problematic results when there are more than two parties in realistic contention for a seat. Furthermore, the UK districting system should not be held up as an exemplar for the United States. The rules do not allow the Boundary Commission to pursue political fairness. Indeed, they empower interested parties to entrench existing advantages. Eliminating the consideration of political factors may seem like a good way of eliminating political manipulation; however, if political inequities do emerge, you cannot deal with them if you are not allowed to consider them.

5

Political Explanations of Partisan Bias

Our argument from the beginning of the book has been that partisan bias can only be explained in political terms. In short, we argue that pro-Republican bias can be found only where the Republicans control the districting process. Furthermore, the degree of partisan bias we observe has increased very significantly in the 2010 districting round following *Vieth v. Jubelirer* (2004), even in states where state legislatures had already drawn biased districts in the previous round.

In this chapter, we test these claims. In Chapter 3, we saw that the degree of partisan bias increased sharply in the districting round following the 2010 Census. We also identified the states where this bias is greatest. In the previous chapter, we considered whether this increase in bias could be explained by demographic factors, such as the urban concentration of Democratic voters or the need to draw majority-minority districts. We found that these factors cannot explain the pattern of bias we observe. Here we return to the story we laid out in Chapter 1. In the 2000 districting round, there were various complaints of partisan gerrymandering. In response to one of these complaints in the case of Pennsylvania, the Supreme Court in *Vieth v. Jubelirer* (2004) gave a clear signal that the courts would not intervene in partisan gerrymandering cases. Following this, state governments pursued partisan advantage in the 2010 districting round to a far greater degree than they had in the previous round.

If this story is accurate, there are two things that we would expect to observe. First, the pattern of partisan bias should follow a political logic. We should find partisan bias in those states where the state government has the ability to pass partisan districting plans and has an incentive to do so. That is to say, we would expect to find bias where one party has control over the entire districting process and where drawing biased districts brings it an advantage (we will see that this is not always the case). Second, we would expect bias to increase between 2000 and 2010 in states where one party has control. That is to say, we expect bias to increase in states where the Republicans controlled the process in both 2000 and 2010, not just in states where the Republicans gained control in 2010.

In terms of the state-by-state pattern of partisan bias, we would expect districting plans to be biased when one party has both the *motive* and *opportunity* pass a plan that advantages it. To have opportunity, the party needs to have complete control of the districting process. This is typically the case when the districting plan is simply passed by the state legislature (possibly subject to gubernatorial veto), and one party controls both chambers and the governorship. As for motive, it might seem that a party would also have an incentive to adopt a biased plan. As we will see, however, this is not the case. When a party is overwhelmingly popular in terms of federal elections in a state, adopting a biased plan brings no benefit and may even be counterproductive. In states that are not electorally competitive, we would not expect to find biased districts, even though one party controls the districting process.

The second thing we expect to observe is that partisan bias increases between 2000 and 2010 where one party controls the process in 2010. Our argument is that state legislatures pushed partisan advantage further after *Vieth*. As we have seen, partisan bias did indeed increase between the 2000 and 2010 districting rounds. However, an alternative explanation is that this was simply the result of the Republicans having control of more states in 2010. Indeed, the Republicans did do extremely well in 2010 and controlled the districting process in more states than in 2000. Furthermore, the Democrats lost control of the districting process in some states, such as California, where districting by the state legislature was replaced by districting by a commission. If our story is true, however, this cannot account for all of the increase in partisan bias. We would expect partisan bias to increase in those states that the Republicans controlled in both 2000 and 2010. Furthermore, in states where the Republicans gained control in 2010, we would expect the level of partisan bias to be higher than we observed in Republican-controlled states in the 2000 round.

The political logic we have proposed to explain the state-by-state pattern of partisan bias raises another question. For motive and opportunity both to be present, it is necessary for one party to control all branches of state government and for the state to be electorally competitive in federal government. This may seem like an unlikely scenario – if the state is electorally competitive, divided government should be likely. However, this scenario is actually very common. Various reasons could be suggested for this. After all, there is no reason to assume that federal and state elections should follow the same patterns – the issues and candidates are different. However, we will suggest that there are institutional reasons that make this disconnect between the state and federal politics more likely. Voter turnout in state elections is lower than at federal elections. Furthermore, elections for many state posts are held when voter turnout is likely to be lower – that is, in nonpresidential years or even odd-numbered years.

DOES POLITICS EXPLAIN WHERE WE FIND PARTISAN BIAS?

We have argued that partisan bias is the result of partisan choices at the state level. If this is the case, then we should only see partisan bias in states where one party has both the *motive* and *opportunity* to bring about a biased plan (see Butler and Cain 1992). We will start by considering the opportunity to create a biased plan, as this is relatively simple. A party has the opportunity to draw districts to its advantage if it completely controls the districting process. If the consent of both parties is required to pass a districting plan, we would not expect either of them to agree to a plan that strongly advantages the other. For one party to control the districting process, two conditions are usually necessary. First, districting must be done through the normal legislative process. If districting is done through an independent or bipartisan commission, one-party control is very unlikely, as these institutions are set up specifically to prevent this. Second, one party must control all the political institutions (the "veto points") necessary to pass a districting plan. If districting is treated as normal legislation, then this will require that the party control both houses of the state legislature and the governorship in states where the governor has a veto. McDonald (2004) finds that these expectations are borne out by the results of the 2000 redistricting cycle. With a few exceptions, he demonstrates that the type of institution and its political orientation can predict the direction of bias of the maps.

It may seem that there would always be a motive for a party to draw biased districts if it has an opportunity to do so. This, however, would be mistaken. Generally speaking, it only benefits a party to draw biased districts – that is, biased in the sense of being asymmetric – when the elections in the state are relatively competitive. Consider the logic of gerrymandering that we laid out in Chapter 3. You create bias by packing your opponents into a small number of districts, where they win by overwhelming margins. You sacrifice these districts to use up your opponents' support so that your party can win a larger number of districts. However, if your party wins (say) 65% of the vote, there is no need to sacrifice any districts. If you just draw every district to be a microcosm of the state (politically speaking), your party will win every district 65–35. Furthermore, this districting plan will be unbiased – if the other party won 65% of the vote, they would win all the seats also. Indeed, drawing a biased districting plan would be thoroughly counterproductive to your party's interest – it would mean concentrating your opponents and possibly giving them an unnecessary seat. The Democrats in Massachusetts and the Republicans in Oklahoma can win every seat in their respective states without having to create biased plans. They simply draw a responsive districting plan and rely on the winner-take-all nature of first-past-the-post elections that gives a strong advantage to the larger party.

Of course, it is not always possible to take full advantage of being the dominant party in terms of the statewide vote. It may be impossible to make every district a political microcosm of the state because the other party is geographically concentrated. Ingenious mapmaking may be able to break up inconvenient concentrations of voters, but there are presumably limits when it comes to large urban areas, rivers, and mountains. If there are large concentrations of minority voters, it may be necessary to draw them as a majority-minority district in order to comply with the Voting Rights Act. Ironically, the very factors that may disadvantage the Democratic Party in competitive states may actually prevent the Republican Party from adopting the optimal districting strategy in states where they are dominant in national elections. It is not obvious what the optimal districting strategy is in a state where one party dominates the statewide vote, but the minority party has concentrations that cannot be "cracked" for some reason. The majority party might create more bias by concentrating its opponents into the district the minority party controls, but it gains little from this – it expects to win the other districts anyway.

We should note that just because a districting plan is unbiased, it is not necessarily uncontroversial. As we noted in Chapter 3, districting plans can be assessed in terms of both their bias and their responsiveness. Even if a districting plan is unbiased (i.e., it treats each party the same if it wins a certain percentage of the vote), parties can still seek advantage by manipulating the responsiveness of the districting plan. If you are the larger party, you benefit from a districting plan that is as responsive as possible, as responsive plans reward the larger party more and may allow it to win every seat. If you are the smaller party, you would probably prefer an unresponsive plan in which both parties are guaranteed as many safe seats as possible. As already noted, an ideally responsive plan is one in which every district is a microcosm of the state. Such plans are by definition unbiased. However, drawing such plans in a state where party support is not evenly spread may require some oddly shaped districts. For example, the Democrats in Massachusetts have long separated Boston into several districts that also take in some rural areas. This serves to "homogenize" the state politically. The Republicans in Utah pursued a similar strategy in the 2010 districting round, dividing the greater Salt Lake City area among all four congressional districts. Such districting practices may be described as gerrymanders by some people.[1] The problem is that there are perfectly legitimate reasons why some states have different levels of responsiveness than others (states that are politically homogenous will typically be more responsive than states where there are large concentrations of the voters of each party), and there is no "correct" level of responsiveness. The ability to gain an advantage by changing the level of responsiveness is an inescapable consequence of having first-past-the-post elections.

We can summarize our expectations in Table 5.1. We expect to find partisan bias when a political party has both the motive and opportunity to create a biased districting plan. A party has the *opportunity* to pass a bias plan when there is single-party control of the redistricting process. If districting requires the approval of another party, it is unlikely that it will agree to a plan that is stacked against it. A party only has a *motive* to create biased plans when the state is relatively competitive in national elections. If national elections are completely one sided, the party may well do better just by drawing unbiased but highly responsive districts. We would expect bias only where we have both single-party control of districting and competitive national elections.

[1] In the case of Utah, the political effect of the districting plan was to take a relatively safe Democratic seat and turn it into a very competitive seat. Prior to 2012, the Republicans won two seats to the Democrats' one. The districting plan was extremely unresponsive (responsiveness = 0.66). In the 2010 round, Utah gained one additional seat. The new districts were far more responsive than the old (responsiveness = 2.78). However, the political effect was that the previously safe Democratic seat was now very competitive. The Republicans took this seat in 2014.

TABLE 5.1. *Expected Bias in Terms of Political Control of Redistricting and Electoral Competitiveness*

	Motive for Bias: Competitiveness in National Elections	*No Motive for Bias:* Noncompetitive in National Elections
opportunity for bias: single-party control over congressional redistricting	HIGH BIAS	LOW BIAS
no opportunity for bias: nonpartisan or bipartisan congressional redistricting	LOW BIAS	LOW BIAS

Opportunity for Bias: Who Determines Redistricting?

Before we can consider whether we observe the patterns of bias we predict, we need to determine who controls the redistricting process in each state. As we discussed in Chapter 2, the Constitution gives state legislatures responsibility for the "Times, Places and Manner of holding Elections" to the House of Representatives (Article 1 §4), although Congress is permitted to overrule them. In practice, this means that state governments decide how congressional districts are drawn (in the next chapter, we consider why Congress has rarely intervened in this). For the majority of states, congressional district maps are drawn by the state legislature and approved by the governor. In Virginia, for instance, congressional redistricting begins in the General Assembly, where a bill must be approved by a majority of both the House of Delegates and the Senate and subsequently signed by the governor. In Maryland, the process is similar except that the governor draws the map, and the state legislature must vote to approve it before it becomes law. These approaches to drawing new congressional districts tend to follow the normal legislative procedure; the proposed district map is treated as a bill that must be approved by the state's lawmaking bodies before becoming law. In delegating the responsibility of redistricting to lawmakers, these states treat redistricting as a political process and thus expose congressional district boundaries to potential partisan manipulation.

Other states cede the task of redistricting to independent commissions outside the normal legislative processes. In 2008, California voters approved a state referendum to adopt the California Citizens Redistricting Commission to draw congressional maps for the 2010 redistricting cycle. Similarly, other states such as New Jersey and Arizona delegate the task of redistricting to independent, bipartisan, or nonpartisan commissions. In general, this approach to redistricting serves to neutralize or insulate a state's political forces from influencing the map drawing and thus reduces the potential for partisan manipulation of the process.

Several states employ a combination of both a commission and the legislature in drawing the maps. In Iowa, a nonpartisan state agency draws the maps, which are subsequently sent for approval by the state legislature. (Traditionally, the legislature's approval is routine and uncontested.) Similarly, in Indiana, the state legislature is given a strict deadline for completing maps; if it fails to approve a plan, an independent commission is convened to draw the districts. Other states subject their redistricting maps to judicial review, either to ensure that racial gerrymandering has not occurred or to satisfy a state constitutional requirement. In Kansas, for instance, the state Supreme Court reviews the maps after a plan has been passed by the legislature. If the legislature cannot agree on a plan, the task falls to a court to do so.

Although there are many subtle nuances and unique differences in how the states approach redistricting, we can broadly group these methods into five categories in terms of who is normally responsible for drawing the congressional maps: (1) the legislature and governor, (2) an independent commission, (3) a commission with the legislature's approval, (4) the legislature with a commission as a backup, or (5) the legislature with a court's approval or with the court as a backup. There is also a sixth category that we must consider: states with only one U.S. House seat allocated to them. In these low-population states with "at-large" districts, such as Alaska and Wyoming, redistricting is rendered unnecessary because the state as a whole is considered one single district. In Table 5.2, we have arranged states according to these six categories.

Of course, this only considers states' congressional redistricting processes in terms of *procedural ideal* – that is, which institutions are tasked with drawing the congressional maps under normal circumstances and contingency plans ("backups") for drawing maps in the event of political gridlock, disagreement, or a failure to meet a deadline for completion. What we are really interested in is who actually controlled the redistricting process – that is, the *realized outcome*. Whether a contingency plan was implemented and a backup institution took control of the process is important for discerning whether there was partisanship influence over the creation of the district boundaries. What matters, then, is who actually drew the maps that were implemented during the 2012 U.S. House elections.

TABLE 5.2. *How Congressional District Maps Are Drawn*

Normal Legislative Process	Independent or Bipartisan Commission	Mixed	No Congressional Redistricting
Alabama	Arizona	*Commission, then approved by Legislature:*	Alaska
Arkansas	California	Iowa	Delaware
Colorado	Hawaii	Maine	Montana
Georgia	Idaho	*Legislature, Commission as a backup:*	North Dakota
Illinois	New Jersey	Connecticut	South Dakota
Kentucky	Washington	Indiana	Vermont
Louisiana		Texas	Wyoming
Maryland[2]		*Legislature, with Court Approval:*	
Massachusetts		Florida	
Michigan		Texas	
Minnesota			
Mississippi			
Missouri			
Nebraska			
Nevada			
New Hampshire			
New Mexico			
New York			
North Carolina[3]			
Ohio			
Oklahoma			
Oregon			
Pennsylvania			
Rhode Island			
South Carolina			
Tennessee			
Utah			
Virginia			
West Virginia			
Wisconsin			

In Indiana, for example, the task of congressional redistricting normally falls first to the state legislature and governor; if they cannot approve a plan within a strict time limit, an independent commission is convened to draw the maps. In 2011, the Republican-led Indiana General Assembly was successful in quickly passing a plan after the release

[2] In Maryland, the governor draws the maps, and the legislature votes to approve them.

[3] In North Carolina, the governor does not hold a veto over the congressional redistricting plans; the legislature alone draws and approves the maps.

of 2010 U.S. Census data, which Governor Mitch Daniels subsequently approved. Ultimately, the backup commission was not necessary. In this regard, the would-be commission played no role in the actual drawing of the district maps; its sole effect was to hasten the legislature to adopt a map quickly at the risk of losing control over the process. As such, we can classify the Indiana congressional redistricting process in terms of two relevant characteristics: (1) the legislature and governor produced and approved the plan, and (2) the process was entirely controlled by Republicans.

Consider also the cases of Florida and Kansas, states that require judicial review of the congressional maps after they are passed by the state legislature and approved by the governor. In Florida, the state Supreme Court quickly approved the legislature's congressional district plans in advance of the 2012 elections, while in Kansas, Republican lawmakers in the state House and state Senate were unable to agree on a single plan. Consequently, the Kansas Supreme Court intervened to draw the maps, which were implemented in advance of the 2012 U.S. House elections. In the case of Florida, it is clear that the Republican-controlled legislature drew the congressional map, which was signed into law by Republican Governor Rick Scott. Conversely, in Kansas, the legislature played no effective role in the final design of the congressional district plans, despite the fact that Republicans controlled both chambers of the Kansas Legislature in addition to the governor's mansion.

As for the rest of the states, Table 5.3 lists the outcome of the 2010 redistricting process in terms of who actually drew the plans and their political affiliations (if any).[4]

Note that for our purposes, we have omitted states with only two congressional seats, such as Idaho and Maine, from our sample.[5] We do so because it is not possible to draw a biased plan in a state with two districts.[6] What is clear from our analysis is that, for the majority of states, a single political party controlled the congressional redistricting

[4] Here we do not consider whether a state's districting plans were subject to the mandatory preclearance requirements of the Voting Rights Act – only whether a state's plans were actually struck down by a federal court and the state was ordered to draw new plans for the 2012 House elections.

[5] These states are Hawaii, Idaho, Maine, New Hampshire, and Rhode Island.

[6] It is not possible to create bias in a two-district state with two parties, but it is possible to manipulate responsiveness. If you "pack" your opponent's supporters in one district, you necessarily pack your supporters in the other district, assuring symmetry. However, if you are the larger party, you will favor drawing both districts to be competitive, whereas the smaller party will favor creating one safe seat for each party.

TABLE 5.3. *Who Actually Drew the Maps? Outcome of 2010 Redistricting Cycle*

Single-Party Government		Divided Government	Other Than Legislature
Republicans:	*Democrats:*	Kentucky	*Commission:*
Alabama	Arkansas	Oregon	Arizona
Florida	Illinois		California
Georgia	Maryland		Iowa
Indiana	Massachusetts		New Jersey
Louisiana	West Virginia		Washington
Michigan			*Court:*
Missouri[7]			Colorado
Nebraska			Connecticut
North Carolina			Kansas
Ohio			Minnesota
Oklahoma			Mississippi[8]
Pennsylvania			Nevada
South Carolina			New Mexico
Tennessee			New York
Utah			Texas[9]
Virginia			
Wisconsin			

process and drew the new maps. Conversely, in only a handful of states, this process was controlled by the courts or an independent commission. Moreover, among the partisans, Republican-led governments vastly outnumbered Democratic governments.

Testing the Political Explanation of Where We Find Partisan Bias

We can now consider whether the states where we observe partisan bias are the same as those predicted by the political explanation we

[7] In Missouri, the Republican legislature overrode a veto from the Democratic governor to pass its maps. In this regard, Republicans controlled the process, so we classify this as "single-party government."

[8] In Mississippi, a deadlocked legislature was not able to pass a redistricting plan. As such, a state court implemented the previous district map for the 2012 U.S. House elections.

[9] The Texas plans have been subject to a number of legal challenges which, at the time of this publication, are yet unresolved. Notwithstanding, for the 2012 U.S. House elections, a U.S. district court implemented an interim district map, PlanC235, which reflected a compromise between Republican state officials and various parties challenging the legislature's map. After the 2012 elections, the Texas legislature formally adopted PlanC235, which was signed into law by Governor Perry and will be used for subsequent U.S. House elections.

summarized in Table 5.1. That is to say, does partisan bias occur only where a party has both the motive and opportunity to pass a biased plan?

Taking the data from the previous section, we classify a state as having the opportunity for political gerrymandering if it meets two conditions. First, districting must be carried out by the state legislature (possibly with a gubernatorial veto). If the districting is done by an independent or bipartisan commission or by the courts, then neither party has the opportunity to draw districts in its favor without challenge by the other party. Second, one party must control all the branches of the government responsible for drawing the districting. That is to say, it must control both houses of the state legislature and (in most states) the governorship. Again, if both parties are required to sign off on a districting plan, it is hard to see how one party can secure a plan that is overwhelmingly in its favor.

A motive for political gerrymandering is present if the state is electorally competitive at the federal level. We define competitiveness in federal elections in terms of popular vote performance in the 2008 presidential election. States with point spreads of less than 25% we consider competitive; all others we consider noncompetitive.[10] While it may be said that this represents somewhat of an arbitrary threshold, for our purposes, it serves as a fairly conservative and simple test for competitiveness. After all, it would be difficult to argue that a state with a presidential point spread exceeding 25% ought to be considered competitive by any definition.[11]

As we can see from Table 5.4, we find almost exactly the pattern we would expect (and predicted in Table 5.1). With very few exceptions, high

10 The exception to this is Illinois. We have classified Illinois as competitive, even though the point spread in the 2008 presidential election was greater than 25%. However, this may have been due to the fact that the senator from Illinois, Barack Obama, was one of the candidates. In general, Illinois is quite competitive in federal elections and, indeed, has had a Republican senator since 2010.

11 In most cases, "competitiveness" is not a dichotomous concept. That different states are comparably more competitive than others in federal elections may suggest that competitiveness is better understood as continuous (perhaps using the presidential point spread or some other measure). However, for our purposes, it makes more sense to treat competitiveness as dichotomous. From the perspective of state lawmakers, there is no middle ground regarding motive to gerrymander; there is either room to grow or there is not. If there is any possibility at all to create more partisan bias in a congressional plan, a motive to gerrymander is present. Thus, only in those extreme cases in which one party dominates federal elections such that it could not reasonably extend its advantages any further through districting is motive not present. We operationalize these cases by including those states with lopsided presidential point spreads.

TABLE 5.4. *States with Partisan Bias Grouped by Motive and Opportunity*

	Competitive in National Elections – *Motive for Bias*	Noncompetitive in National Elections – *No Motive for Bias*
Partisan control – *opportunity for bias*	*Biased:* Alabama, Florida, Georgia, Indiana, Louisiana, Michigan, Missouri, North Carolina, Ohio, Pennsylvania, South Carolina, Tennessee, Virginia, Wisconsin *Unbiased:* Illinois, Nebraska West Virginia	*Biased:* Maryland *Unbiased:* Arkansas, Massachusetts, Oklahoma, Utah
Nonpartisan/bipartisan control – *no opportunity for bias*	*Biased:* Texas *Unbiased:* Arizona, Iowa, Kansas, Nevada, New Jersey	*Biased:* Kentucky, Mississippi *Unbiased:* California, Colorado, Connecticut, Minnesota, New Mexico, New York, Oregon, Washington

levels of partisan bias occur if and only if both motive and opportunity are present. That is to say, we see high levels of partisan bias when one party controls the redistricting process and the state is electorally competitive at the federal level. Of the eighteen states where we find statistically significant levels of partisan bias, fourteen are in the top left quadrant, where opportunity and motive are present. In the other three quadrants (where either motive or opportunity or both are lacking), there are only one or two states with significant evidence of partisan bias and many more states where there is no evidence of partisan bias. Thus, with only a few exceptions, the presence of partisan control of the districting process and electoral competitiveness at the electoral level seem to be both necessary and sufficient conditions for partisan bias. We see partisan bias when a party is able to draw the districts in its favor and has a reason to do this and not otherwise.

We can even explain a couple of the exceptions. Both Texas and Mississippi are classified as not having an opportunity to gerrymander because the districting plans for these states in the 2010 cycle were imposed by the state courts and not by the state legislature. However, in both these cases, the baseline for negotiating districts was set by the previous districts that were drawn by a one-party-controlled legislature. In the case of Mississippi, a court ordered that the previous districts be used in the 2012 elections, which had been drawn by a Republican-controlled state legislature (in the 2014 elections, new districts drawn by the state legislature were used). In the case of Texas, the court imposed districts, but these were based on the districts passed by the Republican-controlled legislature with some accommodations to those challenging them. Once again, the previous districting plan was drawn by a one-party-controlled legislature.

Thus we find that politics does indeed predict where we find partisan gerrymandering. Partisan bias is not something that just happens in more or less random states, perhaps for demographic reasons or because of the need to provide adequate representation to minority voters. Rather, it occurs – indeed it almost *only* occurs – where one party has the power and the incentive to make it happen.

DID STATE LEGISLATURES DISTRICT FOR PARTISAN ADVANTAGE MORE AFTER 2010?

We have shown that we find partisan bias precisely where we would expect it – in states where one party controls the districting process and where it makes sense for this party to draw biased districts. However, we are not just telling a story about where we should find partisan bias but about how it changes over time. We have argued that in the 2010 redistricting round, states pursued partisan advantage to a far greater extent than they had previously. If this is the case, we would expect states to produce more biased districting plans in 2010 than in 2000, even in those states where the political conditions already favored biased districting in 2000. That is to say, we expect partisan bias to increase over time, even after controlling for political factors.

Thus we have to test the alternative hypothesis that partisan bias increased simply because the Republicans were in a stronger position at the state level in 2010 than they were in 2000, and they were able to translate this advantage into favorable districting outcomes. This explanation seems plausible, as the Republicans did indeed do extremely well in 2010. Alternatively, certain Democratic-leaning states moved from legislative control of the redistricting process to some other method. If states that were previously biased toward the Democrats became unbiased, this could increase the bias nationally by removing pro-Democratic gerrymanders that counterbalanced pro-Republican gerrymanders. Again, this explanation appears plausible because some of the states in question (California, New York) are very large. We can test these different explanations by carefully comparing the patterns of change among states and how much difference each made to the national bias.

We can break down the states that contributed to the increased bias toward the Republican Party into three groups. First, there are the states that were already biased in 2002 but became more biased in 2012. Then there are states that were biased toward the Democrats in 2002 but ceased to be biased in 2012. Finally, there are states that only became biased toward the Republicans in 2012, having previously been either unbiased or bias toward the Democrats. We can do the same thing for states that changed in a way that decreased bias toward the Republicans (that is, increased bias toward the Democrats).

If states did indeed gerrymander more aggressively after *Vieth v. Jubelirer* (2004), then we would expect to see more bias in states that were already biased. In these states, the state legislature had already chosen to district in a biased manner. The increased bias cannot be explained by other factors such as change of party control. The situation in the states that became biased in 2012 (but were not previously) is more complex. Certainly some of the change in bias in some of these cases is due to a change of party control of the districting process. However, it may also be partly due to these states pursuing partisan advantage more aggressively than was possible in the previous round. For example, consider a state legislature that was controlled by the Democrats in 2000 but was won by the Republicans in 2010. The Republican-controlled legislature reverses the previous Democratic gerrymander. However, they go further and gerrymander far more effectively than the Democrats did in 2000. We can also consider the effect of various states with districting biased in favor of the Democrats ceasing to be biased.

We classify the various states that contributed to a change in bias in Table 5.5. There are nine states where pro-Republican bias increased from an already biased plan. These tend to be relatively large states and account for 131 House districts. There are only four states that were biased toward the Democrats and became unbiased in 2012. However, these include California, New Jersey, and New York, so the total number of districts is ninety-seven. There are seven states that became biased toward the Republicans in 2012 but had not been previously. These are mostly smaller states and account for fifty-five districts.

TABLE 5.5. *Changes in Bias by State 2002–2012*

States Increasing Bias toward Republicans		
Increased Republican bias in state already biased to Republicans 2002–2010	States that became unbiased, but were biased toward Democrats 2002–2010	States that became biased toward Republican in 2012
Alabama, Georgia, Michigan, Missouri, Ohio, Pennsylvania, South Carolina, Texas, Virginia	California, New Jersey, New York, Oregon	Indiana, Kentucky, Louisiana, Mississippi, North Carolina, Wisconsin, Tennessee
Total 2012 districts: 131 Contribution to change in national bias: (asymmetry): −2.8%	Total 2012 districts: 97 Contribution to change in national bias: (asymmetry): 0.5%	Total 2012 districts: 55 Contribution to change in national bias: (asymmetry): −3.7%
States increasing bias toward Democrats		
Increased Democratic bias in state already biased to Democrats 2002–2010	States that became unbiased, but were biased toward Republican 2002–2010	States that became biased toward Democrats in 2012
	Oklahoma, Utah	
	Total 2012 districts: 9 Contribution to change in national bias: (asymmetry): −0.75%	

In order to test the relative importance of the various groups of states in increasing bias, we need a way to quantify the relative contribution of each group. We did this by first calculating what bias would be using the 2002 districts but accounting for the reapportionment of districts among states that occurred in 2012. (It turns out that this increases bias toward the Republican Party by 0.75% – the states that gained districts tended to be those in which there was already pro-Republican bias.) Then we recalculate bias in the same way, except that we use the 2012 districts for only those states in which we are interested. Thus we can calculate the contribution to the increase in bias from (say) the states that were already Republican biased, but bias increased.

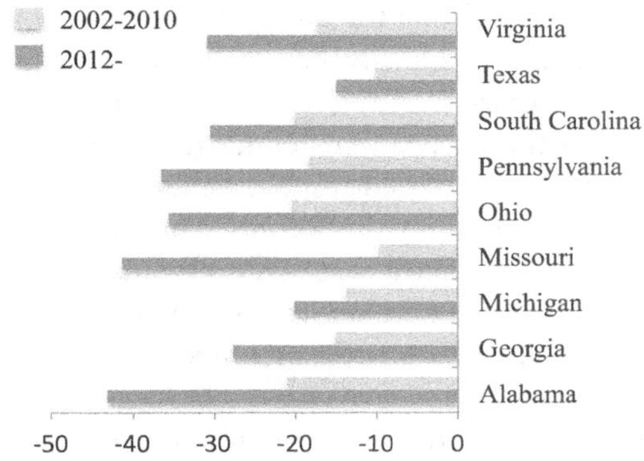

FIGURE 5.1. Increasing bias (asymmetry) in selected states 2002–2010 and 2012.

If it is true that states gerrymander more aggressively after *Vieth v. Jubelirer* (2004), we should see the already-biased states adding to the national bias. This is exactly what we observe. The national bias toward the Republicans increased from 3.4% to 9.4%. The states where bias increased from already-biased districting plans account for an increase of 2.8%. Thus we can conclude that the increase in bias is not just the result of the Republicans doing better in 2010 than in 2000. Even where there was already a biased districting plan in 2000, in 2012, this became more extreme. Figure 5.1 graphs this. We see that the bias in many of these states almost doubled. In 2002, only two states had bias barely above 20%; in 2012, many states had bias in the upper 30s and 40s.

The increase in bias at the national level cannot be explained by the Democrats failing to preserve gerrymanders in states that were biased in their favor in 2002 (such as California and New York). In fact, the 2012 districts in these states actually reduce national bias toward the Republicans relative to the 2002 districts by 0.5%. This seems paradoxical until we consider redistricting in the largest of these states, California. The 2002 districts exhibited substantial bias toward the Democrats, but it was an incumbent-protection gerrymander with very low responsiveness (0.76). Indeed, the Democrats won thirty-four seats in *both* 2008 *and* 2010, despite winning 62% of the two-party vote in the former and only 55% in the latter. Given that the Democrats are dominant in terms of votes in California, this lack of responsiveness was very inefficient in terms of maximizing Democratic seats. In 2008, a voter initiative, Proposition 11, replaced redistricting by the General Assembly with a citizens' commission. As we have seen, the new districting plan for the 2012 election was unbiased but far more responsive (its responsiveness was 1.9 instead of 0.76). While the Democrats lost the bias that was in their favor, the increased responsiveness more than compensated for it. As a result, the Democrats won thirty-eight seats in 2012. It should be noted, however, that these extra seats come at a cost of less security for Democratic incumbents: increased responsiveness and lack of bias mean that for every percentage point the Republican Party gains in votes, it will get approximately one extra seat. Thus eliminating pro-Democratic bias in California had little effect on national bias – the bias toward the Democrats was being used to protect incumbents, not to advantage the Democratic Party nationally.

The states that were biased toward the Republicans in 2012 but were not previously add an estimated 3.7% to national bias. It is hard to break down exactly how much of this is the result of change of party control of the redistricting process and how much is the result of the party that controls the process being willing to gerrymander more aggressively post *Vieth v. Jubelirer* (2004). Consider the cases of North Carolina and Tennessee. In both cases, the 2002 districting plans had a pro-Democratic bias of around 10%. (In the case of North Carolina, this is not quite significant at the 5% level, but it is very close.) In 2010, the Republicans took control of all the relevant decision points in both states (state legislature in North Carolina, state legislature and governor in Tennessee). As expected, the new 2012 districts were biased toward the Republicans instead of the Democrats. However, a 10% bias in favor of the Democrats was not replaced by a 10% Republican bias. Rather, the bias in favor of the Republicans was 27.8% in Tennessee and 36.3% in North Carolina. As was the case with the states that were already biased toward the Republicans, these states districted for partisan advantage far more thoroughly post *Vieth v. Jubelirer* (2004).

Thus we can see that in the 2010 districting round, states districted for partisan advantage more aggressively than they did previously, even when we take into account who had political control of the districting. We may consider why this should be the case. One theory would be that before *Vieth*, the threat that the courts might overturn an egregious gerrymander deterred states from pushing partisan advantage too far. However, the Supreme Court decision in *Vieth v. Jubelirer* (2004) sent a decisive signal that the courts would not intervene in partisan gerrymandering cases. Free from the threat of having their districting plans overturned, state governments drew districts for maximum partisan advantage. If this was the case, we would expect to see the states that were already drawing biased plans in the 2000 districting round go even further, districting for the maximum possible partisan advantage. In states that the Republican Party controlled in 2010 but not in 2000, we would expect plans more biased than those typically seen in the 2000 round. This is what we observe.

One objection to this theory might be that even prior to *Vieth*, there was little threat that the courts would overturn a districting plan on the grounds that it was a partisan gerrymander. It has been widely argued that the standards for partisan gerrymandering set out in the plurality opinion in *Davis v. Bandemer* (1986a) were very hard to meet. Indeed, Justice Scalia in his opinion on *Vieth* argued that the *Bandemer* standard had been ineffective, since no districting plans had been overturned by it. The logic here is questionable – it might be that the possibility of a plan being overturned after *Bandemer* deterred states from adopting egregious gerrymanders, so no plans needed to be overturned. Nevertheless, there was considerable controversy at the time of the *Bandemer* ruling as to whether it would have any effect. Some (for example, Lowenstein 1990) argued that the standard made a successful challenge almost impossible. Grofman (1990, 32), on the other hand, argued that while the standard was high enough to deter frivolous suits, it would allow the courts to discipline the most egregious gerrymanders.

An alternative explanation would be that states gradually learned over two districting cycles that the courts were very unlikely to overturn districting plans on grounds of partisan gerrymandering. Immediately after *Davis v. Bandemer* (1986a), there may have been considerable uncertainty as to how the District Courts would interpret it. However, as more and more cases were brought and none of them succeeded, states might have concluded that there was little risk of a successful legal challenge. As they conclude this, we would expect them to push partisan districting further. In this scenario, we would expect states to district aggressively for partisan advantage in the 2010 cycle, even in a counterfactual world where the Supreme Court refused to hear *Vieth* and let the District Courts decision (to not overturn the Pennsylvania districting plan) stand.

Alternatively, we could explain the increase in partisan bias in terms of a change in the attitudes of the parties that controlled the districting process. For example, it could be argued that the change resulted from the increasing polarization of the Republican Party. Whereas in the past, it could be argued, the Republican Party was happy to engage in bipartisan bargaining, a new, more ideological Republican Party now sought complete control of Congress. There is indeed a very considerable literature suggesting that both political parties have become more polarized (see, for example, McCarty et al. 2006; Layman et al. 2006; Theriault 2008). There seems to be consensus that the political parties have become more polarized, but there is considerable debate on whether this reflects ideological polarization on the part of the public or is simply an elite phenomenon (see Fiorina et al. 2006, 2008; Abramowitz and Saunders 2008; Levendusky 2009).

We cannot discount that the increasing polarization of the Republican Party played a role in the increase in partisan bias we observe. The polarization of parties in Congress did continue to increase through the 2000s (Poole and Rosenthal 2007, 104–109). Furthermore, districting plans have to be passed by the party that controls the districting process at the state level. However, we would note that the parties were already very polarized by the mid-1990s, before the increase in partisan bias in the 2010 districting cycle. Party polarization seems to have increased from 1975 and increased most rapidly in the early 1990s (McCarty et al. 2006; Poole and Rosenthal 2007). According to Poole and Rosenthal (2007, 104–109), by 1994, there was already virtually no overlap between the two parties in the House or Senate (here overlap is defined as the number of members who are ideologically closer in terms of DW-NOMINATE scores to the centroid of the other party than that of their own party). Similarly, they find that the ideological distance between the two parties in the House and Senate increased by around a third between 1975 and 1994 (again using DW-NOMINATE scores), although this distance does continue to increase after 1994.

Of course, we could always explain the increase in partisan bias by some other change in the attitudes of Republican-controlled state legislatures. Perhaps they became more interested in national partisan advantage after 2000. After all, partisan districting could not happen without the participation of parties at the state level. However, what still needs to be explained is the number of states that had already crossed the line in adopting biased districting plans in 2000 and then went on in 2010 to adopt plans that are far more biased. It seems strange to argue that these state legislatures were sufficiently ruthless in 2000 to district for partisan gerrymandering but not ruthless enough to push this all the way. This would suggest that there was something deterring them from districting for maximum partisan advantage in the 2000 districting round.

Whatever the exact sequence of causes that led to partisan bias increasing almost threefold in the 2010 districting round – and it was probably a result of several factors – the basic facts remain the same. State legislatures controlled by one party pushed partisan advantage in districting far further than they did in the previous districting round. This could not have happened if the Supreme Court had acted to prohibit partisan gerrymandering. It does not really matter whether the states pursued partisan advantage in districting without restraint because the Supreme Court had signaled that it would not intervene or whether the states were going to aggressively gerrymander anyway and the Supreme Court did not hinder them. In either case, the high bias we observe could not have happened without the choices of state legislatures to pursue partisan advantage and the choice of the Supreme Court not to prevent them.

WHY ARE SO MANY STATE GOVERNMENTS DOMINATED BY ONE PARTY WHILE COMPETITIVE AT FEDERAL ELECTIONS?

As the previous analysis demonstrates, much of the state level variation in bias can be explained in terms of two variables, which we term "motive" and "opportunity." A party has the opportunity to draw a partisan districting plan when it completely controls the districting process. This usually involves controlling both chambers of the state legislature and the governorship. However, there is only an incentive to produce a districting plan with partisan bias in states that are electorally competitive at the federal level. We would expect this combination to be unlikely – if a state is electorally competitive, we would expect one-party domination of the state government to be infrequent. However, it turns out not to be uncommon at all in recent years. We now turn to the question of why this might be the case.

There is, of course, no reason the outcomes of state and national elections should be the same. After all, different issues and candidates are involved, while state races tend to receive less publicity and media attention than national races do. However, there are institutional reasons that make this configuration (competitive national elections, where state government is dominated by one party) more likely. We observe differential voter turnout rates in state and national elections. Furthermore, the timing of elections in many states increases this differential. Specifically, we argue that the common practice of holding state-level elections in off years leads to systematically lower rates of voter participation compared to state-level elections that run concurrently with presidential-year elections and thus explains why electoral outcomes in many states vary in state and national elections. In most states, a smaller subset of the electorate turns out to vote for state-level offices, which may contribute to one-party dominance at the state level despite partisan competitiveness in national elections – the conditions that provide lawmakers with a motive to create biased congressional district plans.

In order to defend this assertion, we first need to demonstrate that (1) the scheduling of elections influences voter turnout rates – in other words, that there actually is a voter turnout effect in off-year elections – and (2) that this effect is indeed present in the states with the highest levels of asymmetry (where motive and opportunity interact). Although we cannot definitively prove that differential voter turnout rates lead to divergent patterns of electoral competitiveness at the state and national levels, meeting these two burdens will provide us with a plausible explanation for this phenomenon and resolve our theoretical dilemma.

We begin by asking: Is there actually an off-year turnout effect in state-level elections?[12] In order to address this question, we analyze voter participation in state gubernatorial elections. This approach to estimating the off-year effect is intuitive for two reasons: first, all states have a governor who is chosen democratically through regular popular elections. Second, because the governor is the highest elected official in state governance, gubernatorial races are typically the most salient of all state-level elections. Consequently, voter turnout is likely to be at its highest in these races, and any off-year turnout effect will be minimal compared to lower state-level elections. In other words, if we observe an off-year turnout effect in gubernatorial elections, then we can be confident that this effect also impacts voter participation in smaller, less salient state elections to an equal or greater extent.

With regard to gubernatorial election-year scheduling, the states can be grouped into three categories. First, a number of states hold gubernatorial elections every four years concurrently with presidential elections. We dub these states "presidential-year" states. A second group consists of states with off-year gubernatorial elections. In these states, governors serve four-year terms and are elected in even-numbered, nonpresidential years. Our last group, "odd-year" states, includes the five states that hold gubernatorial elections in odd-numbered years, either the year before or

[12] The topic of voter turnout has received a considerable amount of attention within the research on public choice. For instance, Taagepera et al. (2013) demonstrate that much of the variation in voter turnout in democratic elections can be explained in terms of the effective number of parties. This suggests that the two-party system is one factor that may contribute to historically low levels of voter turnout in U.S. elections relative to other democracies. Others (Grofman et al. 1999; Citrin et al. 2003; Martinez and Gill 2005; Hansford and Gomez 2010) have explored the consequences of voter turnout in terms of electoral outcomes.

TABLE 5.6. *Predicted Influence of Gubernatorial Election Years on Voter Turnout*

States with presidential-year elections	HIGH VOTER TURNOUT
States with off-year elections	↕
States with odd-year elections	LOW VOTER TURNOUT

after a presidential election.[13] How do these groups differ with regard to voter turnout?

We would expect scheduling to have an effect on turnout in elections due to the salience of elections. This approach assumes that elections with higher publicity and popular interest will incur greater voter turnout levels and that national elections are on average more salient than state-level elections. Thus, states that hold gubernatorial elections concurrently with presidential elections (which tend to be the most salient elections in American politics and generally have the highest levels of voter turnout) are more likely to yield systematically higher levels of voter turnout compared to other states, as they benefit from the salience of the presidential race.[14] This approach parallels the contributions of Reif and Schmitt (1980), who explain voter turnout levels in terms of the saliency of elections and the perceived importance of the election with regard to voters.[15] In this regard, we expect off-year state elections that run concurrently with national midterm elections to yield lower turnout than presidential-year states but higher turnout than odd-year states, in which there are typically no national elections held. Our theoretical expectations are summarized in Table 5.6.

Now that we have outlined our expectations for the effects of election timing on voter turnout, we can test these predictions. We do so by

13 The one exception to this classification scheme is Vermont, where the governor serves two-year terms. For our purposes, we consider Vermont both a presidential-year state and an off-year state.

14 This is commonly referred to as the "coattails" theory (see Chubb 1988): voter turnout in state and local elections is increased by popular candidates running in high-profile national races.

15 Reif and Schmitt (1980) conceptualize national elections as "first-order elections" because the issues are perceived by voters as being more consequential and significant. They consider local and regional elections "second-order elections" because they are less salient and are perceived as less important to voters. Although Reif and Schmitt (1989) directly apply these concepts to the European context, Percival and colleagues (2007) demonstrate that they are useful for understanding differential turnout in U.S. state elections.

looking at the gubernatorial elections in all fifty states, and we consider voter turnout in the past five gubernatorial elections for each state. For presidential-year states, this period spans elections held between 1996 and 2012; for off-year states, the range is 1994 to 2010; and for odd-year states, we look at elections between 1993 and 2011. We calculate voter turnout in terms of ballots cast and voting-age population (VAP).[16] Although states commonly publish their own voter turnout rates, the methodologies for doing so vary widely from state to state.[17] Our approach to estimating voter turnout may lack the precision of several state measures, but it provides us with an objective, standardized measurement for voter turnout that allows us to make direct comparisons between different states. Thus, for each state gubernatorial election, we calculate turnout as such:

Voter turnout = ballot cast in gubernatorial election/state VAP

Table 5.7 lists the mean voter turnout rates of each of our groups of states spanning the past five elections (see Appendix for an expanded table of the results from each state). The results of this analysis confirm our expectations: *when* state gubernatorial elections are held affects *how many* voters will participate. As is evident, mean voter turnout increases to its maximum in gubernatorial elections that run concurrently with presidential elections and drops to the lowest levels in odd-numbered years. Among the ten states with presidential-year gubernatorial elections, participation was the highest, averaging roughly 57%. The participation rate drops below 50% to roughly 42% in the states with odd-year elections, and we observe the lowest voter turnout in the five states with odd-year gubernatorial elections, where an average of just 37% of the adult population cast votes.[18] This represents a 26% drop in participation from presidential to off years and a 35% drop in participation to odd-year elections.

One possible objection to these results is that we may not be getting an accurate picture of the voter turnout effect insofar as we treat all states as equals. Or perhaps the states with off-year elections share certain

[16] Our VAP estimates are borrowed from the U.S. Census Bureau's biannual Current Population Survey. For states with odd-year elections, we calculate VAP by averaging the VAP estimates for the year before and the year after.

[17] For instance, many states calculate voter turnout as the portion of ballots cast to registered voters. This poses obvious problems with consistency, as the definition of "registered voter" and the criteria for voter registration varies by state.

[18] These differences are statistically significant at the $p = .0001$ level.

TABLE 5.7. *Participation Rates of Voting Age Population in Gubernatorial Elections, 1993–2012*

States with off-year gubernatorial elections	Alabama, Alaska, Arizona, Arkansas, California, Colorado, Connecticut, Florida, Georgia, Hawaii, Idaho, Illinois, Iowa, Kansas, Maine, Maryland, Massachusetts, Michigan, Minnesota, Nebraska, Nevada, New Hampshire, New Mexico, New York, Ohio, Oklahoma, Oregon, Pennsylvania, Rhode Island, South Carolina, South Dakota, Tennessee, Texas, Vermont,[19] Wisconsin, Wyoming	Mean turnout rate 1994–2010 42%
States with presidential-year gubernatorial elections	Delaware, Indiana, Missouri, Montana, North Carolina, North Dakota, Utah, Vermont, Washington, West Virginia	Mean turnout rate 1996–2012 57%
States with odd-year gubernatorial elections	Kentucky, Louisiana, Mississippi, New Jersey, Virginia	Mean turnout rate 1993–2011 37%

structural features unrelated to election year scheduling, such as geographic proximity or candidate selection processes that serve to repress voter participation. If this were the case, we would be forced to have less confidence in the significance of apparent off-year effect we observe. To counter these objections, we turn to the case of Vermont – the only state that elects governors to two-year terms. That Vermont holds gubernatorial elections in both presidential and off years provides us with a natural experiment for gauging the impact of election-year scheduling on voter turnout within a state and a method for allaying our skepticism. After all, the conditions that influence voter turnout in Vermont are equally present during both off-year and presidential-year gubernatorial elections; the sole difference is that during off-year elections, there is not a high-profile presidential election running concurrently. Figure 5.2 plots the gubernatorial election turnout rates in Vermont for the past ten elections (five off-year elections; five presidential-year elections). Without

[19] Vermont is the only state with two-year terms for governor.

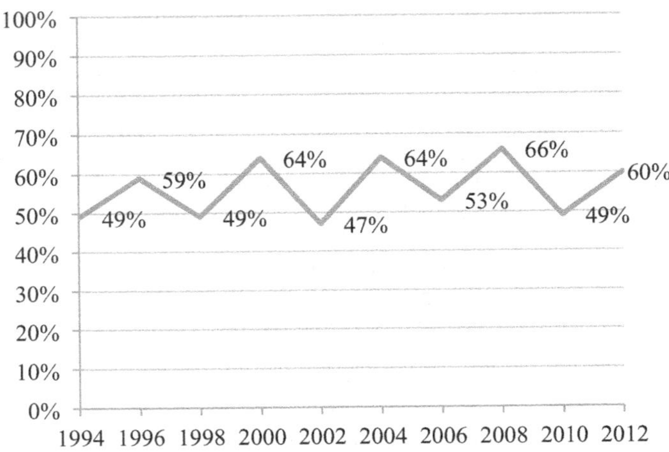

FIGURE 5.2. Participation in Vermont gubernatorial elections, 1994–2012.

exception, voter turnout in gubernatorial races held during presidential election years is higher than in off years. In presidential years, participation averaged roughly 63%, whereas in off years, voter turnout dropped to 49% on average. This decrease of 22% from presidential years to off years is largely consistent with the nationwide average decrease of 26% we observed in our analysis of all fifty states. In short, as Figure 5.2 demonstrates, the wide swings in voter turnout that alternate between presidential and off-year elections provide further evidence for the off-year election effect.

As a second objection to our conclusions, one could argue that our results (Table 5.7) might be skewed by historical anomalies and thus do not signify the presence of an off-year effect in gubernatorial elections. After all, recent historical spikes in voter participation, such as heightened interest in the 2008 presidential race, might serve to increase presidential-year gubernatorial participation rates above their typical levels and thus exaggerate the magnitude of the off-year turnout effect we observe. But this trend cannot simply be dismissed as a historical anomaly. As Figure 5.3 illustrates, for the last twenty years, mean voter turnout has been universally higher in the group of states with presidential-year gubernatorial elections when compared to the groups with off-year and odd-year elections. As is evident, there is a spike in average voter turnout coinciding with the 2008 presidential election, but this increase is negligible and does not represent a statistical outlier that skews the results. As for the off-year and odd-year elections, the data shows definitively that voter turnout has remained stable and consistently low for the past twenty years.

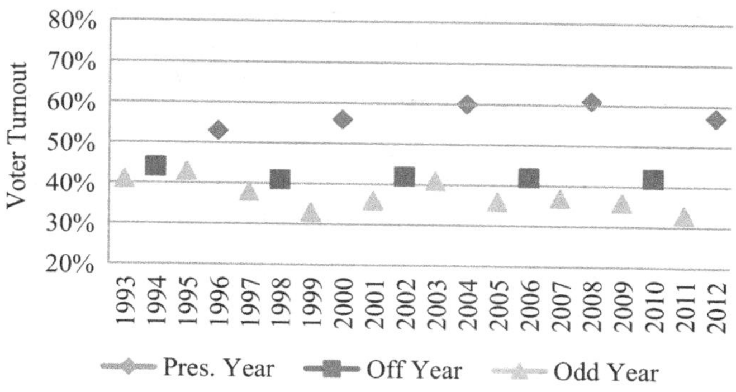

FIGURE 5.3. Voter participation in gubernatorial elections, 1993–2012.

Even when the off-year turnout effect is at its minimum during the election years between 1994 and 1996, the effect is still considerable. Voter turnout in both the off-year and odd-year elections of 1994 and 1995, at 44% and 43%, respectively, were considerably lower than the 1996 presidential-year election average participation rate of 53%.

In sum, our analysis demonstrates that the off-year effect is indeed present in state gubernatorial elections, a result that supports our contention that differential turnout rates in presidential-year and off-year state elections may contribute to the phenomenon of one-party dominance in state elections despite competitiveness in national elections.

In most states where the districting process is controlled by the state legislature, it is necessary to get the districting plan agreed on by both house of the legislature and the governor. Therefore, we need to consider the scheduling of the state legislative elections. In general, the electoral schedules of most state legislatures share common set of features. With the exception of Nebraska, state legislatures are divided into two houses – a lower house and a senate – and typically hold elections in even-numbered years. In most of the lower houses, members serve two-year terms and are elected biannually. State senates are typically composed of representatives with four-year terms and hold "staggered" election schedules, with half of the chamber elected every two years. This pattern holds for a majority of states, but there are a number of exceptions. In both Alabama and Maryland, for instance, legislatures from both houses are elected to four-year terms in even-numbered, nonpresidential years (off years). Conversely, in Georgia, representatives from both houses serve two-year terms and face reelection in even-numbered years. A few states – Louisiana, Mississippi, West Virginia, and Virginia – hold legislative elections in odd-numbered years. Table 5.8 lists the twenty-four states where state legislators

TABLE 5.8. *State Legislatures Tasked with Redistricting: When the Map-Drawers Were Elected*

State		Term Years	Election Schedule	Mapmakers Last Elected
Alabama	Lower	4	off years	2010
	Upper	4	off years	2010
Arkansas	Lower	2	even years	2010
	Upper	4	staggered, even	2008, 2010
Florida	Lower	2	even years	2010
	Upper	4	staggered, even	2008, 2010
Georgia	Lower	2	even years	2010
	Upper	2	even years	2010
Illinois	Lower	2	even years	2010
	Upper	2–4	staggered, even	2008, 2010
Indiana	Lower	2	even years	2010
	Upper	4	staggered, even	2008, 2010
Kentucky	Lower	2	even years	2010
	Upper	4	staggered, even	2008, 2010
Louisiana	Lower	4	odd years	2007
	Upper	4	odd years	2007
Maryland	Lower	4	off years	2010
	Upper	4	off years	2010
Massachusetts	Lower	2	even years	2010
	Upper	2	even years	2010
Michigan	Lower	2	even years	2010
	Upper	4	off years	2010
Missouri	Lower	2	even years	2010
	Upper	4	staggered, even	2008, 2010
Nebraska	Unicam	4	staggered, even	2008, 2010
North Carolina	Lower	2	even years	2010
	Upper	2	even years	2010
Oklahoma	Lower	2	even years	2010
	Upper	4	staggered, even	2008, 2010
Ohio	Lower	2	even years	2010
	Upper	4	staggered, even	2008, 2010
Oregon	Lower	2	even years	2010
	Upper	4	staggered, even	2008, 2010
Pennsylvania	Lower	2	even years	2010
	Upper	4	staggered, even	2008, 2010
South Carolina	Lower	2	even years	2010
	Upper	4	staggered, even	2008, 2010
Utah	Lower	2	even years	2010
	Upper	4	staggered, even	2008, 2010
Tennessee	Lower	2	even years	2010
	Upper	4	staggered, even	2008, 2010
Virginia	Lower	2	odd years	2011
	Upper	4	staggered, odd	2009, 2011
West Virginia	Lower	2	even years	2010
	Upper	4	staggered, even	2008, 2010
Wisconsin	Lower	2	even years	2010
	Upper	4	staggered, even	2008, 2010

participated in drawing the congressional district maps that were implemented during the 2012 U.S. House elections. For each state, we have also included the year during which the legislatures who drew the maps were elected to their chamber. As is evident, the vast majority of state legislators from lower houses were elected in 2010 – an off-year election – and many others were elected during odd-year elections. With regard to state senates, the majority of the representatives were selected in 2010, while a smaller portion was chosen in 2008. In the case of Louisiana, its representatives in both chambers were selected in 2007. If the off-year turnout effect is indeed present in state legislative races, as we have argued, then it is clear that most of the legislators in most states were chosen by a different subset of their districts' electorate than they would have faced in an election held during a presidential year.

Thus we find that different results at the state and federal level is not that surprising. Even though the eligible electorate is the same, the subset of voters who participate is not. In most states, the gubernatorial election is held in off years, when there is not a presidential election. Most state senates are elected for four-year terms with staggered elections. Thus half the state senate is elected in an off-year. State lower-house elections are typically held every two years, so the election that determines who gets to draw the congressional maps alternates between being off year and presidential year every ten years. Thus even in a typical state, many of the elections that determine who gets to draw congressional maps have rather low turnout. Furthermore, in certain states, election timing increases this effect. For example, there are states that elect governors in odd years and where state senators are all elected in off years. Thus the voters that determine who gets to draw the congressional map will often be fewer in number than those that vote in the congressional elections.

CONCLUSION

In this chapter, we have asked whether we can explain where we find partisan bias in terms of political variables. The answer is an overwhelming yes. As we saw in the previous chapter, the patterns of partisan bias we observe cannot be explained by geographic factors such as the urban concentration of Democratic voters or the need to draw majority-minority districts. Rather, partisan bias is a matter of choice by state legislatures. And now we confirm that this choice is a political one. To put it bluntly, we find partisan bias where one party controls the entire districting process and not otherwise. In the 2010 districting round, this party was in the vast majority of cases the Republican Party (Maryland was the only case of a statistically significant Democratic gerrymander). If we take into account whether a party has an incentive to draw biased districts, we can predict partisan bias even better – there is no point for parties that are completely dominant, like the Democrats in Massachusetts or the Republicans in Oklahoma, to draw biased districts, because they win all the seats anyway.

The pattern of changes in partisan bias over time is also consistent with our expectations. States where the Republican Party controlled the entire districting process districted for partisan advantage far more aggressively than in previous districting rounds. We find that partisan bias increases sharply in those states where there was already partisan bias in the 2000 round. In those states that became biased in the 2010 districting round, the level of partisan bias is typically far greater than typically found in the 2000 round. Thus we can conclude that the increase in bias in the 2010 round is not just a result of the Republican Party doing very well in the 2010 elections and controlling more states than it did in 2000 – bias increased strongly in those states the Republicans controlled in both 2000 and 2010. A number of explanations for this are possible. Perhaps it was due to the fact that the Supreme Court had signaled in *Vieth v. Jubelirer* (2004) that it would not intervene in partisan gerrymandering cases. As a result, state legislatures did not have to worry about the threat of legal oversight and pushed partisan advantage to its limits. Alternatively, the Republican Party in various states may have become more determined to pursue national political advantage through redistricting. Or perhaps there was a combination of factors. In any case, state legislatures chose to pursue partisan advantages more aggressively than before, and the Supreme Court chose not to prevent them.

Two other things require mentioning here. First, partisan bias occurs in states where one party controls state government in states that are competitive at the federal level. In other words, a party is using its dominance at the state level to influence or even dominate federal elections to the House of Representatives. This has profound constitutional implications. The United States Constitution is built on the compromise that the House of Representatives represents the people of the United States directly, while the Senate represents the interests of the states. However, now we see parties leveraging their dominance of state government to take control of congressional delegations. This is a fundamental challenge to the Compromise.

Second, we see parties leveraging their dominance in state elections (in which fewer people vote) to influence congressional elections (in which more people vote). That is to say, the balance of power in the House of Representatives is being determined indirectly by the outcome of state elections in which comparatively few people vote. That is to say, we are shifting power from elections in which more people vote to elections in which fewer people vote. Furthermore, those who do vote in the state-level election will probably have little idea that they are determining the makeup of the federal House for the next ten years. This has profound consequences for the practice of democracy in the United States. These questions are considered in depth in the next chapter.

APPENDIX 5A – VOTER TURNOUT (AS A PERCENTAGE OF VAP) IN STATE GUBERNATORIAL ELECTIONS, 1993–2012

TABLE 5.A1. *Voter Turnout (as a Percentage of VAP) in State Gubernatorial Elections, 1993–2012*

State	Election Schedule	t_1	t_2	t_3	t_4	t_5
Alabama	Off year	38	40	42	36	42
Alaska	Off year	54	55	53	51	51
Arizona	Off year	38	30	32	35	36
Arkansas	Off year	40	38	41	37	37
California	Off year	39	36	32	34	37
Colorado	Off year	41	45	44	45	48
Connecticut	Off year	47	41	40	43	43
Delaware	Presidential year	51	57	60	61	57
Florida	Off year	40	35	41	35	38
Georgia	Off year	30	32	33	32	36
Hawaii	Off year	44	48	44	36	39
Idaho	Off year	52	43	43	42	41
Illinois	Off year	36	39	38	37	39
Indiana	Presidential year	50	50	54	58	53
Iowa	Off year	48	46	48	47	50
Kansas	Off year	46	40	41	42	41
Kentucky	Odd year	34	19	36	33	25
Louisiana	Odd year	51	41	44	42	31
Maine	Off year	56	45	48	53	56
Maryland	Off year	38	40	44	43	43
Massachusetts	Off year	48	41	45	46	46
Michigan	Off year	45	42	42	51	43
Minnesota	Off year	52	61	59	57	53
Mississippi	Odd year	43	38	44	35	42

(*continued*)

TABLE 5.A1 (*continued*)

State	Election Schedule	t_1	t_2	t_3	t_4	t_5
Missouri	Presidential year	55	58	64	65	60
Montana	Presidential year	62	62	65	67	63
Nebraska	Off year	50	46	38	46	37
Nevada	Off year	35	33	32	32	37
New Hampshire	Off year	37	36	45	40	45
New Jersey	Odd year	43	40	35	36	37
New Mexico	Off year	40	40	37	39	40
New York	Off year	39	37	33	33	32
North Carolina	Presidential year	48	52	56	62	62
North Dakota	Presidential year	58	64	66	65	60
Ohio	Off year	41	41	38	47	45
Oklahoma	Off year	43	36	41	35	38
Oregon	Off year	53	45	48	49	49
Pennsylvania	Off year	40	34	38	43	41
Rhode Island	Off year	50	42	41	48	42
South Carolina	Off year	35	38	37	34	39
South Dakota	Off year	63	49	58	58	53
Tennessee	Off year	39	24	39	40	34
Texas	Off year	33	27	30	27	28
Utah	Presidential year	50	52	56	51	48
Vermont	Off year	49	49	47	53	49
Vermont	Presidential year	59	64	64	66	60
Virginia	Odd year	38	35	36	36	34
Washington	Presidential year	55	57	61	61	59
West Virginia	Presidential year	44	46	53	51	46
Wisconsin	Off year	43	46	43	51	50
Wyoming	Off year	60	51	50	50	46

6

Constitutional Implications of *Vieth*

The Revenge of the Anti-Federalists

So far we have considered the partisan effects of the redistricting that followed the *Vieth v. Jubelirer* (2004) decision. However, these effects may be short term compared to the constitutional effects of the decision. The redistricting that followed the 2010 Census has indeed strongly advantaged the Republican Party, but after the 2020 Census, districts will need to be redrawn again. It is possible that the current biases will be erased. Indeed, it is even possible that they may be reversed if the Democrats are in a very strong position in state governments and choose to take full advantage of this. However, even if the current partisan advantage is not permanent, *Vieth v. Jubelirer* still represents a fundamental change in the effective constitution of the United States.

What the *Vieth* decision represents is a very clear increase in the power of state governments over national politics. There is now effectively no legal constraint on states employing partisan gerrymandering. We have demonstrated how powerful partisan gerrymandering can be when combined with modern computer mapping technology, even when the districts have to have equal populations. As a result, when one party controls state government, it can guarantee itself a majority on the state's congressional delegation. If this is the case, then it is the state government – and not the voters of the state – that determines the character of the state's congressional delegation. As we have seen, there are eighteen states with significant partisan bias after the 2010 redistricting. Of these, thirteen have an asymmetry of more than 20% and a partisan advantage of more than 10% given a 50/50 election. It is possible in one state (Pennsylvania) for the party that controlled the districting to win thirteen seats out of eighteen in spite of the other party winning a majority of the congressional vote. In these cases, only the strongest swing in support could overturn the bias. Whether this works to the benefit of the Democrats or Republicans in the future, the composition of Congress will be strongly influenced, if not determined, by races for the state legislature and the governor's mansion.

This represents a fundamental change to the Great Compromise that defined the U.S. system of government. The point of the Great Compromise at the Federal Convention was that the House of Representatives would represent the people directly, while the Senate would represent the interests of the states. This, of course, was the result of a compromise between the Federalists, such as Madison, who argued for a *national* conception of government with the legislature being elected directly and proportionally by the people, and the Anti-Federalists who argued for (in modern terminology) a *federal* conception of government, with the legislature being elected through the states. However, as we have seen, the result of the *Vieth* finding is that the House of Representatives, which is supposed to represent the people directly and nationally, now has its composition largely determined by the districting decisions of state governments. This marks a move toward a far more Anti-Federalist conception of government and against the Madisonian principle that at least one house should directly represent the people without the mediation of the states.

The *Vieth* judgment also undermines the one-person, one-vote jurisprudence of the 1960s that followed *Baker v. Carr* (1962), which can be seen in light of the same controversy. This is particularly true of *Wesberry v. Sanders* (1964a), the case that outlawed malapportionment in congressional elections. The Courts' opinion in this case (written by Justice Black) is very much framed in terms of the Great Compromise, and the constitutional debates are cited at length. The House is to be elected by the "People of the Several States," which is taken to mean that all voters be treated equally. The Court finds that this is incompatible with state governments advantaging some citizens over others through the drawing of districts. In this sense, the Court in *Wesberry v. Sanders* (1964a) can be seen as restoring the Great Compromise (and popular election of the House) after years of encroachment by state governments drawing districts with widely varying populations. The *Vieth* decision does not give back to the states the right to draw districts of unequal population, but it does allow them to achieve the same effect by manipulating the boundaries of districts. As such, it does not simply overturn *Davis v. Bandemer* (1986a) but strikes at the spirit of *Wesberry v. Sanders* (1964a).

We also need to consider the effect of the *Vieth* decision on the quality of American democracy. As we have argued, it makes democracy in America more indirect by giving state governments a far greater influence on the composition of the House, the part of government traditionally supposed to represent the People directly. It also allows for striking inequalities to the extent that state governments take advantage of the lack of oversight and engineer districts to advantage some voters over others. There are other democratic values to consider, such as participation, inclusiveness, transparency, and responsiveness. We will consider these later in this chapter.

THE GREAT COMPROMISE AND THE HOUSE OF REPRESENTATIVES

The *Vieth v. Jubelirer* (2004) ruling is constitutionally significant because it increases the power of state governments with regard to the makeup of the House of Representatives. Since the Federal Convention, the House of Representatives is the chamber of Congress that is supposed to represent the People directly, while the Senate represents the interests of the states. This was a result of the "Great Compromise" at the Federal Convention between the Federalists, who wanted a national legislature elected directly by the people in proportion to population, and the Anti-Federalists, who wanted a Congress answerable to, and appointed by, state governments. To the extent that the *Vieth* decision gives state governments control over the part of Congress supposed to represent the people directly, it revises the Compromise in an Anti-Federalist direction.

As is well known, the Federalists at the Federal Convention favored a legislature that would derive its authority directly from the people and not from the state governments. The original plan proposed by Madison (the "Virginia Plan") had a lower chamber directly elected by the people of the various states and an upper chamber elected by the lower from people nominated by the various state legislatures. This was opposed by the representatives of some of the smaller states, and indeed Madison was unable to even hold together the coalition of large states (see Jillson 1988). The New Jersey delegation provided an Anti-Federalist alternative plan, with a unicameral Congress being chosen by state legislatures on the basis of equal representation per state. The eventual compromise, of course, proposed by the Connecticut delegation, was that one chamber would be elected directly proportional to population and one elected by state governments on the basis of equal representation per state.

It is important to realize that this Great Compromise was indeed a compromise between incompatible principles – one person, one vote versus one territory, one vote. While the Compromise has proved remarkably successful, enduring over 200 years, the relative roles of state and national government with regard to the Congress have been repeatedly contested. Indeed, we can see *Vieth v. Jubelirer* as the latest chapter in this history. It is notable that at the time of the Federal Convention, there was considerable skepticism about the Compromise. Hamilton's opposition to the principle of equal representation on June 29 of 1787 is particularly notable, claiming that what was at stake was "a contest for power, not liberty" (Madison 1966).[1] As late as July 14, Madison spoke at the Convention against the equal representation of the states in the Senate, arguing, among other things, that this would allow a minority of the people to negate the will of the majority and also for this minority to extort special advantages from this veto power (Madison 1966). Madison, Hamilton, and the Federalists did, of course, come to support the compromise. However, the discussion of equal representation in the Senate in Federalist 62 (written by Hamilton or Madison) shows considerable reservations. Equal representation of the states in the Senate is portrayed frankly as a compromise between the claims of the large and small states. Given that the small states would not agree to a national legislature proportional to population, the large states faced a choice between the compromise and "a government still more objectionable" (the existing Articles of Confederation).[2] As a result, it was prudent for the large states to accept the Compromise as "the lesser evil."[3]

If the author of Federalist 62 describes accepting equal representation of the states in the Senate as a "sacrifice," we may ask what the Federalists thought they were getting in exchange for this sacrifice. The answer, of course, was a House of Representatives elected on a national basis

[1] Hamilton argued that states were simply "collections of individual men" and that representation ought to be of men, not the artificial bodies they make up.

[2] "A government founded on principles more consonant to the wishes of the larger States, is not likely to be obtained from the smaller States. The only option, then, for the former, lies between the proposed government and a government still more objectionable. Under this alternative, the advice of prudence must be to embrace the lesser evil; and, instead of indulging a fruitless anticipation of the possible mischiefs which may ensue, to contemplate rather the advantageous consequences which may qualify the sacrifice."

[3] It is also notable that the author of Federalist 62 goes on to discount the advantages and justification for equal representation, even though the purpose of the pamphlet is to argue for ratification of the Constitution.

proportional to population. According to Article 1 §2 of the Constitution, the House of Representatives was to be chosen every two years "by the People of the several States." This is exactly the same formula used by Madison in the Virginia Plan. It is notable that the singular "people" is used, as opposed to the "Peoples of the several States." The intention here would appear to be that the House of Representatives represents a single people – the People of the United States – while the Senate represents the various states conceived as separate "peoples."

Two things are notable about the way the House of Representatives is understood in the Federalist Papers. First, the House of Representatives is to provide direct representation of the people without being dependent on the states. Thus in Federalist 39, it is stated that "The House of Representatives will derive its powers from the people of America; and the people will be represented in the same proportion, and on the same principle, as they are in the legislature of a particular State." Thus the House of Representatives represents the principle of national government, not federal, while the Senate does the reverse. In Federalist 52, it is emphasized that the House should not be dependent on the states but only the people. Thus it is unacceptable to allow state legislatures to define the eligibility of voters for House elections because it would have "rendered too dependent on the state governments that branch of the federal government which ought to be dependent on the people alone."

Second, the House of Representatives is to be representative of the people in a popular and egalitarian manner. Thus in Federalist 39, it is argued that for a government to be considered republican, it is necessary for government to "be derived from the great body of the society, not from an inconsiderable proportion, or a favored class of it." It is argued in Federalist 52 that while it is necessary for government in general to have a common interest with the people, "it is particularly essential that the branch of it under consideration [The House of Representatives] should have an immediate dependence on, and an intimate sympathy with, the people." Thus the House of Representatives needs frequent (biennial) elections so that it can immediately reflect the changing interests of the people. It is notable that the Supreme Court in *Wesberry v. Sanders* (1964a) takes the requirement that the House be elected by the "People of the several States" as requiring that representation be accurate and equal and that the Court justifies this with reference to the Great Compromise.

The intention may have been that the House of Representatives would provide direct representation of the people without dependence on the state governments. However, the House was very much dependent on state governments in one vital respect. Article 1§4 gave state legislatures authority over the "Times, Places and Manner of holding Elections for Senators and Representatives," although Congress was given the power to alter these. Although this was not foreseen at the time of the Federal Convention, the ability to determine districts gives state governments tremendous power. In time, this allowed state governments to undermine the principle that the House of Representatives should be directly representative of the people as a whole. The Supreme Court rulings *Baker v. Carr* (1962) and *Wesberry v. Sanders* (1964a) can be seen as restoring this principle by restraining abuses of districting (or failing to redistrict for long periods of time). In this light, *Vieth v. Jubelirer* (2004) relaxes these restraints and once again makes the composition of the House of Representatives dependent on state legislatures.

APPORTIONMENT AND DISTRICTING – THE STATES STRIKE BACK

Thus we are faced with two contradictory principles. On the one hand, the House of Representatives is supposed to represent the people directly, without being dependent on the states. On the other hand, the Constitution gives the states primary authority over how congressional elections are conducted. Article 1§4 of the Constitution states, "The Times, Places and Manner of holding Elections for Senators and Representatives, shall be prescribed in each State by the Legislature thereof; but the Congress may at any time by Law make or alter such Regulations, except as to the Places of chusing Senators." We have seen in previous chapters that the ability to draw districts actually gives state governments tremendous power to influence the composition of the House, totally undermining the idea that the House is not supposed to be dependent on the states. Since the 1960s, however, the Supreme Court has limited the power of state governments to district how they wish and has thus restored the independence of Congress. *Vieth v. Jubelirer* (2004), however, weakened these constraints – while states are still constrained as to the size of districts, they may manipulate their shapes for partisan advantage.

Before we consider this process, we need to ask why it is that the states were granted all this power over elections to the House of Representatives when the intention was that the House was not to be dependent on the states. The answer is twofold. First, gerrymandering (and in particular partisan gerrymandering) was not anticipated. There is no record of it in the debates, and political parties did not yet exist in the modern sense. Second, although Congress was given the power to overrule the states, this power proved ineffective. This was due to various reasons that were not foreseen, such as the emergence of political parties and the rules adopted by the two houses of Congress.

Although Elbridge Gerry was present at the Federal Conventions, there was no discussion of gerrymandering at the debates or in the Federalist Papers. Indeed, the term "gerrymandering" was not coined until the nineteenth century, and the Massachusetts districts that prompted the term actually date to 1812. The concept only really makes sense if there are partisan elections or some other organized cleavage (such as race). Organized political parties only developed after the Convention.

It is notable that Alexander Hamilton in Federalist 59–61 does consider the mischief that states may do to House elections and why this requires that control of elections be shared between the states and Congress. However, the mischief considered does not include manipulation of districts. Hamilton is, in fact, far more concerned with the *time* and *place* of elections rather than with their *manner*. He argues in Federalist 59 that one danger is that states might simply refuse to hold elections and thus undermine the Constitution, which is why Congress needs to be allowed to act if it sees necessary. The kind of manipulation that he considers is manipulation of the time and especially the place of elections; holding elections at inconvenient or distant places might deny some people the right to vote. It is evident that Hamilton is aware of English "rotten boroughs" – an extreme example of malapportionment in which some districts contain only a handful of eligible voters. However, he only mentions this in Federalist 56 in the context of the number of members in the House of Representatives compared to the House of Commons – his argument is that the effective number of representatives in England is smaller than commonly believed because some of these are from unrepresentative "rotten boroughs." He does not present this as a potential strategy for electoral manipulation. James Madison and James Wilson mention rotten boroughs during the debates during the Federal Convention (1966) but only in opposition to the principle of equal representation for states.[4]

The second reason the power of the states over the House was greater than anticipated was that it was unlikely that Congress would overrule the states after the Congress was organized in a partisan manner. For Congress to act, both the House and Senate must agree. If one party is able

[4] James Wilson's comments of June 28 and James Madison's comments on June 29 both compare equal representation of the States to the "rotten borough" in the British House of Commons.

to use its control of state governments to gain control of the House, this party is very unlikely to agree to legislation taking away this advantage. Furthermore, the other party may have a great deal of difficulty keeping its members united to reform House elections, as some of its members may themselves benefit from the existing electoral arrangements. In general, it is difficult to get politicians to vote against the system that elected them. Even if the party that benefits from the manipulation at the state level does not control the House, it may well be able to block action in the Senate. There was, after all, a right to absolute unlimited debate in the Senate until 1917, allowing for a filibuster with a small number of Senators. Even after the 1917 and 1975 reforms of the cloture rule, it is still possible for either party to block legislation in the Senate, except for a few exceptional Congresses in which one party has more than the sixty senators currently required to overcome a filibuster. (The rules of the Senate, of course, also could not be foreseen at the Federal Convention.) As a result, state governments, not Congress, decide on districting plans.

Congress has not intervened directly in the districting process, and the legislation that it has passed regulating how states may district has been infrequent. In 1842, the Apportionment Act included the requirements that House elections be from single-member districts and that these districts be contiguous (Crocker 2012, 4). A potentially far greater constraint on the states was passed in the 1872 Apportionment Act. This required that all districts should have, as nearly as possible, equal population. However, Reconstruction ended soon after, and this was never enforced (Crocker 2012, 4). The requirement of geographical compactness was added to the 1901 Apportionment Act. This was also never enforced, and all these requirements lapsed in 1929. However, in 1967, Congress did restore the requirement that all House elections should be single-member districts.

Given that Congress did not actively intervene in the drawing of House districts, state legislatures were able to draw districts that suited politics at the state level. Sometimes this involved actively drawing districts with a political purpose. Often it simply involved doing nothing. It is possible to create districts that favor rural over urban interests, for example, by simply refusing to redistrict as the population moves to the cities. In time, the population of urban districts becomes a multiple of some rural districts. It is notable that in the absence of judicially mandated redistricting (that is, before the 1960s), those who benefit from the current districts will have a strategic advantage. As long as they are strong enough to be a blocking coalition (that is, control one chamber of the state legislature or the governor's mansion), they can ensure their advantageous districts are maintained. By the time of *Baker v. Carr* (1962), some districts in Tennessee had a population ten times greater than others.

This, of course, completely violated the idea that the House of Representatives is supposed to represent the people directly, without dependence on the states. Given that Congress failed to rectify this, the only other source of redress was the courts. It was not until the 1960s, however, that the courts intervened.

For many years, the Court did not intervene on matters of districting. With *Colegrove v. Green* (1946), this nonaction became a matter of doctrine. This was in response to a complaint from citizens of the State of Illinois that districts were not compact or of equal population, a complaint a district court dismissed. Justice Frankfurter delivered the judgment of the Court and an opinion in which two other justices joined. He argued that the Court could not intervene because the issue was "of a peculiarly political nature, and therefore not meet for judicial determination" (1946, 552). Essentially he argued that the Constitution delegated to the states and Congress the authority to conduct elections however they saw fit and that this was a political question in which the Court was not entitled to intervene. As Justice Frankfurter wrote, "The short of it is that the Constitution has conferred upon Congress exclusive authority to secure fair representation by the states in the popular House, and left to that House determination whether states have fulfilled their responsibility" (1946, 554). Thus the only remedy was for state legislatures or Congress to change the way Illinois was districted. As Justice Frankfurter famously argued, "Courts ought not to enter this political thicket" (1946, 556). The consequence of declaring districting a political question was that the states would continue to control how the House was elected, given that congressional action was extremely unlikely for the reasons we have already discussed.

Sixteen years later, however, in *Baker v. Carr* (1962), the Supreme Court decided that districting was not a "political question" from which the courts were barred. The case dealt with a complaint about the districts of the Tennessee General Assembly, and as with *Colegrove v. Green* (1946), a district court had dismissed the case. However, in *Baker v. Carr* (1962), the Supreme Court found that the district court had been incorrect to do this: the district court had jurisdiction, the plaintiffs had standing, and the complaint that equal protection had been denied was judiciable. This marked an important change in the "political question" doctrine that opened the way for judicial intervention in districting. Writing for the Court, Justice Brennan argued that just because there was a political right at stake did not mean that this was a nonjudiciable "political question" (1962, 209). Instead, a far more restrictive definition of a political question is given, with multiple criteria, the most salient in districting cases being whether there is a practical standard for deciding whether a constitutional right has been violated.[5] In *Colegrove v. Green* (1946), the Court had found that the states and Congress (and thus in practice the states) had *exclusive* authority to district how they wished; in *Baker v. Carr* (1962), it found that the courts could hold the states and Congress to account if districting violated a constitutionally protected right, such as the right to Equal Protection in the Fourteenth Amendment. Justice Frankfurter wrote a notable dissenting opinion, reiterating the position he had taken in *Colegrove v. Green* (1946).

The consequence of *Baker v. Carr* (1962) was that the Supreme Court, in a series of subsequent rulings, imposed national standards on districting, greatly reducing the power of state governments over national politics. On the basis of the Equal Protection clause of the Fourteenth Amendment and (in the case of Congress) Article 1 § 2 of the Constitution, the Court found that all citizens were entitled for their votes to be counted equally and that vote dilution by the drawing of districts amounted to a denial of the right to vote. Thus in *Gray v. Sanders* (1963), the Court found that voting for statewide offices had to be at large; in *Wesberry v. Sanders* (1964a), it found that congressional districts needed to have approximately equal population; and in *Reynolds v. Sims* (1964b), it found that districts in state legislatures similarly could not be malapportioned. These rulings form the basis of the "reapportionment revolution" (Cox and Katz 2002; Ansolabehere et al. 2008).

It is *Wesberry v. Sanders* (1964a) that is particularly relevant to us, as it deals with congressional districting. The Court interprets Article 1 § 2 of the Constitution in a fundamentally egalitarian manner. "We hold that, construed in its historical context, the command of Art. I, § 2 that

5 "Prominent on the surface of any case held to involve a political question is found a textually demonstrable constitutional commitment of the issue to a coordinate political department; or a lack of judicially discoverable and manageable standards for resolving it; or the impossibility of deciding without an initial policy determination of a kind clearly for nonjudicial discretion; or the impossibility of a court's undertaking independent resolution without expressing lack of the respect due coordinate branches of government; or an unusual need for unquestioning adherence to a political decision already made; or the potentiality of embarrassment from multifarious pronouncements by various departments on one question" (1962, 217).

Representatives be chosen 'by the People of the several States' means that, as nearly as is practicable, one man's vote in a congressional election is to be worth as much as another's" (1964a, 7–8). The Court argues that election "by the People" is clearly violated if some people are denied the right to vote. If this is so, then it is also violated if some people's votes are not counted or if they are diluted by ballot stuffing. If this is so, the Court argues, then vote dilution by districting is also unconstitutional. Thus the Constitution "leaves no room for classification of people in a way that unnecessarily abridges this right [the right to vote]" (1964a, 17–18). This argument would seem to apply to any form of vote dilution by districting – that is, gerrymandering as well as malapportionment.

It is notable that the Court very much frames its judgment in *Wesberry v. Sanders* (1964a) in terms of the Great Compromise. Quoting extensively from Madison's *Notes of Debates in the Federal Convention* (1966), Justice Black goes to considerable length to argue that the intent of the Federal Convention was that the House should represent the people directly, while the Senate should represent the states. Thus, "It would defeat the principle solemnly embodied in the Great Compromise – equal representation in the House for equal numbers of people – for us to hold that, within the States, legislatures may draw the lines of congressional districts in such a way as to give some voters a greater voice in choosing a Congressman than others" (1964a, 14). (Note once again that this refers to any districting practice that gives some a greater voice than others, not just malapportionment.) Instead, it is necessary that the people be represented equally and *as individuals*. Justice Black writes, "The House of Representatives, the Convention agreed, was to represent the people as individuals, and on a basis of complete equality for each voter" (1964a, 14). That is to say, the compromise was that the House of Representatives would represent the people directly, without the mediation of the states.

Thus *Wesberry v. Sanders* (1964a) can be seen as a restoration of the Great Compromise after many years of encroachment by the states. The Supreme Court required that districting be done in such a way that every voter was treated equally. No longer could state governments influence or control results by manipulating districts. As a result, the House of Representative would fulfill its intended role of representing the people directly as individuals, without dependence on state governments.

This restoration of the Great Compromise, however, would count for nothing if state governments were allowed to use partisan gerrymandering to achieve the same influence they had previously obtained by drawing unequally sized districts. We saw in Chapter 3 that even if states are forced to draw districts of equal size, they can still largely determine the result by manipulating the shapes of the districts. If states do this, we are back to a situation whereby the states, rather than the people alone, determine the composition of Congress.

Following *Wesberry v. Sanders* (1964a) and *Reynolds v. Sims* (1964b), there was ambiguity as to how the Court would treat partisan gerrymandering. Certainly tolerating partisan gerrymandering would seem to go against the spirit of these cases, especially *Wesberry*. After all, in *Wesberry*, the Court had condemned any district practice that gave one person more of a voice than others. Furthermore, both the *Wesberry* and *Reynolds* judgments relied on the argument that sophisticated discrimination is just as invidious as simplistic discrimination. If malapportionment was in essence no better than denying someone access to the polling station, then surely gerrymandering was no better than malapportionment. If the states had responded to the Court's demand to redistrict in *Wesberry v. Sanders* (1964a) by egregiously gerrymandering, it is entirely possible the Court may have struck down these gerrymanders. However, as we have seen, there is little evidence of partisan bias in congressional districting after 1964 (Erikson 1972; Campagna and Grofman 1990; Jacobson 1990; King and Gelman 1991; Brady and Grofman 1991; Butler and Cain 1992; McDonald 2006; Ansolabehere and Snyder 2008). It was not until *Davis v. Bandemer* (1986a) that the Supreme Court declared unambiguously that partisan gerrymandering was a constitutional violation.

In *Vieth v. Jubelirer* (2004), the Supreme Court did not simply overturn *Davis v. Bandemer* (1986a); rather, in spirit and effect, the *Vieth* decision to a considerable degree undermined the work of *Wesberry v. Sanders* (1964a) and *Reynolds v. Sims* (1964b). As we have seen, the *Vieth* ruling found that complaints of partisan gerrymandering were nonjudiciable – they could not be decided by the courts. This did leave untouched the finding in *Wesberry v. Sanders* (1964a) that the Constitution required that all districts have almost equal population. However, we have already seen in Chapter 3 and Chapter 5 how much power states can have through partisan gerrymandering, even when districts are equal in population. The *Vieth* decision opens up a loophole that once again allows states to control who controls the House of Representatives. *Wesberry v. Sanders* (1964a) found that it was unacceptable "that, within the States, legislatures may draw the lines of congressional districts in such a way as to give some voters a greater voice in choosing a Congressman than others" (1964a, 14). After *Vieth*, this is clearly possible through partisan gerrymandering, if not malapportionment.

It is notable that prior to *Davis v. Bandemer* (1986a), it was not the case that political gerrymandering was *allowed* by the courts. Rather, there was ambiguity. The section cited earlier from *Wesberry v. Sanders* (1964a) certainly suggests the Court would strike down *any* districting plan intended to give some voters a greater voice than others. Furthermore, the Court did strike down a districting plan in *White v. Regester* (1973c) on grounds that it was a racial gerrymander, confirming the principle that a gerrymander could be struck down even if districts had equal population. A state legislature drawing these districts during this period most certainly did have to fear judicial scrutiny. As a result, it is unsurprising that states did not push the envelope in terms of partisan bias. After the *Vieth* decision, however, this changed – there was no longer any reason to hold back for fear of judicial censure. In this sense, *Vieth v. Jubelirer* (2004) did not return us to the situation in 1986 (pre *Davis v. Bandemer*); rather it gave back to state governments much of the power they enjoyed before 1964.

It is interesting that the arguments presented by Justice Scalia in the plurality opinion do hark back to Justice Frankfurter's opinion in *Colegrove v. Green* (1946) and his dissent in *Baker v. Carr* (1962). Justice Scalia revives the doctrine of "political questions" – partisan gerrymandering is a "political question" and therefore nonjudiciable. Of course, Justice Scalia uses this doctrine in a very different way to Justice Frankfurter. Justice Frankfurter in *Colegrove v. Green* (1946) had argued that everything concerning the manner of House elections was a political question because the Constitution gave the states and the Congress jurisdiction over this. Justice Scalia does not rely on this argument but instead on the doctrine of "political questions" set out by the Court in *Baker v. Carr* (1962, 217). In particular, he refers to the standard that a question is political if there is "a lack of judicially discoverable and manageable standards for resolving it" (2004, 277). He argues that while there is such a standard for malapportionment, there is not for political gerrymandering. Interestingly, to do this, he uses another argument reminiscent of Justice Frankfurter's opinion in *Colegrove v. Green* (1946). Justice Frankfurter argued that in the case of districting, there is not a violation of an individual right, but rather a "wrong suffered by Illinois as a polity" (1946, 552).[6] Justice Scalia accepts that malapportionment violates an individual

[6] Justice Frankfurter writes, "This is not an action to recover for damage because of the discriminatory exclusion of a plaintiff from rights enjoyed by other citizens. The basis for the suit is not a private wrong, but a wrong suffered by Illinois as a polity."

right but argues that the claim of partisan gerrymandering rests on a nonexistent collective right to proportional representation (2004, 288). Thus he is able to apply the "political question" doctrine to partisan gerrymandering while accepting that malapportionment is a Constitutional violation. We will return to this argument in the next chapter.

Thus the Court's treatment of congressional districting can be seen within the context of a historic struggle between Federalist and Anti-Federalist visions of government. It was clearly the intent of the Framers that the House of Representatives was to represent the people directly without dependence on state governments, and in exchange, the Senate was to be selected by the states on the basis of equal representation per state. However, the Constitution gives states primary control over the manner of elections, and in a world with political parties, this means that state governments have a great deal of control over the composition of the House. In this light, we can see *Wesberry v. Sanders* (1964a) as a restoration of the Great Compromise at the Federal Convention – the people would elect the House of Representatives on the basis of equality and without the influence of state governments. If this is the case, then *Vieth v. Jubelirer* (2004) moves us back in an Anti-Federalist direction – once again – state governments can draw districts to determine the makeup of Congress.

AMERICAN DEMOCRACY AFTER *VIETH*

We have seen that the *Vieth* ruling has altered the character of representation and democracy in a significant way. It has given state governments far more power to influence national elections. No longer threatened by judicial challenge, they can use their ability to draw districts to full effect. Thus the composition of the House may be influenced as much by the state governments as it is by direct elections. This, of course, violates the Madisonian principle that the House should represent the people directly, unmediated by state government. It also means that a minority may elect a majority, violating the principle of political equality. However, even if the representation provided by the House after *Vieth* is more indirect and less egalitarian, we can evaluate it on other grounds. We can enquire how this more indirect form of democracy will do in terms of participation, responsiveness, and transparency.

First let us consider participation. One problem with indirect democracy is that it may result in fewer people taking part. If this is the case, we are not simply replacing direct representation with a more indirect form, but replacing representation of the people with something that only represents a subset of people. In our example, we go from having a House chosen by the voters in congressional elections to a House with a composition that depends heavily on the smaller group of people who vote in state elections. That is to say, we give disproportionate influence to a minority. In terms of drawing congressional districts, the offices that matter in most states are the governorship and the state legislature. Empirically, it is indeed the case that fewer people vote for these offices than for Congress.

Indeed, as we saw in the last chapter, the timing of many state elections also leads to systematically lower turnout. Turnout is highest in years when there is a presidential election. However, many states hold gubernatorial elections every four years in nonpresidential years. As a result, turnout is lower. Some states even hold gubernatorial elections in odd-numbered years, when there is not even a congressional election to boost turnout. As for elections to the state legislature, most states elect half their senate every two years, with a four-year term. This means that half of the senate will be elected in a nonpresidential year. State assemblies are elected every two years. Thus the state legislature that matters for redistricting is the one elected in the year of the decennial Census (1990, 2000, 2010, etc.). This is elected in a nonpresidential year half the time (as it was in 2010).

We should also be concerned about how representative state legislatures are of the people who actually do vote in state elections. State legislatures often do not just draw congressional districts but draw their own districts as well. In the case of some states, the state constitution places additional constraints on how state legislative districts can be drawn. For example, numerous states have requirements that state legislative districts be contiguous and compact, while no such requirement exists for congressional districts. Nevertheless, if state legislative districts are gerrymandered in a partisan way, then congressional districts are being drawn by state legislatures that themselves may be unrepresentative of their states. This is, of course, an empirical matter. We are not aware of a comprehensive study of partisan bias in state legislatures since Gelman and King (1994a), which looked at districts following the 1990 Census and before.

Another factor to consider is responsiveness. The House of Representatives was intended to be responsive, while the Senate was intended to react more slowly. This is the reason given by the Federalists for the House of Representatives being elected every two years. Federalist 52 argues that very regular elections are necessary so that the House can maintain an "immediate dependence on, and intimate sympathy with, the people." The Senate, on the other hand, is elected in thirds every two years so it does not react quickly to fleeting changes in public opinion. Empirical political scientists have found that these regular elections do in fact promote responsiveness to change in public opinion. For example, Soroka and Wlezien (2010) find that government policy changes more rapidly in response to changes in public opinion in the United States (with legislative elections every two years) than in the United Kingdom, where elections are held every four to five years (see also Erikson et al. 2002).

This responsiveness, however, is undermined if the composition of the House is in large part determined by redistricting that takes place once a decade. It seems that it is possible for state governments in some cases to engineer such bias into the districting map that control of the state delegation is locked in for the ten-year districting cycle. If that is the case, we have gone from the House being up for grabs every two years to it being determined by state elections every ten years. This would mean that the House would no longer fulfill its intended role of reflecting fleeting shifts in public opinion while being balanced by the more stable Senate. Indeed, the House may become less responsive than the Senate.

Finally, there is the issue of transparency. When people go to the polls and vote for governor or state assembly member, they are told that they are voting for governor or state assembly member. They are not told that they are effectively determining the partisanship of the state's congressional delegation for the next ten years. The problem highlighted here is not that the state government has control over the composition of government but that this is not done in an open way. This also creates problems of accountability. If people wish to hold the national government to account, the first opportunity to do this will often be to vote against the controlling party in Congress. If control of the House is effectively already determined by state governments, this line of accountability is compromised.

Indeed, the fact that state governments have this degree of influence over national elections also creates dangers for democracy at the state level. State elections presumably are supposed to allow voters to hold their state government to account for how it has run the state. However, if state elections have a strong influence on congressional elections through districting, then state elections may become proxy national elections. Political parties will probably realize that in order to win control of Congress, they require control of state legislatures and governors' mansions (or at least to deny this to the other party). As a result, in battleground states, we might expect more out-of-state money and campaigning in state-level elections as both parties realize that they cannot afford to lose state level races. This may make it more difficult for state-level elections to fulfill their intended purpose of holding state officials accountable for the conduct of state government. The consequence of allowing state governments to determine national House elections may be to make state elections effectively national elections, albeit in a convoluted and opaque manner.

CONCLUSION

This chapter has considered the historical and constitutional significance of the Supreme Court's ruling in *Vieth v. Jubelirer* (2004). In short, the constitutional significance of the *Vieth* rulings is that it gives state governments far more power over the composition of Congress. States can now draw congressional districts however they choose, provided they have equal population, return a single representative, and are not racial gerrymanders. As a result, if state governments so choose, they can largely determine the composition of their congressional delegation.

This has to be understood in terms of a tension that has existed with the Constitution since the Federal Convention. The Constitution was a compromise between two competing visions of government. On one hand, there was a Federalist vision based on the idea of a single nation and a single legislature elected directly by the people as individuals. On the other hand, there was an Anti-Federalist vision based on the idea that there should be a union of states, with each state retaining equal weight regardless of population. The Great Compromise that emerged from this was that the House of Representatives should be elected directly by the people by population, without the mediation of state governments, while the Senate should be elected by the states.

Although the intent may have been to have the House of Representatives represent the people directly, the Constitution also gave state governments the means to undermine this aim. States have primary control over the conduct of House elections. Once politics was organized in terms of political parties (something not completely foreseen at the Convention), it was possible for the dominant party in a state to organize House elections to its benefit. For various reasons, the oversight of Congress did little to prevent this (not least because the representatives elected had little incentive to change a system that had, in fact, elected them). As a result, the composition of the House of Representatives was very much dependent on state governments.

Wesberry v. Sanders (1964a) can be seen as a restoration of the Great Compromise. Indeed, this is the way the Supreme Court portrayed its own decision in this case. The Supreme Court removed from state governments the means by which they could determine the composition of their state's House delegation. Most notably, all districts would have to have the same population. However, the language and the argument of the ruling also appeared to prohibit more subtle forms of manipulation, such as gerrymandering. There appears to have been little partisan bias in congressional districting in this period. State governments did not appear to try to use partisan gerrymandering to achieve the outcomes that malapportionment had produced, and if they had, the Court might well have struck the offending districts down. The case *Davis v. Bandemer* (1986a) confirmed that partisan gerrymandering was a constitutional violation.

If *Wesberry v. Sanders* (1964a) was a restoration of the Great Compromise, then *Vieth v. Jubelirer* (2004) marked a step back in an Anti-Federalist direction. States once again have the means to determine the character of their state's House delegation. They cannot manipulate outcomes by drawing districts of differing populations; however, they can achieve the same ends by other means. We have seen that if a state can draw districts as it wishes, the constraint that the districts have to be of equal size does little to hinder them. It is still possible to produce districts that give 70% of the seats to the party that won fewer votes.

We can also consider the consequence of the *Vieth* ruling for democracy in America. Clearly the character of American democracy is changed. The Madisonian principle that at least one chamber of the legislature directly represent the people without the states as intermediaries is clearly violated. The majority rule principle – a majority of voters should be able to elect a majority of representatives – is clearly violated, as is the principle that all voters have equal voice. There are other consequences. If the composition of the House is largely determined in state elections, then fewer people will take part in this, as turnout in state elections is generally lower than that for federal elections. Furthermore, the reason the Constitution demands House elections every two years is so that the House may reflect the immediate concerns of the people. If the composition of the

House is determined by a state districting process that takes place every ten years, then this accountability is lost. Finally, the fact that the outcome of federal House elections may be largely determined by elections that are supposed to be for state offices leads to a system that is both opaque and poses significant dangers for state democracy.

7

Answering Justice Scalia's Challenge to Equality

Does Equal Protection Imply Majority Rule?

So far we have considered the effects and the significance of the *Vieth v. Jubelirer* (2004) ruling and the redistricting that followed it. We have found that it gives state governments a very powerful tool to manipulate election outcomes. Indeed, by drawing districts (in)appropriately, a state legislature can turn a minority of voters into an overwhelming majority of the state's federal House delegation. Now, however, we turn to the case itself and, in particular, how the finding may be challenged in the future. We find that this hinges on a fundamental question of political philosophy: Does the United States Constitution require that the House of Representatives respect the majority rule principle? That is, is it required that a majority of voters be able to elect a majority of representatives?

Writing for a plurality of the Court on *Vieth v. Jubelirer* (2004), Justice Scalia argued that the Court should not consider complaints of partisan gerrymandering because no standard exists for adjudicating such cases. That is to say, there is no standard that can be derived from the Constitution and then be practically applied to determine whether unconstitutional partisan gerrymandering has occurred. A fifth Justice (Justice Kennedy) agreed that no such standard currently existed but held out hope that one might be found. This defines the task for anyone who may wish to challenge the *Vieth* ruling. It is necessary to find a standard that is both required by the Constitution and provides a practical test that rules out partisan gerrymandering.

The majority rule principle is an obvious candidate for such a standard of political fairness. It is clear that partisan gerrymandering violates the majority rule principle. As we saw in Chapter 3, in some states, it is necessary for one party to win 58% of the vote to win a majority of the state's congressional delegation. Furthermore, as was also demonstrated in Chapter 3, we clearly have the technology to determine whether a districting plan has a systematic tendency to violate the majority rule principle – this was provided by Gelman and King (1994b).

Majority rule is also a basic principle of political fairness. Indeed, it is often argued that it is synonymous with democracy. For example, Robert Dahl begins chapter 2 of *A Preface to Democratic Theory* by documenting the idea that majority rule and democracy are equivalent in Locke, Rousseau, Jefferson, and Lincoln. Essentially, if you wish to treat everyone equally, then majority rule is the only game in town. As Brian Barry (1979) put it, if you eliminate inequalities based on the *quality* of people, all you have left is *quantity*. There is even a formal mathematical proof of this principle (May 1951).

The majority rule principle has also been central to many people's understanding of the American system of government. As we saw in the last chapter, at the Constitutional Convention, many of the delegates (the Federalists in particular) argued that majority rule was essential to free government. The House of Representatives, in particular, was supposed to represent this principle. These arguments are noted in the Supreme Court's "one person, one vote" decisions, most notably *Wesberry v. Sanders* (1964a). Madison in Federalist 58 argued that in the absence of majority rule, "the fundamental principle of free government would be reversed. It would no longer be the majority that would rule: the power would be transferred to the minority." When discussing Federalist 10, it is often the need to prevent majority tyranny that is emphasized. But it should not be forgotten that in Federalist 10, Madison assumes that the "Republican principle" – that is, majority rule – will provide an adequate defense against minority tyranny. As Abraham Lincoln argued in his first inaugural address, "Unanimity is impossible; the rule of the minority, as a permanent arrangement is wholly inadmissible; so that rejecting the majority principle, anarchy or despotism in some form is all that is left."

Justice Scalia, however, in his opinion on *Vieth v. Jubelirer* (2004, 288), denies that the Constitution provides any right to majority rule – at least in the sense that a majority of voters should be able to elect a majority of representatives. (Could there be another sense?) This is a crucial part of his argument that there is no standard for adjudicating political gerrymandering cases. The reason that there is no constitutional right to the majority rule principle in elections, according to Justice Scalia, is that the Constitution only provides the right of equal treatment to individuals, not to groups. He argues that the majority rule principle, as articulated by the plaintiffs in *Vieth*, inevitably depends on the claim that a group has a right to fair representation and that the Constitution grants no such right.

If it is the case that majority rule is not constitutionally mandated because it is based on a group rights claim, then it is hard to see how it could be possible to find a standard that outlaws partisan gerrymandering. Justice Scalia's argument is potentially decisive because surely all standards of political fairness would be vulnerable to the same critique. And without a constitutionally justified standard based on a concept of political fairness, it is hard to see how it is possible to prohibit partisan gerrymandering.

However, we will argue that it is, in fact, possible to justify the majority rule principle based solely on an individual right to equal treatment. The intuition is exactly the same as the intuition underlying the idea that majority rule is synonymous with democracy. That is, if you treat all individual voters equally, then the only way to settle a question is to let the majority have its way. It turns out that this principle is as logically valid for elections to a legislature as it is for decisions within a legislature. The equal treatment of individuals logically implies that a majority of individuals must be able to elect a majority of representatives. Given that the equal treatment of individuals can be constitutionally grounded, so can the majority rule principle.

Thus we will show in this chapter that it is possible to derive a standard from the Constitution that prohibits partisan gerrymandering. This standard is no more complex than the standard of majority rule. The next section will lay out the details of Justice Scalia's challenge to the majority rule principle. The following section will demonstrate that the majority rule principle can be logically derived from the equal treatment of individuals. The final section will show that the majority rule standard can be implied in a manageable way – in fact, it logically implies a partisan symmetry that can be tested using the same techniques that we have used in Chapter 3 to measure partisan bias.

JUSTICE SCALIA'S CHALLENGE TO THE MAJORITY RULE PRINCIPLE

We hold that the argument about the unconstitutionality of partisan gerrymandering after *Vieth* hinges on one crucial question: Is it possible to derive the majority rule principle – the principle that a majority of voters should be able to elect a majority of representatives – from an individual right of equal treatment? If this is so, then we can derive the majority rule principle from the right to equal protection and the requirement that the House of Representatives be elected by the people. Given that partisan gerrymandering violates the majority rule principle, it violates constitutional rights. Of course, in his *Vieth* opinion (2004, 288–290), Justice Scalia vigorously denies that the majority rule principle can be derived from individual – as opposed to group – rights.

To understand why the majority rule principle is important in this context, we need to consider the construction of the claim that political gerrymandering is unconstitutional, and also Justice Scalia's objection to it. The claim that partisan gerrymandering violates constitutional rights is derived from the claim that the Constitution guarantees an equal right to vote and to have one's vote counted equally. There are two sources for this claim: Article 1 §2 and the Equal Protection Clause of the Fourteenth Amendment.

The Supreme Court in *Wesberry v. Sanders* (1964a, 7–8) found that "the command of Art. I, 2, that Representatives be chosen 'by the People of the several States' means that as nearly as is practicable one man's vote in a congressional election is to be worth as much as another's." The Court found that this implies that if congressional elections are held by district (as opposed to statewide), then the districts must be of equal size.

In *Reynolds v. Sims* (1964b), the Court found that citizens had a right to have their votes counted equally, based on the equal protection clause of the Fourteenth Amendment.[1] The Court found that the right to vote is protected by the Constitution (1964b, 554). Given that refusing to allow someone to vote is a constitutional violation, then so is diluting the value of their vote by other means, such as ballot stuffing and not counting certain votes. If these are constitutional violations, then so is diluting someone's vote via unequally sized districts. The Court concludes that "the right of suffrage can be denied by a debasement or dilution of the weight of a citizen's vote just as effectively as by wholly prohibiting the free exercise of the franchise" (1964b, 555). It is also notable that the Court in *Reynolds v. Sims* (1964b, 565) very definitely makes the connection between equal protection and the majority rule principle – the principle that a majority of voters should be able to elect a majority of representatives:

[1] The exception to this is, of course, Senate elections, for which the Constitution explicitly demands that elections be held by the states.

Logically, in a society ostensibly grounded on representative government, it would seem reasonable that a majority of the people of a State could elect a majority of that State's legislators. To conclude differently, and to sanction minority control of state legislative bodies, would appear to deny majority rights in a way that far surpasses any possible denial of minority rights that might otherwise be thought to result. Since legislatures are responsible for enacting laws by which all citizens are to be governed, they should be bodies which are collectively responsive to the popular will. (1964b, 565)

The claim that partisan gerrymandering is a constitutional violation is an extension of the claims made in *Wesberry v. Sanders* (1964a) and *Reynolds v. Sims* (1964b). If diluting a person's vote by drawing unequally sized districts violates their right to vote, then surely so does cleverly manipulating the shapes of districts to achieve the same effect. After all, *Reynolds v. Sims* (1964b, 563) finds that the Constitution forbids "sophisticated as well as simple-minded modes of discrimination,"[2] and that "Weighting the votes of citizens differently, *by any method or means*, merely because of where they happen to reside, hardly seems justifiable" (1964b, 563, italics added). It took the Court a considerable amount of time to explicitly confirm this logic that partisan gerrymandering could indeed be a constitutional violation, but it eventually did so in *Davis v. Bandemer* (1986a).

Of course, this argument is precisely what Justice Scalia seeks to refute in his opinion on *Vieth v. Jubelirer* (2004). He argues that it is not possible to extend the argument from the unconstitutionality of disenfranchisement and malapportionment in *Wesberry* and *Reynolds* to the unconstitutionality of partisan gerrymandering. The reason is that there does not exist a standard that the Court can use to decide partisan gerrymandering cases. In the case of malapportionment, there is a clear standard – whether the population of each district is approximately the same. With partisan gerrymandering, there is no such standard. Given that the courts do not have a clear standard, they have no business acting. Rather, such issues should be considered nonjudiciable "political questions." Thus Justice Scalia can conclude, "Our one-person, one-vote cases, see *Reynolds* v. *Sims,* 377 U. S. 533 (1964); *Wesberry* v. *Sanders,* 376 U. S. 1 (1964), have no bearing upon this question, neither in principle nor in practicality" (2004, 290).

The use of the "political question" doctrine by Justice Scalia seems reminiscent of the arguments of Justice Frankfurter, who argued that in

[2] Citing *Lane v. Wilson*, 307 U.S. 268, 275.

Colegrove v. Green (1946) and his dissent on *Baker v. Carr* (1962), all districting issues in general should be considered nonjudiciable. However, there are important differences. Justice Scalia does not rely on Justice Frankfurter's dissent in *Baker v. Carr* (1962), but rather on the definition of a "political question" given in the Court's opinion in that case. The Court in *Baker v. Carr* (1962, 217) gives six reasons an issue can be considered a nonjusticiable, political question. Justice Scalia concentrates on the second: "a lack of judicially discoverable and manageable standards for resolving it" (2004, 277). By arguing that this applies to political gerrymandering, Justice Scalia is able to accept the finding in *Wesberry* and *Reynolds* that malapportionment is unconstitutional while preventing the extension of the logic of these cases to partisan gerrymandering. As we have seen, this gives back to state governments considerable power to manipulate the results of congressional elections.

Thus according to Justice Scalia, the challenge for anyone making a complaint about partisan gerrymandering is to find a suitable standard for determining whether such gerrymandering is present. This standard must be both judicially "discoverable" and "manageable." To be judicially "discoverable," it must be possible to show that the standard can be derived from a constitutionally protected right. To be judicially manageable, it must be possible for the courts to use the standard in a practical way to decide cases. Justice Scalia notes that a majority of the Court in *Davis v. Bandemer* (1986a) was unable to agree on such a standard and argues that the existing standards that have been proposed fail both these tests. Furthermore, he argues that the failure to find a suitable standard over a considerable period of time suggests that no such standard exists.

We can now see the importance of the majority rule standard. The majority rule standard – that a majority of voters should be able to elect a majority of representatives – is perhaps the simplest and, in our view, most promising candidate for a standard for deciding partisan gerrymandering cases. Indeed, we believe it may be the only standard that can meet the challenge of both being derived from the Constitution and producing a viable practical test. Furthermore, the arguments that Justice Scalia makes against the majority rule principle (that it is derived from group rights while the Constitution only protects individual rights) applies equally to other proposed standards, such as that put forward in the plurality opinion on *Davis v. Bandemer* (1986a).

It is notable that the plaintiffs in *Vieth v. Jubelirer* (2004) did not rely on the standard proposed by the plurality in *Bandemer* but proposed their own standard based on the majority rule principle. (In addition to the requirement that a districting plan make it likely that a majority will not be able to elect a majority of representatives, they also require that there be systematic "packing and cracking" and that intent be present.) The plurality standard from *Bandemer* requires that the plaintiffs show that "the electoral system is arranged in a manner that will consistently degrade a voter's or a group of voters' influence on the political process as a whole" (1986a, 132). It is not sufficient that the plaintiff show that the districting makes it more difficult for a group to win elections; it is necessary to show that the group can expect to be ignored by those who are elected. Needless to say, this will prove very difficult to demonstrate. It is hardly surprising that the *Vieth* plaintiffs chose to advance their own standard based on majority rule.

Justice Scalia critiques the majority rule standard proposed by the *Vieth* plaintiffs at some length (2004, 284–290). He argues that the majority rule principle cannot serve as a standard for deciding political gerrymandering cases because it cannot be derived from any constitutionally protected right – that is, it is not "constitutionally discoverable." This is because the majority rule principle makes a claim about the rights of a group, not an individual. It claims that a majority group should be able to elect a majority of representatives. Justice Scalia argues that the Constitution only grants rights of equal protection to individuals, not to groups. In the case of malapportionment, there is a clear violation of an individual right – some people's votes are weighted more heavily than others. However, Scalia argues, this is not the case when a majority is able to elect a majority of representatives – here only a (nonexistent) group right has been violated.

Thus Justice Scalia, after noting that the standard proposed by the plaintiffs would only invalidate a district plan if is prevents a majority of voters from electing a majority of representatives, argues,

> . . . we question whether it is judicially discernible in the sense of being relevant to some constitutional violation. Deny it as appellants may (and do), this standard rests upon the principle that groups (or at least political-action groups) have a right to proportional representation. But the Constitution contains no such principle. It guarantees equal protection of the law to persons, not equal representation in government to equivalently sized groups. It nowhere says that farmers or urban dwellers, Christian fundamentalists or Jews, Republicans or Democrats, must be accorded political strength proportionate to their numbers. (2004, 288)

To the extent that existing arguments for the unconstitutionality of partisan gerrymandering rely on a group right to proportional representation,

Scalia's argument appears decisive. There is no dispute that the Constitution does not enumerate a right to proportional representation for groups. Furthermore, the plaintiffs in *Vieth v. Jubelirer* (2004) appear to rely on just such a claim, simply asserting that a majority partisan group ought to have the right to elect a majority of representatives. Similarly, the argument made for partisan symmetry by four political science professors in *LULAC v. Perry* is that it allows us to determine whether "a districting plan unfairly burdens the representational rights of a *particular political group*" (King et al. 2006, 4, italics added).

However, we argue that Justice Scalia was incorrect to argue that a right to group proportional representation is *necessary* to justify the majority rule standard. Using recently published results in social choice theory, it is possible to justify the majority rule standard strictly on the equal treatment of individual voters. It can be shown that the equal treatment of all individual voters logically implies the majority rule standard – a majority of the voters must be able to elect a majority of representatives. Or to put it another way, in partisan elections, it is not logically possible to treat all voters equally without treating all parties equally as well.

Justice Scalia has set the challenge of providing a standard for political gerrymandering cases that is both judicially discoverable and judicially manageable. We argue that the majority rule principle can provide a standard that satisfies both criteria – it can be derived from constitutionally protected rights, and it provides a workable test. If we can show that the majority rule principle can be derived from individual rights of equal treatment, then it can be justified in terms of the right to equal protection in the Fourteenth Amendment. Furthermore, it can be justified in terms of the right to equality implied by the Article 1 §2 requirement that the House of Representatives be elected by the people. We will see that the majority rule principle also logically implies a test that can be practically applied and is thus judicially manageable. This is the partisan symmetry standard proposed by Gelman and King (1994b) and advocated by King et al. (2006) in an amicus brief on *LULAC v. Perry* (2006). This, incidentally, also provides the basis for the empirical measures of partisan bias in Chapter 3 of this book. The next section demonstrates how the majority rule principle can be justified in terms of the equal treatment of individuals and can thus be derived from constitutionally protected individual rights. The section after that demonstrates how the partisan symmetry test can be derived from the majority rule principle and can thus provide a test of partisan gerrymandering that is both judicially discernable and manageable.

DERIVING THE MAJORITY RULE PRINCIPLE FROM INDIVIDUAL RIGHTS TO EQUAL PROTECTION

The formal result that this argument is based on comes from Hout and McGann (2009a, 2009b). Roughly speaking, this result states that if an electoral system for a legislature treats all voters equally and satisfies some other necessary qualities, then it must give more seats to the party that wins more votes. In a two-party system, the larger of the two parties must have a majority of the vote and, if it receives more seats than its rival, must have a majority of seats. Thus political equality implies the majority rule standard. The importance of this result is that it allows us to get from liberal political equality – the equal protection of individuals – directly to the principle that a majority of voters should be able to elect of majority of representatives.

This does require two assumptions. First, we consider the composition of the legislature as a whole as opposed to considering just the individual districts. We can justify this both by appealing to Article 1§2 of the Constitution and on the grounds that the output of the legislature does in fact depend on the action of the legislature *as a whole* and not just on its individual parts. Second, we have to consider the partisan balance of the legislature as an important part of the *results* of congressional elections. This is justified not because we assign rights to partisan groups, any more than we assign rights to demographic or religious groups; this is justified because the U.S. Congress *as a matter of fact* organizes itself along partisan lines. We turn next to the detailed justification of these two assumptions.

Assumptions

For the argument developed here to go through, it is necessary that voters have a right to equal protection in regard to the results of congressional elections as a whole and that it is legitimate to consider the partisan balance of power an important part of that result. We doubt it would be difficult to convince political scientists, political journalists, or politicians that we do in fact have partisan elections and that the overall balance of power in Congress as a whole matters. The day after the election, newspaper headlines are likely to read "Republicans retake House" or "Democrats retain House." It is not likely (parodying the law review article cited by Justice Scalia) that they will read, "There were separate elections between separate candidates in separate districts, and that is all there is!" Contrary to the assertion by the same authors, political parties do not just "compete for specific seats"; they also compete for control of the House. (To be fair to Lowenstein and Steinberg, 1985, they are correct in asserting that parties do not compete for statewide vote totals and that we cannot simply infer a party's statewide support by adding up the district totals.)

It may seem like common sense that we have partisan elections in which the overall result matters. This, however, does not automatically mean that there is a constitutional basis for considering the House of Representatives in such a manner. Indeed, the Supreme Court has denied that results of congressional elections *as a whole* can be used as evidence of unconstitutional partisan gerrymandering. The plurality opinion in *Vieth v. Jubelirer* (2004) is particularly assertive about this. However, all the dissenting opinions other than that of Justice Breyer also accept this point. In fact, the plurality in *Davis v. Bandemer* (1986a) comes to the same conclusion. To establish a violation of the Equal Protection clause, it is necessary to produce a district-specific claim.

Let us first consider why it is appropriate to consider the composition of the House as a whole. What we are faced with here are two differing conceptions of representation. When we consider the House as a whole, we are thinking of it as a single deliberative body representing the people. If its overall composition is stacked against me, then I have been wronged. We can contrast this to what we might call an "atomistic" or "district-based" view of representation.[3] Provided the process by which I elect my Representative passes muster, I have received equal protection. I cannot argue that the overall process by which Congress is elected discriminates against me. It is as if each representative is treated as a separate, individual magistrate as opposed to a member of a representative body. The assumption seems to be that because I only get to vote for the member from my district, that member and that member alone represents me, as opposed to the House as a whole.

There are two lines of argument for considering the House of Representatives as a single legislative body rather than as a collection of district representatives. The first is derived from Article 1§2 of the Constitution and applies specifically to the House; the second is drawn from more general considerations of political philosophy and applies to legislatures generally (including, potentially, state legislatures). Turning to Article 1§2, we can see that this certainly describes elections to the House in

[3] See also Weissberg's (1978) distinction between dyadic and collective representation.

collective terms: "The House of Representatives shall be composed of Members chosen every second Year by the People of the several States." Interestingly, it does not even say "the Peoples of the several States," but rather uses the single collective noun "people" – that is, the people of the United States. There is nothing here to support the view that an individual voter is only represented by their representative and thus does not have a stake in the composition of Congress as a whole. Rather, the House of Representatives *as a whole* is to be chosen by the people *as a whole*. Indeed, districts are not even mentioned in Article 1 – Article 1§4 gives states authority over the "Times, Places and Manner" of elections but gives the United States Congress the power to overrule them.[4]

In the Federalist Papers, likewise, we see the House of Representatives described as a single national legislature representing the people as a whole. After all, as is argued in Federalist 39, the House of Representatives represents the principle of national government, while the federal principle (that is, territorial representation) is represented by the Senate. Thus Federalist 39 states, "The House of Representatives will derive its powers from the people of America; and the people will be represented in the same proportion, and on the same principle, as they are in the legislature of a particular State." Similarly in Federalist 52, it is argued, "As it is essential to liberty that the government in general should have a common interest with the people, so it is particularly essential that the branch of it under consideration [the House of Representatives] should have an immediate dependence on, and an intimate sympathy with, the people." Once again, the conception of representation is collective – the House as a whole needs to be bound to the people as a whole in relations of dependence, sympathy, and common interest.

The Supreme Court in *Wesberry v. Sanders* (1964a) reiterates the same arguments. The Great Compromise led to the House representing the people directly and the Senate representing the states. As stated, this is taken to imply a very high level of political equality in House elections, with every voter being weighted equally. The district principle is not privileged in any way in *Wesberry v. Sanders* (1964a). District elections are not constitutionally necessary and are only permitted to the degree that they do not interfere with the principle that one person's vote be weighted equally to another's. The Court notes that this principle "is

4 There is also variation in the way that states choose to discharge this responsibility, from direct adoption by the legislatures to districting commissions, with governors having various degrees of veto power (see McDonald 2004).

followed automatically, of course, when Representatives are chosen as a group on a statewide basis, as was a widespread practice in the first 50 years of our Nation's history" (1964a, 8). States may, if they wish, elect representatives by district, but only as long as this does not frustrate the requirement that the House be chosen "by the People of the various States." As a result, states may not "draw the lines of congressional districts in such a way as to give some voters a greater voice in choosing a Congressman than others" (1964a, 14).

Thus a strong case can be made for considering the composition of the House as a whole based on Article 1§2 of the Constitution. In addition to this, we can also argue that it is necessary to consider the composition of the House as a whole based simply on its nature as a legislature. After all, it is the performance of the House *as a whole* that affects my well-being. The House as a whole deliberates and passes laws, not individual members. The output of the House is legislation, and this is intrinsically a collective good. Whether the House passes laws that protect me or do me harm depends not on me having a personal representative, but rather on the entire body. The need to consider the composition of the House as a whole does not depend on its mode of election but on its nature as a collective decision-making body.

It is possible for me to have the ability to elect my representative in a fair and proper manner but for the legislature as a whole to be stacked against me. Consider the following scenario. The districting and election administration of the district in which I live are beyond reproach. However, there are serious abuses (whether malapportionment, gerrymandering, or outright fraud) in other districts. This results in massive misrepresentation, so that my representative and those of similar opinion are outvoted. Indeed, because of the overwhelming artificial majority in the legislature created by the abuses, my representative and those of similar opinion are irrelevant to policy and law making. By the standards of all the *Vieth v. Jubelirer* (2004) opinions except that of Justice Breyer, I cannot claim that I have been denied equal protection – I am able to elect *my* representative. Presumably someone in the other districts could claim that their right to equal protection had been violated, unless the abuse was gerrymandering. I, however, cannot because I do not have a district specific case (my district is fine) and I cannot make a case based on the overall composition of Congress. Nevertheless, it appears preposterous to claim that I have received equal protection when the composition of Congress is stacked against me and I can reasonably expect my representative to be completely ignored.

It is also notable that the Supreme Court has not always endorsed an atomistic, "district-based" conception of representation. For example, writing for the plurality of the Court in *Georgia v. Ashcroft* (2003, 482) – in fact, for the very same plurality as in *Vieth v. Jubelirer* (2004) – Justice O'Connor argues that, "Indeed, in a representative democracy, the very purpose of voting is to delegate to chosen representatives the power to make and pass laws" (2003, 482). That is to say, the purpose of voting is to influence the provision of the collective good of policy, not just to provide districts with appropriate representation. As a result, it is possible to balance the benefit to minority populations from having influence in a broader number of districts against having an almost guaranteed ability to elect a group member in a smaller number of districts (2003, 479–481). Maximizing influence as opposed to preserving representation can produce very different assessments (Lublin 1997; Epstein et al. 2007). Of course, *Georgia v. Ashcroft* (2003) dealt with the Voting Rights Act as opposed to the Fourteenth Amendment (see Grofman 2006). Nevertheless, there is clear tension between two incompatible conceptions of representation.

Given that it is appropriate to consider the overall composition of the House of Representatives, let us turn to why it is appropriate to think of it in partisan terms. This is a more difficult task. The Constitution does not mention parties any more than it mentions districts. We may often take it for granted that we have partisan elections in the United States. Justice Scalia, however, in the section quoted earlier argues that parties have no special status – they are simply social groups comparable to farmers or Christian fundamentalists (2004, 288). Nevertheless, there seems to be something different about the partisan nature of the House. We can talk about the Democrats or the Republicans winning the House. We would not talk about men, Protestants, or non-Southerners winning the House in the same sense. The question is, what is it that makes elections to the House of Representatives objectively partisan, as opposed to party just being one demographic description amongst others?

The reason we can consider the partisan composition of the House as part of the *result* of a House election is the House *as a matter of fact* organizes itself along partisan lines. This partisan organization of the House is an objective institutional fact. If this partisan result is systematically biased against certain individuals, or if certain individuals are not given a fair opportunity to influence this result, then they can reasonably claim that they have been denied equal protection. They could also claim that the House has not been chosen by the people in the strongly egalitarian sense advanced by the Supreme Court in *Wesberry v. Sanders* (1964a).

The partisan balance of power in the House of Representatives has a number of direct institutional consequences about which voters have a right to be concerned. Members caucus in the House of Representatives on the basis of party. The majority party chooses the Speaker of the House. Which party has a majority will influence the distribution of committee assignments and, in particular, committee chairs. The majority party will have a number of procedural advantages in terms of control of the Rules Committee and the Calendar (see Cox and McCubbins 1993, 2005; Boyce and Bischak 2002). Which party has a majority determines certain significant national posts and is likely to have a strong influence on the character of legislation passed.

In fact, elections to the House of Representatives would still be partisan even if there were no partisans in the electorate. Imagine that the entire population was independent and no one had a partisan group identity. Provided that the legislature still organized itself on partisan lines, we still ought to care about the partisan balance in Congress. The Democrats or Republicans would not be identifiable groups in the electorate who could demand the right to elect members of their group – everyone would decide each election on its merits. However, the partisan balance would still matter – it would determine how the House of Representatives was organized. The newspapers the morning after the election would still report that the Democrats or Republicans had captured or retained the House.

Neither is the partisan nature of House elections dependent on party-line voting in the House. The level of party discipline in the House has varied over the years, although it has never gone away altogether. If there is very strong party-line voting, the output of the legislature will be almost completely determined by its partisan composition. However, even if this is not the case, as long as the parties can remain cohesive long enough to organize the House, the partisan composition of the House will determine the leadership, the committee assignments, and other structures such as the rules and the Calendar. These factors will affect the legislative output of the House, even if members do not always vote on party lines.

Thus a strong case can be made for both considering the results of House elections *as a whole* (as opposed to a series of unrelated district elections) and for considering these results in partisan terms. The results need to be considered as a whole because the output of the House (legislation) is intrinsically a collective good and is determined by the entire

House, not by individual members. The results need to be considered in partisan terms because the House *as a matter of fact* organizes itself along partisan lines. If someone were denied an equal opportunity to influence the partisan composition of the House as a whole, it would seem reasonable for the person to claim that he or she did not enjoy the equal protection of the law and that the House was not chosen by the people. Given these assumptions, we can proceed to the formal, social choice theoretic argument.

Individual Rights and the Majority Rule Standard

We may now turn to the formal result. Stated intuitively, if we treat everyone equally, then in a two-party system, the results must respect the *majority rule* standard – if a party wins a majority of the vote, it must get at least 50% of the seats. More precisely, if we treat every individual voter equally, and we do not discriminate against specific parties or candidates on the basis of their names, and we do not punish parties for winning more votes than they need, then if a party wins more votes than another party, it must win as many seats, if not more. In a two-party system, this produces the majority rule standard. In technical language (to be explained in what follows) if a seat allocation system is anonymous, neutral, and nonnegatively responsive, then it must satisfy the plurality ranking property. The importance of this result is that the standard that a minority of voters cannot elect a majority of representatives does not have to rest on a principle of group representation. Rather, it can be justified strictly in terms of equal treatment of individuals.

The result comes from Hout and McGann (2009a, 2009b). It is Proposition 1 in both of these articles. It is based on an earlier result from Hout, Swart, and Veer (2006). The Hout and McGann articles go farther than we need, introducing further assumptions to produce a justification of proportional representation based on a *liberal* conception of individual equality. We do not need or rely on these additional assumptions for the argument in this chapter.

The result does require that we think of the election result in terms of a *seat allocation function*. A seat allocation function is just an abstraction that takes the vote of each individual voter and returns an allocation of seats to each party. How it does this is left open. For example, it could divide the voters into districts and award a party a seat for each district in which it has the largest number of votes. This, of course, is how the current electoral system in the United States works. Alternatively, it could count up all the votes and award seats proportionally. Or it could combine the two or do something completely different. A seat allocation function is thus an abstraction that can accommodate the details of any electoral system. However, it does consider the election result *as a whole* and considers it in terms of seat allocations to parties. This is why it was necessary to argue that it is justified to view the election result in this way. It should be noted that a seat allocation rule does not capture everything that an electoral system may do. For example, district elections do not just determine how many seats each party gets but also who gets to fill those seats. However, as was argued in the last section, the partisan balance is surely an important – perhaps the most important – aspect of these results. On those grounds, it is possible to make the argument that if someone is denied an equal role in determining this aspect of the result, they have been denied equal protection.

We can now turn to the axioms required by the result. The idea of political equality is captured by two axioms, anonymity and neutrality. If a seat allocation function is to treat all voters equally, it must be anonymous. This means that it does not discriminate between voters based on their names. If we change the names of the voters, this does not change the results. An obvious example of a seat allocation system that is not anonymous is a system that gives some people more votes than others. However, there are many more subtle ways that electoral systems can discriminate between voters and thus violate anonymity.

Neutrality means that a seat allocation rule does not discriminate between candidates or parties on the basis of their names. If we exchange the names of two parties, then we must also exchange their seat allocations. Alternatively, if all the people who voted for Party A suddenly change their votes to Party B, and all the Party B voters vote for Party A, then Party A must win the seats that Party B previously won and vice versa. Neutrality is a minimal requirement of any democratic electoral rule. It is satisfied by the electoral systems of all liberal democracies, including the United States. It does not prevent certain parties being advantaged in terms of where their support comes from. It only prevents the explicit advantaging of certain parties purely in terms of their identities.

The final axiom we need is a technical one – nonnegative responsiveness. This means that a party cannot be penalized for winning extra votes when it retains all its previous support and nothing else changes. Suppose that a party wins the votes of certain voters and is awarded certain seats. Suppose then that the same party retains the support of all those voters and no one else changes their vote except for some voters who switch their vote to the party we are considering. Then nonnegative responsiveness means that the party must get at least as many seats as before. It should be noted that nonnegative responsiveness does not mean that a party with more votes than another party necessarily gets at least as many seats. It only prevents the perverse outcome where a party is punished for adding voters when nothing else changes. This is a minimal requirement that is met by every reasonable *single-vote* electoral system, including the first-past-the-post system used in the United States, although a case can be made for relaxing it when considering ordinal voting systems (where voters rank order the candidates as opposed to voting for only one).[5]

If an electoral system satisfies the requirements of political equality (anonymity and neutrality) and the commonsense requirement of nonnegative responsiveness, then it can be shown that it must satisfy the weak plurality ranking property. The weak plurality ranking property means that if one party wins more votes than another party, it must receive at least as many seats. In a two-party system, this means that the minority party cannot be awarded a majority of the seats.

The proof that anonymity, neutrality, and nonnegative responsiveness imply the plurality ranking property is given in Hout and McGann (2009a, Proposition 1, 2009b). Here we can consider the intuition behind the formal proof. We proceed in two steps. First, I demonstrate why anonymity and neutrality imply something called the cancellation property. Then we show that if we add nonnegative responsiveness to this we get the weak plurality ranking property. The cancellation property is the property that if two parties have the same vote total, they must be allocated the same number of seats. Let us see why anonymity and neutrality imply this property. Consider the voter profile in Table 7.1. This lists each voter and places an X under the party chosen by the voter. Thus Voter 1 votes for Party A, Voter 2 for Party B, Voter 7 for Party C, and Voter 8 abstains. There may be any number of voters, but in this example we only consider the first eight. First let us consider a situation, as in Table 7.1, in which two parties have the same number of votes. Let us suppose that the cancellation property is not true and that one party

[5] Multiple vote systems such as plurality runoff and single transferable vote violate nonnegative responsiveness in some cases. This is because it is possible for a party to increase its support and cause another party to be eliminated in that round than otherwise would be the case. As a result, the party faces a stronger competitor in a later round and loses a seat.

TABLE 7.1. *Voting Profile for Three Parties. Party A Gets Same Number of Votes as Party B, but Let Us Suppose That It Gets More Seats*

	Party A	Party B	Party C
Voter 1	X		
Voter 2		X	
Voter 3	X		
Voter 4		X	
Voter 5	X		
Voter 6		X	
Voter 7			X
Voter 8			
Etc.			

gets more seats than the other (let us assume Party A gets more seats, for the sake of argument). We can show that this is impossible if anonymity and neutrality are respected.

First, let us change the names of all the voters who vote for Party A and Party B. Each voter who votes for Party A gets the name of a voter who voted for Party B and each voter who voted for Party B gets the name of someone who voted for Party A. Thus Voter 1 is renamed Voter 2 and Voter 2 is renamed Voter 1. Alternatively, we could think of this as each voter who voted for Party A now voting for Party B and each voter who voted for Party B now voting for Party A. (Given that the number of voters for each party is assumed equal, the voters match up one to one.) This gives the voting profile in Table 7.2. If the electoral system respects

TABLE 7.2. *The Names of the Voters Have Been Rearranged from Table 7.1, but by Anonymity, Party A Must Still Get More Seats Than Party B*

	Party A	Party B	Party C
Voter 2	X		
Voter 1		X	
Voter 4	X		
Voter 3		X	
Voter 6	X		
Voter 5		X	
Voter 7			X
Voter 8			
Etc.			

TABLE 7.3. *The Names of Party A and B Have Been Exchanged. Note: By neutrality, the party now known as Party B must get more seats than Party A. However, this profile is identical to that in Table 7.1, where Party A gets more seats. This is a contradiction. It shows that if a party has the same number of votes as another party, it must (given our assumptions) get the same number of seats*

	Party B	Party A	Party C
Voter 2	X		
Voter 1		X	
Voter 4	X		
Voter 3		X	
Voter 6	X		
Voter 5		X	
Voter 7			X
Voter 8			
Etc.			

anonymity, this changing around of the voters can make no difference to the result. Therefore Party A must still be allocated more seats than Party B.

Next let us change the names of the parties. Let Party A now be called Party B and Party B now be called Party A. This gives us the voting profile in Table 7.3. By neutrality, if we change the names of the parties, this is not allowed to change the allocation of seats. The party previously known as Party A (now known as Party B) must win more seats than the party now known as Party A (previously Party B). That is to say, if Party B gets the support of all the voters who previously supported Party A, by neutrality, Party B must get all the seats that were previously allocated to A. Thus Party B must now receive more seats than Party A.

The problem is that if we look at Table 7.3, we see that it is identical to Table 7.1, except that the order of the rows and columns is different. If we rearrange the rows and columns of Table 7.3 without changing who votes for whom, we end up with a voter profile identical to Table 7.1 (Voter 1 votes for Party A, Voter 2 votes for Party B, etc.). By anonymity and neutrality, with the votes in Table 7.3, Party B must get more seats than Party A. But Table 7.3 is identical to Table 7.1, and we started by assuming that in Table 7.1, Party A gets more seats than Party B. What we have shown is that if Party A gets more seats than Party B despite having the same number of votes, then Party B must also get more seats than Party A. This is obviously impossible. The only way out of this contradiction is to assign the same number of seats to parties with the same number of votes. This is the cancellation property.

By adding the requirement of nonnegative responsiveness, we can go from the cancellation property to the weak plurality ranking property. The weak plurality ranking property requires that if one party wins more votes than another party, it must get at least as many seats as it. Suppose we have a voting profile in which Party A gets more votes than Party B. Now suppose that some of Party A's voters abstain, so that the vote totals for Party A and Party B are identical. By the cancellation property (which we have already shown can be derived from anonymity and neutrality), the two parties must receive an equal number of seats. Now let the abstaining voters go back to supporting Party A. By nonnegative responsiveness, Party A cannot be disadvantaged by this; it still must have at least as many seats as Party B. This is the weak plurality ranking property. If there are only two parties, this is equivalent to the majority rule standard (the party that receives a majority of the vote should receive at least half the seats in a two-party system).

The significance of this result is that it shows that the *majority rule* standard for electoral districting can be derived solely from the principle of the equal protection of individual voters. It does not depend on the principle that equally sized groups are entitled to equal representation, a principle that is not to be found in the Constitution. Rather, it is based on the requirement that individual voters receive equal protection in determining the overall result of the election. Given that the House of Representatives is institutionally partisan, this provides a standard of electoral justice that can be derived from Article 1§2 of the Constitution and the Equal Protection Clause of the Fourteenth Amendment.

APPLYING MAJORITY RULE AS A JUDICIALLY MANAGEABLE STANDARD: THE SYMMETRY TEST

We argued in the last section that the majority rule standard can be derived from the equal treatment of individual voters. This in turn can be derived from the requirement that the House of Representatives be elected by the people and from the equal protection of individual voters. However, if political gerrymandering is to be adjudicated in the courts, it is necessary to provide a standard that is not only judicially *discernable* – derived from a Constitutionally protected right – but also judicially *manageable*. That is to say, there needs to be a method to determine whether unconstitutional political gerrymandering has occurred in a specific case.

In the plurality opinion in *Vieth v. Jubelirer* (2004, 288), Justice Scalia argues that the plaintiffs would be unable to provide a manageable standard, even if their proposed standard was judicially discernable (2004, 288). In his concurring opinion, Justice Kennedy notes that the Court has not been shown a "statement of principled, well-accepted rules of fairness that should govern districting" (2004, 308), although he leaves open the possibility that one may be found.

Of course, until we have a viable judicially discernable standard, the question of judicial manageability is moot. However, in the last section, we laid out the case for the majority rule standard being such a standard. Given this, we can consider how this standard can be implemented. There already exist well-established techniques for measuring whether the majority rule standard is violated. For example, given established patterns of voting, we can calculate the probability that a given districting plan will result in a majority of voters not electing a majority of Representatives.

One complicating factor, however, is that districting plans are produced by each state, while the justification of the majority rule standard in the previous section applies to the House of Representatives as a whole. This is a direct consequence of Article 1 of the Constitution. Section 2 states that the House of Representatives shall be elected by the "People of the several States." Section 4, on the other hand, gives states authority over the "Times, Places and Manner" of elections, although it gives Congress the power to overrule them. We thus need to produce a standard that can be applied to state districting plans that ensures that the majority rule standard is respected nationally.

Requiring that each state's districting plan satisfy the majority rule standard does not guarantee that a majority of voters nationally will be able to elect a majority in the House of Representatives. To ensure this, we require a stricter standard at the state level, that of partisan symmetry. Partisan symmetry is defined as the requirement that "the electoral system treat similarly-situated political parties equally, so that each receives the same fraction of legislative seats for a particular vote percentage as the other party would receive if it had received the same percentage" (King et al. 2006, 4–5).[6] This standard was proposed in an amicus brief by King et al. (2006) for the case *LULAC v. Perry* (2006). As a result, there is a well-developed, peer-reviewed technology for implementing it.

6 That is to say, if Party A wins 60% of the vote to Party B's 40% and gets fourteen seats out of twenty, Party B would have to get fourteen seats if it was to win 60% of the vote.

Let us turn now to how the partisan symmetry standard can be constitutionally justified. The previous section showed that the majority rule standard is a logical consequence of the requirement that the House be elected by the people and the equal protection of all voters and thus can be justified in terms of the Constitution. If partisan symmetry is, in turn, a necessary condition for satisfying the majority rule standard, then any violation of partisan symmetry implies a violation of the election of the House by the people and the equal protection of voters. All that remains is to show that partisan symmetry in statewide districting is a necessary condition for the majority rule standard to apply to Congress as a whole.

In the case of the justification of the majority rule standard in the last section, the partisan outcome that matters is the balance of Congress nationally – that is, who holds a congressional majority. We have argued that the balance of the parties is an inescapable part of the result, not because voters think of themselves as partisans but because Congress organizes itself along party lines. That is, the partisan nature of the result is an *institutional fact*. However, this argument applies to Congress as a whole, not to the individual state delegations. Who has a majority in Congress has major institutional and political consequences; who has a majority of the (say) Pennsylvania delegation does not, at least not to the same degree. If we are to treat all U.S. citizens equally, then it is necessary that a majority of voters nationally should be able to elect a majority of representatives.

However, the constitutionality of state districting plans has to be judged on a state-by-state basis. While we have a decentralized system in which each state draws its own districts (that is, if the power of Congress to overrule the states is not invoked), states cannot be required to draw their districts based on how they expect other states to draw theirs. In principle, we could maintain national partisan majority rule by having the courts force states to coordinate so that the biases in different states cancel out. In effect the courts would have to order one state to make its districting biased in favor of Party A in order to balance out the bias in favor of Party B in another state. This would be a revolutionary change, effectively nationalizing the districting process. Given that this is unlikely to be acceptable, the only alternative is to demand that all states district in such a way that they would be unbiased in their own right. Only by doing this can we guarantee that a national majority of voters can elect a national majority of representatives.

Partisan symmetry is a necessary condition of a state districting plan that ensures that a majority of U.S. voters can elect a majority of representatives and thus ensures that all voters are equally protected. Clearly, the weaker quality of the majority rule standard at the state level is also necessary. If state districting plans are biased so that a minority can elect a majority of a state's delegation, it is obviously possible that a national minority may be able to elect a congressional majority. However, the majority rule standard at the state level is clearly not enough. Imagine that we had a districting plan that gave a majority of a state's delegation to whichever party won a majority of the state's vote. However, suppose this districting plan resulted in Party A winning sixteen seats out of twenty if it won 55% of the statewide vote but only gave Party B eleven seats out of twenty if it won 55%. If such a districting scheme was generalized nationally, it could clearly give Party A a majority in Congress even if it only won a minority of the votes. To ensure that the party that wins the national vote gets a majority of the seats, it is necessary that both parties be treated equally in the event that they win 55% of the vote – that is, we must require symmetry.

Symmetry at the state level is a necessary condition for guaranteeing a national majority can elect a congressional majority, but it is not a sufficient condition: this requires the stronger condition of statewide proportionality. The problem with statewide proportionality is that achieving this might require overhauling the entire U.S. electoral system. Even if statewide proportionality is not practical in the context of the United States, statewide symmetry clearly is – many state districting schemes have satisfied it (see Gelman and King 1994a, 546). And although statewide symmetry does not guarantee that a national voter majority will elect a majority of seats, it does severely reduce the scope for bias nationally.

Thus we can see that partisan symmetry is a necessary consequence of ensuring that a majority of voters can elect a majority of representatives, which is itself a necessary consequence of the election of the House by the people and the equal protection of individual voters. Partisan symmetry has the added advantage of being clearly measurable. In fact, the technology to measure it is already well developed and peer reviewed (see King and Browning 1987; Gelman and King 1994b, 1994a, 1990; King et al. 2006). It is the same technology that we use to measure partisan bias in Chapter 3.

The technique involves calculating the number of seats each party would win at different level of support. It is not assumed that the relative pattern of support for the parties across districts remains constant; rather, the degree to which it remains constant can be estimated from the data. Thus we can take account of that fact that some of the variation is the result of idiosyncratic factors like candidate quality and scandals, which are undeniably important in House elections. It is then possible to create a measure of bias – this is defined as the average level of asymmetry as party support goes from 45% to 55% (Gelman and King 1994a, 545). While the overall level of support for each party fluctuates between elections, we would expect the relative pattern of support across districts to remain somewhat stable – strong Democratic districts remain Democratic and strong Republican districts remain Republican. However, if this is not the case empirically, this will be reflected in the estimates. The Gelman/King measure of bias/symmetry indeed has all the features that Hastie (2011, 7–8) would ask for in a "legal number."[7]

It is certainly possible to calculate the symmetry of a districting scheme after the event using the election results. However, it is also possible to calculate the symmetry of a new districting scheme before it is implemented. Using GIS software, it is possible to apportion the election results (by polling station) among census tracts and calculate what the results would have been using the new districts. This does not require any new technology – districting consultants and political parties already do exactly this in the process of drawing districts. There is now even open-source software available (Altman and McDonald 2011a), and the same authors maintain a website that provides online interactive tools (www.publicmapping.org). The methodology for assessing partisan symmetry does not appear to be controversial among political scientists or practitioners. Indeed, as Grofman and King (2007, 15) point out, the expert witnesses for both the plaintiff and the defendant in *LULAC v. Perry* (2006) "were in remarkable agreement about the partisan implications of the plans whose partisan bias they investigated." Indeed, in his dissenting opinion, Justice Stevens (2006, 465–466) used the counterfactual results of the state's expert (Professor Gaddie) to show that the proposed plan violated the symmetry standard.

We can consider objections to symmetry as a manageable standard. In the plurality opinion in *Vieth v. Jubelirer* (2004, 288–290), Justice Scalia argues in principle that it will not be possible to find a manageable standard for partisan gerrymandering. This is for two reasons. First, he argues that it is not possible to identify a partisan majority, because there are no statewide House elections but simply a variety of district

[7] That is, they are reliable (we get the same result if we redo the analysis), equitable (similar cases are treated similarly), accurate (correspond to the thing being measured), predictable, and produce just results in individual cases.

elections, all of which depend to some degree on local or candidate-specific factors. However, the partisan symmetry standard does not rely on showing which party won a statewide majority of the vote in a particular election. Instead, it shows that we would expect a districting scheme to violate symmetry given reasonable and empirically testable assumptions and thus give a party that has a minority of the vote an opportunity to win a congressional majority.[8] It is, after all, the districting scheme that is being challenged, not the particular election. Furthermore, the method explicitly quantifies the degree to which election results are the result of local or candidate-specific factors and takes this into account when generating the measure of bias.

Second, Justice Scalia argues that there is no possibility of relief, short of completely overhauling the U.S. electoral system. The response to the second objection would be that the remedy is simply to require a districting scheme that does not violate symmetry. This is clearly feasible, as many state districting schemes have in fact managed to satisfy the symmetry standard (see Gelman and King 1994a, 546). It should also be noted that none of the criteria proposed in Grofman and King (2007) require *absolute* symmetry but merely approximate symmetry within some margin of error. Of course, even the most fairly drawn districts may on occasion give a majority of seats to a party that has won a minority of votes, as Justice Scalia correctly points out (2004, 290). However, the fact that no districting scheme will behave perfectly in all circumstances does not change the fact that some districting schemes are far worse than others. What makes a districting scheme unfair is not occasionally producing a bad result; what makes it unfair is that we expect it to be systematically biased in favor of one party or another. The fact that even the fairest districts may give the wrong result (say) once every hundred years does not mean that we have to tolerate a districting scheme that (say) gives two-thirds of the seats to the minority, overturns larger majorities, or systematically advantages one party on a regular basis.[9]

[8] It should be noted that the assumption that patterns of party voting remain approximately stable is not an "assumption" that can be accepted or rejected at will. Rather, it is a fact about the world that needs to be measured empirically.

[9] The example of Pennsylvania in 2000, which Justice Scalia (2004, 290) cites, is indeed the kind of "error" we need not be too concerned about. The Democrats won 50.6% of the vote but only received ten seats out of twenty-one. The election was essentially a tie in terms of votes cast, and the seat allocation to both parties was as close to even as possible.

It might be objected that the symmetry measure is based on counterfactual reasoning. However, it is entirely appropriate that a *measure* of electoral fairness be based on counterfactual reasoning, because the *concept* of fairness in a contest is inherently counterfactual. Rules are not unfair because they happen to produce a particular outcome in a particular case; they are unfair because of the outcomes that they *would* produce under different conditions. Whether I *happen to* win a lottery has no bearing on whether the lottery is fair; whether a lottery is fair depends on what would have happened if the world had turned out differently, that is, on whether I had the *opportunity to* win that I was promised. A baseball game in which one team has to hit the ball 400 feet for a home run while the other team has to hit it 500 feet is unfair (assuming no justifying circumstances), even if in a particular game no batter hits the ball 400 feet or more. It is unfair because if (hypothetically) the ball had been hit 450 feet, the two teams *would* have been treated differently. The two teams did not have the same opportunity to score a home run.

Justice Kennedy in the plurality opinion on *LULAC v.* Perry (2006, 420) adroitly notes that the measure depends "on conjecture about where possible vote-switchers will reside." This is inescapable for any measure because the *actual results* in a district-based election system depend on where voters live. It is in the nature of district-based electoral systems that 50 voters changing their votes in one district may change the result, while 50,000 voters changing their votes in another district may have no effect at all. What the symmetry measure assumes is that the relative pattern of support for parties remains relatively stable compared to what it has been in the recent past. This appears to be the case empirically, and the extent to which this is not so is reflected in the estimates of bias. This assumption of approximately uniform partisan swing (see King 1989, 796–798) does not appear to be controversial among political scientists – as mentioned before, there was little disagreement amongst the expert witnesses of the opposing parties in *LULAC* as to the effects of the districting plan under different levels of support for the two parties.

Justice Kennedy (2006, 420) also argues that the amici fail to provide a standard for deciding how much partisan asymmetry is too much. In response, Professors Grofman and King (2007, 5) echo Justice Stevens's (2006, 468) opinion that it is the place of the Court, not social scientists, to set the standards for what is constitutional and what is not. However, the amicus brief (2006) certainly does provide workable standards that the Court could choose to adopt. For example, the Court could adopt a quantitative standard – Justice Stevens (2006, 468) suggests that the Court could adopt a 10% deviation from symmetry standard, similar to the 10% standard for malapportionment. Another alternative suggested by the amici is that a districting plan be considered unfair if it deviates from symmetry by at least one whole seat. Social scientists can provide a precise measure of how unfair a districting plan is, just as an expert witness on DNA evidence can provide a precise estimate on the probability of a false identification; neither, however, can tell a court exactly how much uncertainty constitutes reasonable doubt.

It should be noted that the "intents prong" of the standard for political gerrymandering has not been mentioned here, although it was part of the standard adopted by the plurality in *Davis v. Bandemer* (1986a) and part of the standard proposed by the plaintiffs in *Vieth v. Jubelirer* (2004). This is because an intents prong is not strictly necessary, given that we have an objective measure of electoral fairness. If we can show that a districting plan violates the rights of individual voters in its effects, it does not matter whether this injustice came about by design or historical accident. The intent to gerrymander would be at most an aggravating circumstance. We can compare this to the way that cases of malapportionment are dealt with. Since *Wesberry v. Sanders* (1964a), congressional districts need to have approximately similar populations. Differences in population are a violation, regardless of whether there was intent. Indeed, historically, many cases of malapportionment came about through inaction, by simply failing to redraw districts while population distributions changed (see Cox and Katz 2002; Ansolabehere and Snyder 2008). Similarly, there is evidence that inaction combined with population shifts can produce severe partisan bias (Gelman and King 1994a). Electoral fairness is not something that occurs "naturally"; it has to be actively pursued.

Various justices in the case of *LULAC v. Perry* (2006) responded favorably to the partisan symmetry test proposed to the amici (2006). For example, Justice Stevens commended it as being "a helpful (though certainly not talismanic) tool in this type of litigation" (2006, 468).[10] However, based on social science results that were not yet published at the time of *LULAC v. Perry* (2006), it can be argued that it is considerably more than this. Rather than simply being one potential test among many, partisan symmetry is a *necessary condition* for a districting scheme that

[10] Justice Souter, joined by Justice Ginsberg, does not "rule out the utility of a criterion of symmetry as a test" (2006, 483). Justice Kennedy does not completely dismiss the usefulness of the measure, although he concludes that "asymmetry alone is not a reliable measure of unconstitutional partisanship" (2006, 420).

provides equal protection to all individual voters. While partisan symmetry ostensibly measures fairness to parties (which is not constitutionally protected), it is logically entailed by the equal protection of individual voters, which does enjoy constitutional protection. If partisan symmetry is violated, then we can conclude with no further evidence that individual voters are not being treated equally in a way that may substantially change the composition of Congress or even change the overall result of the election.

CONCLUSION

In *Vieth v. Jubelirer* (2004), a majority of Supreme Court justices agreed that the courts cannot intervene in cases of partisan gerrymandering because there currently exists no standard for adjudicating such cases that can be derived from the Constitution and applied in a manageable way. We propose such a standard. It is nothing more complex than the majority rule principle – the principle that a majority of the voters should be able to elect a majority of representatives. Majority rule is, of course, fundamentally tied to the idea of political equality and democracy (see, for example, Dahl 1956, 1989). It is also a value with a long history in American political thought, from the Federalists through to the Supreme Court's one-person, one-vote decisions such as *Wesberry v. Sanders* (1964a) and *Reynolds v. Sims* (1964b). It is, however, a standard that Justice Scalia explicitly rejects as a suitable standard for adjudicating complaints of partisan gerrymandering.

The challenge posed by Justice Scalia is a fundamental one. He argues that the Constitution only grants rights of equal treatment to individual citizens, not to groups. He argues that the majority rule standard has no constitutional basis because it relies on the idea that the larger group has a right to the most seats, and no such right is enumerated in the Constitution. Justice Scalia aims this critique at the majority rule standard proposed by the plaintiffs in *Vieth*. However, it would appear to apply equally to almost any standard that would invalidate partisan gerrymandering. After all, partisan gerrymandering is almost by definition a political – that is to say, collective – wrong. To prohibit it surely requires a standard of political fairness.

We, however, show that the majority rule principle does not necessarily depend on political groups having a right to fair representation. Rather, the majority rule principle can be justified strictly in terms of the equal treatment of individual voters. This means that it can be justified in terms of individual constitutionally protected rights. Our argument relies on a recently published result in mathematical social choice theory. However, the intuition is the same as the reason majority rule is intrinsic to democratic government: if you treat all individuals equally, you cannot make decisions based on anything but quantity. Parties and groups of partisans may not have a right to fair treatment. However, if we have partisan elections, it is not logically possible to treat every voter equally without also treating each party equally.

Once we have established that the majority rule principle is logically required by the equal treatment of individual voters, it is straightforward to provide it with a constitutional justification. Equal protection of citizens is required by the Fourteenth Amendment. Furthermore, the Supreme Court in *Wesberry v. Sanders* (1964a) found that Article 1§2 (that the House of Representatives is to be "elected by the People of the several States") also implies equal treatment of voters. Once we have established that the majority rule principle can be constitutionally justified, we can show that it generates judicially manageable tests that can allow courts to determine whether unconstitutional partisan gerrymandering is present. One such standard is the partisan symmetry principle developed by Gelman and King (1994b), which provides the basis for the empirical results presented in this book. We can thus provide a standard for outlawing partisan gerrymandering that is both judicially discernable and manageable.

8

Conclusion

Vieth, *Majority Rule, and* One Person, One Vote

The Supreme Court's decision in *Vieth v. Jubelirer* (2004) and the partisan districting that followed the 2010 Census raise fundamental questions about American democracy. They force us to reconsider the principles of majority rule, equal protection, and one person, one vote. In an immediate sense, the current level of partisan gerrymandering challenges the principle of majority rule, in that control of the House may depend as much on how the districts are drawn as on how people vote, and a minority may often dominate a majority. However, the consequences of the Supreme Court's ruling are more profound than who controls the House for the next decade. The *Vieth* decision undermines the one-person, one-vote jurisprudence of the 1960s that began with *Baker v. Carr* (1962). The decision respects the finding in *Wesberry* and *Reynolds* that all districts have to have equal population. However, this requirement means little or nothing if state legislatures are able to use partisan gerrymandering to achieve the same ends. The fact that state legislatures can to a substantial degree fix the outcome of House of Representatives elections also subverts the Madisonian principle that at least one branch of the legislature should be chosen directly by the people. This marks a major change in the effective constitution of the United States.

However, before considering the broader significance of *Vieth* and the partisan bias that followed the 2010 districting round, we need to summarize the empirical findings of this book. We can confirm that partisan bias increased sharply in the 2010 districting round. We find that the bias of the House of Representatives in 2012 was around 9% (measured by asymmetry). Roughly speaking, this means that if there were a 50/50 vote split, one party would win 55% of the seats, while the other would get

45%. This compares to a 3% bias in the 2000 districting round. In many individual states, the bias is far, far greater. There are numerous states where the asymmetry is between 30% and 40%. Or, alternatively, one party can win between two-thirds to three-quarters of the seats with only half the votes. The immediate political implication of this bias is that the House of Representatives is likely to remain under Republican control for the next decade. The degree of bias is such that it would require a Democratic victory on the level of 2008 to overhaul it.

We can debunk various myths about partisan gerrymandering. The first myth is that there is little at stake in redistricting except to the individual legislators affected. It was widely argued before and after *Vieth* that partisan gerrymandering had little effect on the overall political picture. There *was* some truth in this. Between the redistricting that followed the reapportionment revolution of the 1960s and the *Vieth* ruling, there seems to have been little partisan bias in House districting. In some states, this may have been because one party did not control the whole districting process. In other states, the threat that the courts would overturn a blatant partisan gerrymander may have acted as a deterrent. However, after the 2010 districting round, it is clear that the level of partisan bias is far greater and can determine control of the House of Representatives.

A second myth we have debunked is that partisan gerrymandering is self-limiting because a district drawer has to trade off partisan advantage against the protection of incumbents. Alternatively, it has been argued that geographical constraints mean that it is not possible to achieve massive bias. We have shown both these propositions to be false. If it is possible to concentrate your opponents' supporters in districts where they win 80% or more of the vote, it is possible to create a large number of seats for your party that are safe enough. There is a trade-off between creating bias and creating safety, but if you can "pack" your opponents' supporters tightly enough, you can satisfy both goals. With the help of modern geographical information systems that can map political data down to the census tract, it is quite possible to achieve the required "packing." Indeed, numerous states have done just this.

A final myth to dispel is that partisan bias is an inevitable result of demographic factors such as the fact that Democratic voters are concentrated in urban areas or the need to draw majority-minority districts to comply with the Voting Rights Act. We have shown that it is quite possible to draw districting plans without partisan bias, even in the states with the largest urban concentrations. It turns out that we do not find significant partisan bias in the most urban states, such as California,

New York, New Jersey, and Illinois. Furthermore, these states comply with the Voting Rights Act, and California has more majority-minority districts than does any other state. In many of the states where we do find partisan bias, we can find alternative districting plans that are unbiased or at least far less biased than the plan the state adopted. If states could have adopted an unbiased plan but chose a highly biased plan instead, this is a *choice* the state has made; it is not something imposed on the state by demographic factors.

Of course, this is not to say that demographic and geographic factors do not have a considerable effect on what kind of districting plans are possible. For example, the Voting Rights Acts requires that if there are compact concentrations of minority voters that can be drawn into congressional districts, these districts must be drawn. Similarly, if there are large geographic urban concentrations of Democratic voters, then it is easy to draw districts that "pack" them into overwhelmingly Democratic districts. Pro-Republican gerrymanders become easier, and pro-Democratic gerrymanders become harder. Consider the case of Illinois. The Democrats controlled the redistricting process and seem to have aimed at partisan advantage – they certainly drew some very oddly shaped districts. However, the most that they could achieve is a districting plan that is approximately unbiased. Given the concentration of Democratic voters in Chicago, it would have been very easy to draw a plan with a strong Republican bias. Generally speaking, strong urban concentrations of Democrats make it easier to draw districting plans that favor the Republicans. However, many Republican-controlled states still managed to draw highly biased plans without the help of such urban concentrations. The case of North Carolina is illustrative – its districting plan is one of the most biased in the nation, but to accomplish this, it was necessary to draw an array of the most oddly shaped districts.

However, while demographic and geographic factors may make it easier or more difficult to draw biased districts, they cannot explain why partisan bias is so much greater in the 2010 districting round than in the 2000 districting round. The fact that Democrats are concentrated in urban areas is not new, but the level of partisan bias is. Clearly the Democrats did not all move to urban areas in 2010. In fact, it appears that it is the Republicans who are becoming more concentrated in relative terms. When we consider data at the county level, the concentration of Republican voters appears to be catching up with that of Democratic voters. As a result, it should be easier to draw unbiased districts in 2010 compared to in 2000, not more difficult. The increase in the number of majority-minority districts also cannot explain the increase in bias. It is true that the number of majority-minority districts has increased, but the increase has not, for the most part, occurred in the states where bias increased.

The one thing that does explain where we find partisan bias in districting is politics. We find that the statistically significant partisan bias occurs *almost exclusively* in those states where there is both a political motive and a political opportunity. That is, it occurs where one party controls the entire districting process but where the state is politically competitive enough that gerrymandering brings an advantage. (There is nothing to be gained from having partisan bias in a state where your party is overwhelmingly strong. You can just benefit from the fact that first-past-the-post elections favor the larger party.)

Political control explains where we find partisan bias. However, it cannot explain the increase in partisan bias between 2002 and 2012. Rather, there has been a change in the behavior of state legislatures – they are now pursuing partisan advantage in districting more aggressively. That is to say, the increase in bias in 2012 is not simply the result of the Republican landslide in the 2010 elections. It is true that this gave the Republicans control of the districting process in many states. However, the Republicans also were in a very strong position in state government in 2000, and this did not result in the same level of partisan bias. Furthermore, in those states the Republicans controlled in both 2000 and 2010, they proposed plans with far more bias in 2010. That is, the 2010 round produced far more partisan bias, even after partisan control is taken into account. Whether this is because state legislatures felt less constrained after the *Vieth* ruling removed the threat of districting plans being overturned or whether it was simply because parties at the state level have become more focused on the pursuit of partisan advantage, *something* has changed. It may well be that state legislatures are now districting for partisan advantage to almost the maximum degree possible.

Having established what has happened empirically following the *Vieth* ruling, we can go on to consider its significance. The *Vieth* ruling fundamentally undermines the one-person, one-vote jurisprudence of the 1960s. The Supreme Court's rulings in cases such as *Wesberry v. Sanders* (1964a) and *Reynolds v. Sims* (1964b) did not simply establish that malapportionment was unconstitutional and that all districts needed to have approximately the same population. They established fundamental principles of political equality. They asserted that the right to equal protection and the fact that the House was to be "elected by the People of the several States" meant that every vote needed to be weighted equally. This in turn implied majority rule and the principle that vote dilution *by any means* amounted to disenfranchisement. This would certainly appear to rule out partisan gerrymandering. After all, in both judgments, the Court argued that subtle means of discrimination were as invidious as obvious means. Indeed, preventing malapportionment would do little good if states could simply produce the same outcomes through the more subtle means of gerrymandering.

The Supreme Court's judgment in *Vieth v. Jubelirer* (2004) effectively eviscerates *Wesberry* and *Reynolds* without overturning either of them. In *Colegrove v. Green* (1946) and his dissent to *Baker v. Carr* (1962), Justice Frankfurter argued that all questions of districting are beyond the competence of the courts to rule on because the Constitution assigns these tasks to the state legislatures and Congress – that is, they are nonjusticiable, "political questions." Justice Scalia in his *Vieth* opinion revives the "political question" doctrine but in a rather different way than Justice Frankfurter. Closely following Justice O'Connor's concurring opinion in *Davis v. Bandemer* (1986a),[1] Justice Scalia in *Vieth* argued that partisan gerrymandering was nonjusticiable in terms of the standards laid out not by Justice Frankfurter but by the Court in *Baker v. Carr* (1962). He argued that the reason that partisan gerrymandering was nonjusticiable was that there was not a "judicially discoverable and manageable standard" for adjudicating such cases. While there clearly was such a standard for deciding whether malapportionment was present, there was not, Justice Scalia argued, for partisan gerrymandering. This allows Justice Scalia to leave *Wesberry* and *Reynolds* intact while preventing them from being extended to cases of partisan gerrymandering. This, of course, opens up a loophole that totally undermines the egalitarian intent of these judgments. State legislatures can simply use partisan gerrymandering to engineer the outcomes that in the past they would have obtained by malapportionment.

Indeed, this process can be seen in an even broader historical context. At the Federal Convention, Madison and the Federalists argued for a legislature elected directly by the people, while the Anti-Federalists proposed a legislature selected by the state governments. The eventual compromise, of course, was that the House of Representatives was to represent the

[1] Justice O'Connor's opinion was concurring in that it agreed with the position of the Court to deny relief to the plaintiff. Justice O'Connor, however, strongly objected to the most notable finding of the Court, that partisan gerrymandering was justiciable.

people directly, while the Senate was to represent the states. However, the fact that the state legislatures had primary control over the administration of House elections undermined the principle of direct representation in the case of the House. For example, massive discrepancies in the population represented by each House member undermined the principle of proportionality to population that the House was supposed to embody. The one-party Democratic South was one consequence of this.

One person, one vote was in a sense a restoration of the Great Compromise. Indeed, this is exactly how the Supreme Court represented its decision in the case of *Wesberry v. Sanders* (1964a), which prohibited malapportionment in federal House districts and established the principle that all votes were to be weighted equally. Election by the people was taken to mean that the House was to represent the people directly and equally as individuals. The judgment in *Vieth*, however, undoes this work. By allowing partisan gerrymandering, it allows state governments to once again manipulate the process. State legislatures, by drawing the districts, can engineer outcomes in House elections and have a decisive effect on the composition of the state's federal House delegation. Indeed, there is a danger that the House of Representatives will become more a creature of state interests than the Senate. This is what we mean by the *revenge of the Anti-Federalists*.

This increased power of state governments has a profound effect on the effective constitution of the United States. The House of Representatives was supposed to directly and equally represent the people of the United States. Instead, elections are anything but equal. As we have seen, some voters are advantaged over others, and it is quite possible for a minority to elect a substantial majority of representatives. Federalist 52 emphasizes that the House of Representatives needs to accurately represent the interests and sympathies of the people as a whole. For this reason, it needs to be elected every two years so that it is responsive to the changing opinions of the people. Instead, the composition of the House is now largely determined by state legislative elections every ten years (the elections that take place in the year of the census). Furthermore, these are elections in which most people do not vote, and indeed typically have lower turnout than federal elections. The composition of the popular house of the legislature of the most powerful nation in the world is largely determined by elections that are supposed to be about matters of the administration of state government.

While it can be argued that the *Vieth* judgment undermines the democratic nature of American government, it turns out the crucial point of the argument in *Vieth* rests on a central concern of political philosophy and, indeed, the theory of democracy. The reason partisan gerrymandering is nonjusticiable, according to both Justice Scalia's *Vieth* opinion and the concurring opinion by Justice Kennedy, is that there does not exist a standard to adjudicate these cases. Such a standard would need to be both derived from a constitutionally protected right and practically applicable. If we accept the majority rule principle – the principle that a majority of voters should be able to elect a majority of representatives – then it is not difficult to measure this, as we have demonstrated. However, Justice Scalia does not accept that the majority rule principle can be derived from the right to equal treatment.

There is, of course, a long history in political philosophy of the idea that political equality and majority rule are almost synonymous (see Dahl 1956, 1989). Indeed, there is even a mathematical proof that political equality logically implies majority rule. However, Justice Scalia, following Justice O'Connor's dissent in *Davis v. Bandemer* (1986a), argues that the majority rule principle cannot be derived from any individual right. Rather, the principle that a majority should be able to elect a majority rests on an alleged group right to proportional representation. The Constitution grants no such right to groups. The Constitution only grants equal protection to individual citizens.

This critique appears at first to be decisive. The Constitution, indeed, does not enumerate a group right to proportional representation, and it is hard to see how it is possible to come up with a standard for partisan gerrymandering that does not rely on some concept of group justice. However, we have shown that it is possible to derive the majority rule principle strictly from the equality of individual voters. This relies on results in mathematical social choice theory that were not published when *Vieth v. Jubelirer* was adjudicated. We can show that if we treat all individual voters equally, it is logically necessary that a majority of voters must be able to elect a majority of representatives. To put it intuitively, if we have partisan elections, it is not possible to treat voters equally without treating parties equally. Of course, this assumes that we have partisan elections. But we do *as a matter of fact* have partisan elections. Our elections are partisan as a matter of institutional fact. Our elections are partisan not because individual voters happen to be partisans (as opposed to Catholics or farmers or whatever other demographic description you may choose) but because Congress and elections are organized on the basis of political party.

If this is so, then finding the standard the Justices demand is simply a matter of restoring the principle that all Americans are politically equal.

POSTSCRIPT – JULY 2015

Since the completion of the manuscript, several developments have occurred that warrant consideration and mention. The most obvious is the 2014 congressional election. However, several court decisions and filings at several levels also deserve to be addressed. Here we first briefly discuss the 2014 election and then turn to the important judicial decisions that concern congressional redistricting in a host of ways. None of these developments, however, would lead us to alter the main findings of the book.

THE HOUSE OF REPRESENTATIVES AND THE 2014 ELECTION

The outcome of the 2014 midterm elections is consistent with what the model presented in this book predicts. That is to say, the gains in seats that the Republicans made are approximately what we would predict given their gains in votes. In 2014, the Republicans won 53% of the House vote nationwide and won 57% of the seats as a result. This represented a net gain of thirteen seats over 2012, when they won 53% of the seats from 49% of the vote. The model presented in Chapter 3 actually predicts that the Republicans would win 58% of the seats if they won 53% of the national vote, but the actual outcome of 57% is well within the margin of error. Thus we continue to be confident in our prediction that the Democrats would have to win around 54% of the vote to win a House majority.

The 2014 results demonstrate how interpreting the result of one election can be misleading. It is not unusual with first-past-the-post elections for one party to win 57% of the seats from 53% of the vote. This is quite consistent with unbiased districts and the well-known tendency for first-past-the-post elections to reward the larger party. However, our analysis reveals that this is not what is happening here. If the Democrats were to win 53% of the vote, they would not win 57% of the seats. In fact, our analysis suggests that the Republicans would continue to have a majority (albeit a small majority) in the House. There is no doubt that the Republicans would have won control of the House in 2014 with virtually any districts, unless those districts were very heavily gerrymandered in favor of the Democrats. However, this does not change the fact that many districting plans exhibit high degrees of partisan bias and that the Democrats will require a landslide victory in the popular vote to have a chance of regaining control of the House. In effect, decisions taken by state governments at the beginning of the decade are determining the composition of the House of Representatives.

LITIGATION

Significant redistricting litigation has occurred or continues in Alabama, Arizona, Florida, Texas, North Carolina, and Virginia. This in general does not challenge the basic landscape governing partisan gerrymandering cases – since *Vieth v. Jubelirer* (2004), partisan gerrymandering is effectively nonjusticiable unless the plaintiff can identify a new standard. The one exception is the case of Florida, where state law prohibits partisan gerrymandering. Litigation there is ongoing.

In Alabama, two companion cases, *Alabama Democratic Conference v. Alabama* (2014a) and *Alabama Legislative Black Caucus v. Alabama* (2014b) concerned redistricting of state House and Senate districts in Alabama. When Alabama redrew its state house and state senate boundaries, it focused on typical redistricting objectives like incumbent protection, compactness, minimal change, and avoiding a split of precincts or counties. However, Alabama also privileged two specific goals: minimizing district population deviation to less than 1% of the ideal and, most importantly for the litigation, the avoidance of any diminution in the ability of racial minorities to elect their preferred candidate. Alabama sought to satisfy section 5 of the Voting Rights Act of 1965 (52 USC sec. 10304(b)) by retaining the same proportion of the black populations in the existing majority-minority districts. After a bench trial, the three-judge district court ruled for the state and found that the new district boundaries did not create a racial gerrymander in violation of the Fourteenth Amendment's Equal Protection Clause. The decision had four distinct dimensions. First, while both appellants argued the redistricting as a whole constituted improper racial gerrymandering, the *Conference* also argued that four specific districts constituted improper racial gerrymandering (Senate Districts 7, 11, 22, and 26). However, second, the bench found that the *Conference* lacked standing, so the claims about the four districts were not properly before the court. Moreover, third, the court also determined race was not the predominant motivating factor in the design of the districts, so there could be no violation. Further, fourth, ruling in the alternative, the court determined that even if race was the predominant factor, the use of race here was narrowly tailored to achieve a compelling state interest (avoiding retrogression under section 5) and therefore could survive strict scrutiny.

In March of 2015, the Supreme Court vacated the opinion and remanded it for further consideration. In a 5–4 opinion, Justice Breyer determined the district court erred by considering the state as a whole and ignoring specific claims about specific districts. Breyer also determined that the district court erred in claiming a waiver of a right to challenge specific districts because there was also a challenge to the scheme as a whole, erred in its determination that the *Conference* lacked standing, erred in its assessment of the predominance of racial factors, and that the final alternative holding is based on a misunderstanding of the law.

The vacate-and-remand order for the Alabama cases led to a vacate-and-remand order for both *Dickson v.* Rucho (2014c), a challenge to the persistently gerrymandered North Carolina map based on explicit racial balancing, and *Cantor v.* Personhuballah (2015b), which was similar litigation over the 3rd Congressional District in Virginia.

In Arizona, the Supreme Court determined that the ballot initiative process can transfer the obligation for districting to a nonpartisan commission without violating the constitutional requirement that the state legislature shall prescribe the time, place, and manner of elections. In *Arizona State Legislature v. Arizona Independent Redistricting Commission* (2015a), the state legislature argued that the word "legislature" in the Elections Clause (Art. 2 USC sec. 2a) in the Constitution could only mean the official body that makes laws in the state. Justice Ginsburg wrote the 5–4 opinion that determined that at the time of the drafting of the Constitution, "legislature" would have been more broadly understood as the power to make laws, not the specific narrow institution. Accordingly, nothing in the Constitution prohibits the states from providing for direct democracy even when the topic is the format of elections.

In Florida, the plaintiffs in *The League of Women Voters of Florida etc. et al. v. Ken Detzner et al.* (2015d) argued that the congressional redistricting plan violated Article III, Section 20 of the Florida Constitution, which explicitly forbids districting plans or districts that are "drawn with the intent to favor or disfavor a political party or an incumbent." After a lengthy trial, the trial judge found that Districts 5 and 10 were improperly drawn, and therefore the redistricting map as a whole was unconstitutional. The Florida Supreme Court affirmed the trial court's finding that the 2012 map was unconstitutionally drawn to favor the Republican Party and incumbents. The Court identified eight districts (5, 13, 14, 21, 22, 25, 26, 27) that the legislature needed to redraw in order to move to a constitutionally permissible map. The Court further instructed the legislature to conduct the process transparently, preserve all communications about the redraw, consider alternate plans from all available sources, and attempt to achieve "fairness." The Court relied on evidence of compactness measures, including the Reock or circle dispersion method and the Area/Convex Hull method. At the time of this writing, the legislature has been given 100 days to redraw the map as directed, and the Florida Supreme Court has retained jurisdiction pending the redraw effort. We do not yet know what the outcome will ultimately be or whether the final Florida Supreme Court decision may be challenged in the federal system. Accordingly, although the litigation bears close monitoring, at this point the only certainty is that the Court would have had an even better assessment of the degree of gerrymandering had it considered compactness and bias.

Finally, the Supreme Court has granted cert to a case that has the potential to radically transform redistricting. In *Evenwel v. Abbott* (2015c), the Court will decide whether the three-judge district court correctly decided that the Equal Protection Clause principle of one person, one vote allows states to use the total population rather than require states to use only eligible voters in the calculation. This case will either solidify the status quo, in which the proper number is population, or radically shift redistricting analysis by requiring parity among potential voters. Although it seems unlikely the Court would embrace a count structure that excludes all those not eligible to vote, including children and those otherwise not eligible to vote, should the Court embrace that approach, it would have serious consequences for redistricting.

Bibliography

Cases Cited

Abrams v. Johnson, 521 US 74 (1997).

Alabama Democratic Conference v. Alabama, No. 2:12-cv-1081-WKW-MHT-WHP (2014a).

Alabama Legislative Black Caucus v. Alabama, No. 2:12-cv-00691 (M.D. Ala.), No. 13–395, No. 13–895 & No. 13–1138 (S. Ct.) (2014b).

Arizona State Legislature v. Arizona Independent Redistricting Commission, No. 2:12-cv-01211 (D. Ariz.) & No. 13–1314 (S. Ct.) (2015a).

Baker v. Carr, 369 US 186 (1962).

Bush v. Vera, 517 US 952 (1996a).

Cantor v. Personhuballah No. 3:13-cv-00678 (E.D. Va.), No. 14–518, & No. 14–1504 (S. Ct.) (2015b).

Citizens United v. Federal Election Commission, 558 US 310 (2010).

Colegrove v. Green, 328 US 549 (1946).

Committee for a Fair and Balanced Map v. Illinois State Board of Elections, No. 1:11-cv-05065 (N.D. Ill.) (2011a).

Davis v. Bandemer, 478 US 109 (1986a).

Dickson v. Rucho, No. 11-CVS-16896 (N.C. Super Ct., Wake County), No. 201PA12, No. 201PA12-2, & No. 201PA12-3 (N.C. Sup. Ct.), No. 14–839 (Sup. Ct.) (2014c).

Easley v. Cromartie, 532 US 234 (2001).

Evenwel et al. *v. Abbott* et al., USSC (Docket No. 14–940) (lower court USDC W. Distr. TX). (2015c).

Gaffney v. Cummings, 412 US 735 (1973a).

Georgia v. Ashcroft, 539 US 461 (2003).

Gomillion v. Lightfoot, 364 US 339 (1960).

Gray v. Sanders, 372 US 368 (1963).

Hunt v. Cromartie, 526 US 541 (1999).

Johnson v. DeGrandy, 512 US 997 (1994).

Karcher v. Daggett, 462 US 725 (1983).
Kirkpatrick v. Preisler, 394 US 526 (1969).
League of Women Voters of Florida v. Detzner, No. 2012-CA-002842 (Fla. Cir. Ct., Leon County) & No. SC13-252 (Fla. Sup. Ct.) (2015d).
LULAC v. Perry, 548 US 399 (2006).
Miller v. Johnson, 515 US 900 (1995).
Mississippi Republican Executive Committee v. Brooks, 469 US 1002 (1984).
Mobile v. Bolden, 446 US 55 (1980).
Radogno v. Illinois State Board of Elections, No. 1:11-cv-04884 (N.D. Ill.) & No. 11–1127 (Sup. Ct.) (2011b).
Reynolds v. Sims, 377 US 533 (1964b).
Romo v. Detzner, consolidated case nos. 2012-CA-412 & 2012-CA-490 (2014d).
Shaw v. Hunt, 517 US 899 (1996b).
Shaw v. Reno, 509 US 630 (1993).
Shelby County v. Holder, 570 US (2013).
Smiley v. Holm, 285 US 355 (1932a).
South v. Peters, 339 US 276 (1950).
Thornburg v. Gingles, 478 US 30 (1986b).
Vieth v. Jubelirer, 541 US 267 (2004).
Wesberry v. Sanders, 376 US 1 (1964a).
White v. Regester, 412 US 755 (1973c).
White v. Weiser, 412 US 783 (1973b).
Wood v. Broom, 287 US 1 (1932b).

Works Cited

Abramowitz, Alan I., and Kyle L. Saunders. 2008. Is Polarization a Myth? *Journal of Politics* 70 (2):542–555.
Abrams, Samuel J., and Morris P. Fiorina. 2012. "The Big Sort" That Wasn't: A Skeptical Reexamination. *PS: Political Science and Politics* 45 (2):203–210.
Altman, Micah, Karin MacDonald, and Michael McDonald. 2005. From Crayons to Computers – the Evolution of Computer Use in Redistricting. *Social Science Computer Review* 23 (3):334–346.
Altman, Micah, and Michael P. McDonald. 2010. The Promise and Perils of Computers in Redistricting. *Duke Journal of Constitutional Law and Public Policy* 5:69–159.
Altman, Micah, and Michael P. McDonald. 2011a. BARD: Better Automated Redistricting. *Journal of Statistical Software* 42 (4):1–28.
Altman, Micah, and Michael P. McDonald. 2011b. Redistricting Principles for the Twenty-First Century. *Case Western Reserve Law Review* 62:1179.
Altman, Micah, and Michael P. McDonald. 2013. A Half-Century of Virginia Redistricting Battles: Shifting from Rural Malapportionment to Voting Rights to Public Participation. *University of Richmond Law Review* 47:771–831.
Altman, Micah, and Michael P. McDonald. 2014. Redistricting by Formula: An Ohio Reform Experiment. http://ssrn.com/abstract=2450645.

Altman, Micah, and Michael P. McDonald. 2015. Paradoxes of Political Reform: Congressional Redistricting in Florida. In *Jigsaw Puzzle Politics in the Sunshine State*, edited by S. C. McKee. Gainesville: University of Florida Press.

Ansolabehere, S., J. Rodden, and J. M. Snyder. 2008. The Strength of Issues: Using Multiple Measures to Gauge Preference Stability, Ideological Constraint, and Issue Voting. *American Political Science Review* 102 (2):215–232.

Ansolabehere, Stephen, and James M. Snyder. 2008. *The End of Inequality: One Person, One Vote and the Transformation of American Politics*. 1st ed., *Issues in American Democracy*. New York: Norton.

Ballotpedia. 2015. *Ballotpedia: An Interactive Almanac of American. Politics* 2015 [cited July 21, 2015]. Available from http://www.ballotpedia.org.

Barry, Brian. 1979. Is Democracy Special? In *Philosophy, Politics and Society, 5th Series*, edited by P. Laslett and J. Fishkin. New Haven, CT: Yale University Press.

Bell, Peter, and David Wasserman. 2012. Minority Districts Multiply: The Number of Congressional Districts with a Majority of Nonwhite Residents Has Tripled Since 1982. *National Journal*, **April 13, 2012. News.yahoo.com/since-1982-minority-congressional-districts-tripled-graphic-083421594.html.**

Bhaskar, Roy. 1989. *The Possibility of Naturalism: A Philosophical Critique of the Contemporary Human Sciences*, 2nd ed. New York: Harvester Wheatsheaf.

Bishop, Bill, and Robert G. Cushing. 2008. *The Big Sort: Why the Clustering of Like-Minded America Is Tearing Us Apart*. Boston: Houghton Mifflin Harcourt.

Borisyuk, Galina, Ron Johnson, Colin Rallings, and Michael Thrasher. 2010. Parliamentary Constituency Boundary Reviews and Electoral Bias: How Important Are Variations in Constituency Size. *Parliamentary Affairs* 63 (1):4–21.

Borisyuk, Galina, Ron Johnson, Michael Thrasher, and Colin Rallings. 2010. A Method for Measuring and Decomposing Electoral Bias for the Three-Party Case, Illustrated by the British Case. *Electoral Studies* 29 (4):733–745.

Boyce, John R., and Diane P. Bischak. 2002. The Role of Political Parties in the Organization of Congress. *Journal of Law Economics & Organization* 18 (1):1–38.

Brace, Kimball. 2004. Technology and Redistricting: A Personal Prospective on the Use of Technology in Redistricting over the past Thirty Years. In *The Brookings Institute Conference on Congressional Redistricting*. Washington, DC.

Bradlee, Dave. 2014. Dave's Redistricting App. Available from http://gardow.com/davebradlee/redistricting/launchapp.html.

Brady, David W., and Bernard Grofman. 1991. Sectional Differences in Partisan Bias and Electoral Responsiveness in United-States House Elections, 1850–1980. *British Journal of Political Science* 21:247–256.

Butler, David, and Bruce E. Cain. 1992. *Congressional Redistricting: Comparative and Theoretical Perspectives, New Topics in Politics*. New York, Toronto: Macmillan Pub. Co.; Maxwell Macmillan Canada.

Caliper. 2014. Maptitude. Available from http://www.caliper.com/mtredist.htm.

Cameron, Charles, David Epstein, and Sharyn O'Halloran. 1996. Do Majority-Minority Districts Maximize Substantive Black Representation in Congress? *American Political Science Review* 90:794–812.

Campagna, Janet, and Bernard Grofman. 1990. Party Control and Partisan Bias in 1980s Congressional Redistricting. *Journal of Politics* 52 (4):1242–1257.

Chen, Jowei, and Jonathan Rodden. 2013a. *Report on Computer Simulations of Florida Congressional Districting Plans*. www.redistricting.lls.edu/files/FL%20romo%2020130215%20chen.pdf, *unpublished working paper*.

Chen, Jowei, and Jonathan Rodden. 2013b. Unintentional Gerrymandering: Political Geography and Electoral Bias in Legislatures. *Quarterly Journal of Political Science* 8:239–269.

Chubb, John E. 1988. Institutions, the Economy, and the Dynamics of State Elections. *American Political Science Review* 82 (1):133–154.

Citrin, Jack, Eric Schickler, and John Sides. 2003. What if Everyone Voted? Simulating the Impact of Increased Turnout in Senate Elections. *American Journal of Political Science* 47 (1):75–90.

Colomer, Josep. 2004. It's Parties that Choose Electoral Systems (or Duverger's Laws Upside Down). In *Annual Meeting of the Public Choice Society*. Baltimore, MD: Public Choice Society.

Cox, Gary W., and Jonathan N. Katz. 2002. *Elbridge Gerry's Salamander: The Electoral Consequences of the Reapportionment Revolution, Political Economy of Institutions and Decisions*. Cambridge; New York: Cambridge University Press.

Cox, Gary W., and Mathew D. McCubbins. 1993. *Legislative Leviathan: Party Government in the House, California Series on Social Choice and Political Economy*. Berkeley: University of California Press.

Cox, Gary W., and Mathew D. McCubbins. 2005. *Setting the Agenda: Responsible Party Government in the U.S. House of Representatives*. Cambridge; New York: Cambridge University Press.

Crocker, Royce. 2012. Congressional Redistricting: An Overview. In *CRS Report for Congress*. Washington, DC: Congressional Research Service.

Curtice, John. 2010. So What Went Wrong with the Electoral System? The 2010 Election Result and the Debate About Electoral Reform. *Parliamentary Affairs* 63 (4):632–638.

Dahl, Robert. 1956. *A Preface to Democratic Theory*. Chicago: University of Chicago Press.

Dahl, Robert. 1989. *Democracy and Its Critics*. New Haven, CT: Yale University Press.

Daily Kos. 2015. Redistricting California with 47 reasonably compact strong Dem seats (and only 6 GOP seats). Daily Kos 2015 [cited July 21, 2015]. Available from http://www.dailykos.com/story/2015/07/03/1397966/-Redistricting-California-with-47-reasonably-compact-strong-Dem-seats-and-only-6-GOP-seats.

Dunleavy, Patrick. 2005. Facing Up to Multi-Party Politics: How Partisan Dealignment and PR Voting Have Fundamentally Changed Britain's Party System. *Parliamentary Affairs* 58 (3):503–532.

Economist. 2002. How to Rig an Election. *The Economist*, April 25, 2002, www.economist.com/node/1099030.

Electoral Reform Society. 2010. *The UK General Election 2010 in Depth: Report and Analysis*. London: ERS.

Engstrom, Richard N. 1995. Voting Rights Districts: Debunking the Myths. *Campaigns and Elections* 16:24–46.

Epstein, David, Michael C. Herron, Sharyn O'Halloran, and David Park. 2007. Estimating the Effect of Redistricting on Minority Substantive Representation. *Journal of Law Economics & Organization* 23 (2):499–518.

Epstein, David, and Sharyn O'Halloran. 1999. Measuring the Electoral and Policy Impact of Majority-Minority Voting Districts: Candidates of Choice, Equal Opportunity, and Representation. *American Journal of Political Science* 43:367–395.

Erikson, Robert S. 1972. Malapportionment, Gerrymandering, and Party Fortunes in Congressional Elections. *American Political Science Review* 66 (4):1234–1245.

Erikson, Robert S., Michael MacKuen, and James A. Stimson. 2002. *The Macro Polity, Cambridge Studies in Political Psychology and Public Opinion*. New York: Cambridge University Press.

Fiorina, Morris P., Samuel J. Abrams, and Jeremy C. Pope. 2006. *Culture War? The Myth of a Polarized America*. New York: Pearson Longman.

Fiorina, Morris P., Samuel J. Abrams, and Jeremy C. Pope. 2008. Polarization in the American Public: Misconceptions and Misreadings. *Journal of Politics* 70 (2):556–560.

Fisher, Stephen D., and John Curtice. 2006. Tactical Unwind? Changes in Party Preference Structure and Tactical Voting in Britain between 2001 and 2005. *Journal of Elections, Public Opinion and Parties* 16 (1):55–76.

Forest, Benjamin. 2005. The Changing Demographic, Legal, and Technological Contexts of Political Representation. *Proceedings of the National Academy of Sciences of the United States of America* 102 (43):15331–15336.

Gardner, James. 2004. A Post-*Vieth* Strategy for Litigating Partisan Gerrymandering Claims. *Election Law Journal* 3 (4):643–652.

Gelman, Andrew, and Gary King. 1990. Estimating the Electoral Consequences of Legislative Redistricting. *Journal of the American Statistical Association* 85 (410):274–282.

Gelman, Andrew, and Gary King. 1994a. Enhancing Democracy through Legislative Redistricting. *American Political Science Review* 88 (3):541–559.

Gelman, Andrew, and Gary King. 1994b. A Unified Method of Evaluating Electoral Systems and Redistricting Plans. *American Journal of Political Science* 38 (2):514–554.

Goedert, Nicholas. 2014. Gerrymandering or Geography? How Democrats Won the Popular Vote but Lost the Congress in 2012. *Research and Politics* 1: 1–8.

Grigg, Delia, and Jonathan N. Katz. 2005. *The Impact of Majority-Minority Districts on Congressional Elections* presented at Midwest Political Science Association Meeting 2005, Chicago: MPSA.

Grofman, Bernard. 1990. Towards a Coherent Theory of Gerrymandering: Bandemer and Thornburg. In *Political Gerrymandering and the Courts*, edited by B. Grofman. New York: Agathon Press.

Grofman, Bernard. 2006. Operationalizing the Section 5 Retrogression Standard of the Voting Rights Act in the Light of *Georgia v. Ashcroft*: Social Science Perspectives on Minority Influence, Opportunity and Control. *Election Law Journal* 5 (3):250–282.

Grofman, Bernard, and Lisa Handley. 1991. The Impact of the Voting Rights Act on Black Representation in Southern State Legislatures. *Legislative Studies Quarterly* 16:111–127.

Grofman, Bernard, and Gary King. 2007. The Future of Partisan Symmetry as a Judicial Test for Partisan Gerrymandering after *LULAC v. Perry*. *Election Law Journal* 6 (1):2–35.

Grofman, Bernard, Guillermo Owen, and Christian Collet. 1999. Rethinking the Partisan Effects of Higher Turnout: So What's the Question? *Public Choice* 99 (3–4):357–376.

Hansford, Thomas G., and Brad T. Gomez. 2010. Estimating the Electoral Effects of Voter Turnout. *American Political Science Review* 104 (2):268–288.

Hasen, Richard L. 2004. Looking for Standards (in All the Wrong Places): Partisan Gerrymandering Claims after *Vieth v. Jubelirer*. *Election Law Journal* 3 (4):626–642.

Hasen, Richard L. 2011. The Supreme Court's Shrinking Election Law Docket, 2001–2010: A Legacy of *Bush v. Gore* or Fear of the Roberts Court? *Election Law Journal* 10 (4):325–333.

Hastie, Reid. 2011. The Challenge to Produce Useful "Legal Numbers." *Journal of Empirical Legal Studies* 8 (S1):6–20.

Hirsch, Sam. 2003. The United States House of Unrepresentatives: What Went Wrong in the Latest Round of Congressional Redistricting. *Election Law Journal* 2 (2):179–216.

Hout, Eliora van der, and Anthony J. McGann. 2009a. Liberal Political Equality Implies Proportional Representation. *Social Choice & Welfare* 33 (4):617–620.

Hout, Eliora van der, and Anthony J. McGann. 2009b. Proportional Representation within the Limits of Liberalism Alone. *British Journal of Political Science* 39:735–754.

Hout, Eliora van der, Harrie de Swart, and Annemarie ter Veer. 2006. Axioms Characterizing the Plurality Ranking Rule. *Social Choice & Welfare* 27 (3).

Ingraham, Christopher. 2014. America's Most Gerrymandered Congressional Districts. *The Washington Post*, May 15, 2014.

Issacharoff, Samuel, Pamela S. Karlan, and Richard H. Pildes. 2012. *The Law of Democracy*. 4th ed. Eagan, MN: Foundation Press.

Jacobson, Gary C. 1990. *The Electoral Origins of Divided Government: Competition in US House Elections, 1946–1988*. Boulder, CO: Westview Press.

Jacobson, Gary C. 2013. Partisan Polarization in American Politics: A Background Paper. *Presidential Studies Quarterly* 43 (4):688–708.

Jillson, Calvin C. 1988. *Constitution Making: Conflict and Consensus in the Federal Convention of 1787*. New York: Agathon Press.

Johnson, Kevin R. 2003. *Mixed Race America and the Law: A Reader*: New York: NYU Press.

Johnson, Ron, Charles J. Pattie, David Rossiter, Danny Dorling, Iain MacAllister, and Helena Tunstall. 2007. New Labour's Landslide and Electoral Bias: An Exploration of Differences between the 1997 UK Election Result and the Previous Thirteen. *British Elections and Party Review* 9 (1):20–45.

Johnson, Ron, David Rossiter, and Charles J. Pattie. 2006. Disproportionality and Bias in the Results of the 2005 General Election in Great Britain: Evaluating the Electoral System's Impact. *Journal of Elections, Public Opinion and Parties* 16 (1):37–54.

King, Gary. 1989. Representation through Legislative Redistricting: A Stochastic Model. *American Journal of Political Science* 33 (4):787–824.

King, Gary, and Robert X. Browning. 1987. Democratic Representation and Partisan Bias in Congressional Elections. *American Political Science Review* 81 (4):1251–1273.

King, Gary, and Andrew Gelman. 1991. Systemic Consequences of Incumbency Advantage in United-States House Elections. *American Journal of Political Science* 35 (1):110–138.

King, Gary, Bernard Grofman, Andrew Gelman, and Jonathon Katz. 2006. Brief of Amici Curiae Professors Gary King, Bernard Grofman, Andrew Gelman, and Jonathan N. Katz, in Support of Neither Party. *For the case of LULAC v. Perry.*

Ladewig, Jeffrey W., and Matthew P. Jasinski. 2008. On the Causes and Consequences of and Remedies for Interstate Malapportionment of the US House of Representatives. *Perspectives on Politics* 6 (1):89–107.

Layman, Geoffrey C., Thomas M. Carsey, and Juliana Menasce Horowitz. 2006. Party Polarization in American Politics: Characteristics, Causes, and Consequences. *Annual Review of Political Science* 9:83–110.

Levendusky, Matthew S. 2009. *The Partisan Sort: How Liberals Became Democrats and Conservatives Republicans*. Chicago: University of Chicago Press.

Levitt, Justin. 2014. *Color by Numbers: The New Misreading of the Voting Rights Act*. Rochester, NY: Loyola-LA Legal Studies Paper.

Lowenstein, Daniel. 1990. Bandemer's Gap Gerrymandering and Equal Protection. In *Political Gerrymandering and the Courts*, edited by B. Grofman. New York: Agathon Press.

Lowenstein, Daniel, and Jonathan Steinberg. 1985. The Quest for Legislative Districting in the Public Interest: Elusive or Illusory. *UCLA Law Review* 33 (1):1–75.

Lublin, David. 1997. *The Paradox of Representation: Racial Gerrymandering and Minority Interests in Congress*. Princeton, NJ: Princeton University Press.

Madison, James. 1966. *Notes of Debates in the Federal Convention of 1787 Reported by James Madison*. Athens: Ohio University Press.

Martinez, Michael D., and Jeff Gill. 2005. The Effects of Turnout on Partisan Outcomes in US Presidential Elections 1960–2000. *Journal of Politics* 67 (4):1248–1274.

May, Kenneth. 1951. A Set of Independent Necessary and Sufficient Conditions for Simple Majority Decision. *Econometrica* 20:680–684.

McCarty, Nolan, Keith Poole, and Howard Rosenthal. 2006. *Polarized America: The Dance of Ideology and Unequal Riches*. Cambridge, MA: MIT Press.

McDonald, Michael P. 2004. A Comparative Analysis of U.S. State Redistricting Institutions. *State Politics and Policy Quarterly* 4 (4):371–396.

McDonald, Michael P. 2006. Seats to Votes Ratios in the United States. In *Plurality and Multi-Round Electoral Systems. Center for the Study of Democracy*. Irvine: University of California Press.

McDonald, Michael P. 2011. The 2010 Midterm Elections: Signs and Portents for the Decennial Redistricting. *PS-Political Science & Politics* 44 (2):311–315.

McDonald, Michael P. 2013. Geography Does Not Necessarily Lead to Pro-Republican Gerrymandering. In *Huffington Post*, July 1, 2013. www.huffingotn.com/Michael-p-mcdonald/geography-does-not-necess_b_3530099.html.

McKee, Seth C., and Jeremy M. Teigen. 2009. Probing the Reds and Blues: Sectionalism and Voter Location in the 2000 and 2004 U. S. Presidential elections. *Political Geography* 28 (8):484–495.

New York Times. 2004. Elections with No Meaning. *The New York Times*, February 21, 2004 www.nytimes.com/2004/02/21/opinoin/elections-with-no-meaning.html?_r=0.

Niemi, Richard G., Bernard Grofman, Carl Carlucci, and Thomas Hofeller. 1990. Measuring Compactness and the Role of a Compactness Standard in a Test for Partisan and Racial Gerrymandering. *Journal of Politics* 52 (4):1155–1181.

Nir, David. 2008. Presidential Results by Congressional District, 2000–2008. Swing State Project 2008 [cited July 21, 2015]. Available from http://www.swingstateproject.com/diary/4161/presidential-results-by-congressional-district-20002008.

Nir, David. 2012. Daily Kos Elections' presidential results by congressional district for the 2012 and 2008 elections. Daily Kos 2012 [cited July 21, 2015]. Available from http://www.dailykos.com/story/2012/11/19/1163009/-Daily-Kos-Elections-presidential-results-by-congressional-district-for-the-2012–2008-elections.

Percival, Garrick L., Mary Currin-Percival, Shaun Bowler, and Henk van der Kolk. 2007. Taxing, Spending, and Voting: Voter Turnout Rates in Statewide Elections in Comparative Perspective. *State and Local Government Review* 39 (3):131–143.

Perkins, Alec. 2014. *FairDistrict.US* 2014 [cited November 6, 2014]. Available from fairdistrict.us.

Poole, Keith T., and Howard Rosenthal. 2007. *Ideology and Congress*. New Brunswick, NJ: Transaction Publishers.

The Public Mapping Project, Michael Altman, Michael P. McDonald, and Azavea. 2014. *District Builder*. www.publicmapping.org.

Puppe, Clemens, and Attila Tasnadi. 2009. Optimal Redistricting under Geographical Constraints: Why "Pack and Crack" Does Not Work. *Economics Letters* 105 (1):93–96.

Rae, Douglas. 1967. *The Political Consequences of Electoral Laws*. New Haven, CT: Yale University Press.

Reif, Karlheinz, and Hermann Schmitt. 1980. 9 2nd-Order National Elections – a Conceptual-Framework for the Analysis of European Election Results. *European Journal of Political Research* 8 (1):3–44.

Shotts, Kenneth W. 2001. The Effect of Majority-Minority Mandates on Partisan Gerrymandering. *American Journal of Political Science* 45 (1):120–135.

Soroka, Stuart Neil, and Christopher Wlezien. 2010. *Degrees of Democracy: Politics, Public Opinion, and Policy*. Cambridge; New York: Cambridge University Press.

Stephanopoulos, Nicholas O., and Eric M. McGee. 2015. Partisan Gerrymandering and the Efficiency Gap. *University of Chicago Law Review* 82:831. http://ssrn.com/abstract=2457468.

Taagepera, Rein, Peter Selb, and Bernard Grofman. 2013. How Turnout Depends on the Number of Parties: A Logical Model. *Journal of Elections, Public Opinion and Parties* (forthcoming):1–21.

Taagepera, Rein, and Matthew Shugart. 1989. *Seats and Votes: The Effects and Determinants of Electoral Systems*. New Haven, CT: Yale University Press.

Tam Cho, Wendy K., James G. Gimpel, and Iris S. Hui. 2012. Voter Migration and the Geographic Sorting of the American Electorate. *Annals of the Association of American Geographers* 103 (4):856–870.

Theriault, Sean M. 2008. *Party Polarization in Congress*. New York: Cambridge University Press.

Thrasher, Michael, Galina Borisyuk, Colin Rallings, and Ron Johnson. 2011. Electoral Bias at the 2010 General Election: Evaluating Its Extent in a Three-Party System. *Journal of Elections, Public Opinion and Parties* 21 (2):279–294.

Tufte, Edward. 1973. The Relationship between Seats and Votes in Two-Party Systems. *American Political Science Review* 67 (2):540–554.

Weissberg, Robert. 1978. Collective vs. Dyadic Representation in Congress. *American Political Science Review* 72 (2):535–547.

Wolf, Stephen. 2012. What if We Had Non-Gerrymandered Redistricting Nationwide? The Daily Kos, August 6, 2012 [cited July 21, 2015]. Available from http://www.dailykos.com/story/2012/08/06/1115538/-What-if-We-Had-Non-Partisan-Redistricting-Nationwide.

Index